THE UNHEROIC HERO

THE UNHEROIC HERO
in the Novels of
Stendhal, Balzac
and Flaubert

RAYMOND GIRAUD

Rutgers University Press

New Brunswick, N. J.

1957

843.09
D 44 u

35326
September, 1957

Preface

Like many other writers of their century, Stendhal, Balzac and Flaubert had the unhappy conviction that the old aristocratic ideal of heroism was absurd in a predominantly bourgeois society. Yet in their novels about contemporary life appear characters who, though unheroic, define a new concept of heroism in the novel. These heroes, in whom some of the most acute moral problems of our own time are prefigured, are not romantic villains or anti-heroes but complex, sensitive individuals adrift in an expanding, vulgarized society. They are tempted by its promise of success, but suspicious of what they think success implies. They are the product of a mixture of the novelist's sympathy and self-expression, on the one hand, and his response to the demands of realism, on the other. This book is an attempt to understand them and, through them, an enduring literary effect of hostility toward the bourgeois in the nineteenth century.

The translations from the French are my own. Only a few verses of poetry are left in the original language—those I thought might suffer too outrageously if turned into English.

I wish to thank Pierre-Aimé Touchard and Mme Magali Marsan for their kindness in permitting me to quote from *Dionysos, Apologie pour le théâtre* and *La Bataille romantique*.

I should also like to acknowledge the courtesy of Harcourt, Brace and Company, who have permitted me to quote from T. S. Eliot's *Notes Toward the Definition of Culture.*

Much of *The Unheroic Hero* was originally contained in a dissertation presented in Yale University. I owe a heavy debt to all who helped me in the early days of composition, particularly to Jean Boorsch, Kenneth Douglas and Georges May, who read and criticized the manuscript. Very special thanks must go to Erich Auerbach, who combined all moral and intellectual virtues in his encouragement and guidance of my work. It would be impossible to express adequately my gratitude to Henri Peyre. If there is a glint of truth or life in these pages, it can only be a reflection of his genius. But, if I were to try to share the responsibility for this book, it could only be with my wife.

RAYMOND GIRAUD

NEW HAVEN, CONNECTICUT
OCTOBER, 1956

Contents

Chapter

I The Writer and the Bourgeoisie in
   Nineteenth Century France 3

   THE BOURGEOIS BEFORE 1830 13
   THE NEW SITUATION OF THE WRITER 27
   PUBLICATION AND THE BOURGEOIS PUBLIC 37
   THE UNHEROIC BOURGEOIS HERO 47

II Stendhal—The Bridge and the Gap Between
    Two Centuries 53

    LUCIEN AT BLOIS—A MORAL COMEDY 59
    A PROBLEM IN THE REPRESENTATION OF REALITY 66
    THE DUPLICITY OF THE STENDHALIAN HERO 71
    "LE NATUREL" 78
    MIXED FEELINGS ABOUT MONEY 82
    STENDHAL AND THE PROFESSION OF LETTERS 87

III Balzac the Great Compromiser 93

     BALZAC AND THE PROFESSION OF LETTERS 93
     REPRESENTATION OF THE BOURGEOIS 99

CÉSAR BIROTTEAU   101
CÉSAR BIROTTEAU—A "NEW" BOURGEOIS   109
PEASANT HANDS AND BOURGEOIS FEET   115
SOCIAL CHANGE   119
DEPUIS 1830 . . .   123
RATHER VICE THAN BOURGEOIS VIRTUE   127

IV   Gustavus Flaubertus Bourgeoisophobus   132
FLAUBERT'S "VOCATION" FOR ART   133
THE "EDUCATION SENTIMENTALE"   140
FRÉDÉRIC MOREAU—"HOMME TE TOUTES
LES FAIBLESSES"   150
ADULTERY: AN ASPECT OF ROMANTIC AMBIGUITY   152
DREAMS: A ROMANTIC RETREAT FROM REALITY   157
LOVE AND MONEY   162
THE "BOURGEOIS"   170
FLAUBERT AND THE BOURGEOIS PUBLIC   177
IN AND ABOVE THE BOURGEOISIE   181

V   Anti-Bourgeois Sentiment and Mass Culture   185
THE UNHEROIC HERO   185
PESSIMISM AND THE TRIUMPH OF THE
"BOURGEOIS"   190
FROM THE BOURGEOIS TO THE MASS-MAN   196
THE AMERICAN CENTURY?   200

Notes   215
Bibliography   225
Index   237

THE UNHEROIC HERO

I · The Writer and the Bourgeoisie in Nineteenth Century France

Ohé! les bourgeois! les philistins damnés!
GÉRARD DE NERVAL

Since the end of the Napoleonic era, almost every literary manifestation of discontent with contemporary French society has reflected a new, modern kind of hostility for the bourgeois. The French bourgeois had often been slighted and ridiculed under the *ancien régime*, but he had never been scorned, insulted and attacked so loudly and so violently as in the middle decades of the nineteenth century. This new anti-bourgeois feeling was not simply a strong echo of earlier sentiment; it was the product of all the political, social and economic changes that had combined to transform French society and, with it, the situation of the writer, the artist and the intellectual. Nostalgia for the past and resentment of cultural change created feelings of solitude and superiority among the writers of the romantic generations and was responsible for hostility, discontent and frustration in their attitude to society and the way they chose to represent it in works of art.

Elements of the situation of which early hostility to the bourgeois was symptomatic persisted throughout the century and still endure today. In France and elsewhere, for over a hundred years now, important groups of writers, artists and

intellectuals have repudiated and been repudiated by democratic bourgeois society and have been both afflicted and
stimulated by feelings of isolation, superiority and revolt.
Romantics, realists, symbolists, surrealists and, most recently,
existentialists—all, for one reason or another, and to varying
degrees, have confronted amused, shocked, hostile or uncomprehending bourgeois publics, and have been moved to assume
postures of defense or attack, or, obsessed by an ideal of uncompromising purity, have retreated to lonely ivory towers of
despair and inaction.

The great social and literary importance of the early phases
of this hostility has too often been subordinated to its trivial
and anecdotal side. We are too easily tempted to remember
mainly the stories of Théophile Gautier's red vest and Mero-
vingian locks and of Gérard de Nerval's rumored strolls
through the Luxembourg gardens with a lobster on a leash, as
though hostility to the bourgeois were mainly a juvenile sport,
a comic sympton of the decay of romanticism or of the birth
of art for art's sake.

It is true that Bohemian efforts to shock the bourgeois have
commonly been undertaken by youthful enthusiasts and mal-
contents, who have then often mended their ways and made
their peace with a society that maturity led them to accept.
And it may also be true that the nineteenth century hostility
toward the bourgeois—like other violent and indefinable passions—was strongest and cruelest among the young, the post-
Napoleonic generation, whose heart was armed

> With virulent hatred and pity morose
> For the bourgeoisie, Napoleon's code, and prose.[1]

For that matter, even a much older poetic tradition supports
the idea of flaming youth, infused with rebellious liquors, excessively frank, excessively indignant and excessively foolish.

Confronted with problems of sincerity, justice and success in a world that their elders seem to have appropriated for themselves, young men have always felt frustrated and impotent, unheard, unappreciated and alone.

Nineteenth century anti-bourgeois sentiment, however, represented much more than an outburst of peevish spite or the Bohemian sowing of wild oats. Like the bearded devotees of "existentialist" jazz clubs around Saint-Germain-des-Prés, the writers of the second romantic generation, the epigones of the great generation of Hugo, Vigny and Lamartine, often seem silly and childish, insincere poseurs and pranksters in the complicated and sometimes grotesque attitudes they adopted to keep the world of their bourgeois parents, professors and public at a distance. Yet, despite the youth of the famous Jeune-France, or Petit Cénacle, in which the young Nerval and Gautier, among others, manifested their early devotion to Art, the enemies and critics of the bourgeois did not fall neatly into any age group. Moreover, their attack on the bourgeois was serious, a moral indictment of their century rather than a mere mischievous fashion. For all their superficially scandalous behavior, the fiercest bourgeois-haters of the nineteenth century were, with a few rare exceptions, true moralists, who, although they may never have preached from a pulpit, an editorial box or a university chair, did not retreat to an ivory tower, but were, on the contrary, fatally attracted to the contemporary scene and the social, economic and political problems that became so pressing after the July Revolution.

The year 1830 is a pivotal date in the new bourgeois century, separated from the *ancien régime* by far more than the mechanical renewal of the calendar. The turning of a century or the isolation of a year of political change may seem an arbitrary pretext for the definition of a new era. Even the famous *mal du siècle*, formerly so intimately associated with Chateaubriand and Musset, seems really to have constituted a

century-long moral crisis that began in the middle of the
eighteenth century.[2] But what stamped the new era with its
original character was the overwhelming conviction of the
nineteenth century writer that he lived in a new world and a
new society. As we today are so conscious of living in what
we call the twentieth century, though mindful of our romantic
heritage, so were the survivors of the Revolution and the
Napoleonic wars aware of the pastness and irretrievability of
the eighteenth century, even though its tradition weighed
heavily upon them.

There is much to be said in favor of the argument that the
nineteenth century was not clearly launched in France before
the reign of Louis-Philippe.[3] After Louis XVI's violent death
in 1793, the agony of the Bourbons was prolonged until 1830,
when the bourgeoisie officially took possession of French
politics, burying definitively the idea of government by the
king. The existence of a numerous proletariat, announced by
Sismondi and the Saint-Simonians, had first come into public
view in 1831, when the uprisings of textile workers in Lyons
inspired hostility toward the bourgeois government of Louis-
Philippe, even on the part of otherwise conservatively inclined
observers. Though he did not share the misery of the working
class, or even subscribe to the hopes of republicans or the
ideals of democrats, an intellectual of those days could nevertheless feel humiliated by the behavior of important groups
within the bourgeoisie and, in sentiment at least, dissociate
himself from the aggressively materialistic culture that had, in
the words of Sainte-Beuve, made money its god.

The July Revolution was indisputably a triumph for those
"bourgeois dynasties" (as Beau de Loménie has called them)
that had dominated French politics from the time of the Con-
vention to the final exile of Napoleon and the election of the
ultraroyalist Chambre des introuvables.[4] The "Orleanist bourgeoisie" did not wait till 1830 for all its wealth and its power,

but an official seal was affixed to its social prestige and its political responsibility when it captured the monarchy and helped a bourgeois king to mount the throne. From 1830 on, not only the government, but all aspects of French life, the entire culture of the nation, rapidly acquired a middle-class flavor. Even under the limited government of the two preceding Bourbons, it is inconceivable that anyone should have written, as Henry Monnier did, some years later: "The bourgeoisie is everything today. The aristocracy no longer exists and there is still no democracy; there is only the bourgeoisie." [5]

Doubtless, this conviction was not born unaided in the public mind. The Carlist opposition, it has been said, first described the new government as bourgeois in the hope of depreciating it in the public esteem, "because of the derogatory connotation that reminiscences of another age caused people to attach to the word." Repeating the idea in newspapers, salons, literature, and on every possible occasion, the legitimists seem to have done their best to help the expression "bourgeois monarchy" acquire currency in France.[6] On the other hand, the socialists were certainly no less alert to the triumph of the bourgeoisie, which, the *Globe* asserted in March 1831, had already been effected under the Restoration.[7]

Louis-Philippe and his umbrella were not the only symbols of the character of the July Monarchy. Anti-bourgeois writers of the early thirties also denounced a general bourgeois drift in all areas of French society. Extremists like Gautier were willing to except only themselves and their own intimate circle of friends from what they considered a nation homogeneously composed of smug, philistine bourgeois. "The bourgeois! That meant just about everybody: bankers, brokers, notaries, merchants, shopkeepers and others, anyone who wasn't part of the mysterious *cénacle* and who earned his living prosaically." [8]

Vigny found the newly mushrooming industries of the

country ugly. Liberals were disappointed by the policies of the new regime. Socialists were horrified by the government's severe repression of workers' demands for social justice. A more general and broadly moral complaint was that money, together with the practical and material values for which it stood, was acquiring a new and overwhelming importance. Men of letters recognized and resented the imposition of commercial bourgeois standards in areas of life that had previously been (or seemed) exempt. Not only the narrowly bourgeois era that followed the July Revolution, but all of the century seemed suspect, corrupt and inferior. Chateaubriand's early description of the sensitive modern's "disgust for his century"[9] was elaborated by Stendhal, who called the century "boring" and "morose," by Balzac, who attacked its hypocrisy, and by Musset, who found it "impious" and "tasteless." Later, Leconte de Lisle would condemn, in terms that suggest Flaubert,

le siècle assassin
De toute passion vigoureuse et profonde.[10]

Most specifically denounced, of course, was the importance of money, "the worship of the golden calf," as Balzac called it, in what Vigny termed "this society based on gold." The world had become a place, wrote Leconte de Lisle, where men die stupidly while filling their pockets. A letter of his, written in 1839, sums up the late romantic *l'art pour l'art* idea that the culture of the century was inseparable from the bourgeois triumph: ". . . this century in which everything that is beautiful, everything that is noble and great, meets only contempt and disgust . . . which recognizes nothing but gold for its God, and which crushes underfoot all adoration for the true and the beautiful."[11]

Bourgeois himself, the late romantic writer despised his own class for the position of dominance it had reached by 1830.

He looked back with nostalgic regret to an earlier time when the French bourgeoisie had been more imitative of the aristocracy or had modestly kept to its place. Flaubert in particular might have found T. S. Eliot's description of the evolution of the middle classes in England in close accord with his own conception of French social history.

> At the stage of dominance of *bourgeois* society (I think it might be more exact to say here "upper middle class society") there is a difference applying particularly to England. However powerful it was—for its power is now commonly said to be passing—it would not have been what it was, without the existence of a class above it, from which it drew some of the ideals and some of its criteria, and to the condition of which its more ambitious members aspired. This gives it a difference in kind from the aristocratic society which preceded it and from the mass-society which is expected to follow it.[12]

Like Eliot, a Stendhal, a Vigny, a Flaubert, might be accused of having wanted to turn the clock back, for they were all troubled by the crystallization of what they regarded as a new and disappointing society in which they found premonitory symptoms of what is now coming to be called the age of the mass-man. Like many twentieth century critics of mass culture, they too were uneasy about the formation of a large new petty bourgeois reading public and resented the concomitant changes in the economics of book publishing and the effect these changes had on their personal situation in society. They felt exposed to a public vitiated by the spirit of the times, a public they could not entirely respect, but on which their success depended. We shall later have occasion to return to the resemblances between the anti-bourgeois writers of the nineteenth century and the "maladjusted" nonconformist intellectuals of the twentieth, with their common feelings of superiority and isolation in society and their common inability to produce novels peopled by confident and cheer-fully "engaged" young heroes.

However violently and harshly a writer attacked the bour-geoisie, he could not easily escape the central condition of his own life: He was a bourgeois too. He was in the curiously ambiguous position of having, for the most part, grown up in a bourgeois household and of having acquired considerable sympathy for many bourgeois virtues and ideals, and even the habit of exercising them. On the other hand, through some quirk of fate, he had been fired with the ambition to enter a profession that, thanks to his romantic heritage, he thought was dedicated to values irreconcilable with those of his family, his class and his century. Bound to the bourgeoisie by his origin and by tastes and needs inculcated in him since child-hood, such a writer felt himself split in many ways and prey to numerous disagreeable feelings of solitude, insufficiency, guilt, shame and resentment. There was in the nineteenth cen-tury a veritable flood of confessions of self-division and am-bivalence. Did not that same Gérard de Nerval who prayed God to let him create a universe all his own where he might be master of his "eternal dream" also confess he was "alas! the son of a century stripped of illusions, who had to touch be-fore he could believe"? [13]

The effect such feelings have produced in literature is far richer and far more interesting than a simple gallery of cari-catural portraits of the bourgeois, and far deeper and subtler than the familiar arrogant expressions of contempt and hatred. Not only frustrated minor poets and playful Bohemians but also the most eminent literary figures of the century owed some of the complexities of their work to their divided feel-ings about the new bourgeois world. Among them were Stendhal, Balzac and Flaubert. Spaced a generation apart, each of them inherited his childhood image of the bourgeois and grew up to create a new and more unfavorable portrait as both bourgeois society and the artist's conception of his work evolved in the course of the century.

It is in the novel, and particularly the novel that portrays contemporary life, that the question of the "bourgeois" is most brutally present. My aim has been not so much to expatiate on the personal feelings of the writer toward the real living bourgeois as to observe the ways in which his attitude and consciousness of his situation in society have affected his characterization of heroes drawn from his conception of the bourgeois world around him. That is why Stendhal, Balzac and Flaubert will be the major objects of study in the chapters that follow. They are the great novelists of the century, and, moreover, they are the creators of hero types that are responsive in a negative way to the great changes that the bourgeoisie produced in nineteenth century France.

All three of these men have been called "realists," and all three were romantics. Yet both labels are too vague and too confining for them all. In this particular context, we might say that a realistic novelist is one who cannot ignore the candidacy of the bourgeois for serious, even heroic, treatment in a novel. This requirement is met by Stendhal, Balzac and Flaubert, but it is met with doubts, reserves, hesitations and some resentment. In this, we might say, they show their romantic qualities. Their heroes are thus products of conflicting forces within the novelists themselves. They tell us little of what we may want to know objectively about the living bourgeoisie of the July Monarchy or the Second Empire. But they do tell us a great deal about how these individual writers came (or failed to come) to terms, in their work, with the society in which they lived and how the very concept of the literary hero was subtly altered in reaction to social change.

Harry Levin has mentioned, as an example of the weak or unadventurous literary protagonist, the hero "whose bourgeois environment affords little scope for exploits and passions on the epic or the romantic scale." [14] This was indeed one of the reasons for Stendhal's and Flaubert's discontent. We can go a step further, however. The reason for a romantic novelist's impatience with such a bourgeois was that he wanted to sympathize with his hero. Any novelist writing in the path opened by Rousseau and eighteenth century sentimentalism was bound to be troubled by the question of the degree of sympathy he could accord to his hero. His uncertainty and anguish were especially acute when the hero was bourgeois and had to get along in a bourgeois environment. In grappling with this problem, Stendhal, Balzac and Flaubert succeeded in producing complex and delicately shaded portraits of heroes who were both bourgeois and unbourgeois, whose situation was comparable to that of the writer and whose action was inspired by his own temptations to compromise and concession. Toward such heroes the novelist could be both tender and cruel, suggesting hidden pity and fear. Thus, the realistic-romantic novel could become a modern tragedy, into which the writer poured his personal feelings of discontent and in which he expressed his inability to ally himself wholeheartedly with the conditions of his own life.

There is clearly something Hamlettian about these new heroes, and the vogue of Hamlet in France is surely more than a mere by-product of literary cosmopolitanism. As a symbolic figure of indecision and inaction, the lonely prince of the Renaissance, so addicted to self-reproach and self-justification, found a spiritual home among the spiritually homeless postromantic generations of French artists and intellectuals. Yet the sense of loneliness and estrangement, with its accompanying paralysis of heroic action, establishes only a coincidental bond of sentimental union between the melancholy Dane and such curious reluctant bourgeois types as Lucien Leuwen, Lucien de Rubempré and Frédéric Moreau. To understand these modern heroes of Stendhal, Balzac and Flaubert, we must try to see them through the artist's own eyes, and, to do so, must reconstruct his conception of contemporary bourgeois society and his situation in it.

The Bourgeois Before 1830

The new opposition of writers, artists and intellectuals to the bourgeoisie developed in an atmosphere in which two other kinds of opposition were influential: the traditional opposition of the aristocracy and the nascent hostility of the proletariat. It was not new to define the bourgeois by opposing him to other groups, like the aristocracy, the clergy and the military, but the way in which he was opposed to both the artist and the worker was unprecedented, for it was determined by a combination of social and literary conditions that had never existed before.

Nevertheless, the word "bourgeois" had in its long history accumulated a rich deposit of meanings and values that inevitably affected later conceptions. The nineteenth century hostility toward the bourgeois was certainly facilitated and even to some extent guided and channeled by attitudes and concepts inherited from pre-Revolutionary times.

As early as the twelfth and thirteenth centuries, the bourgeois had become the victim of satirists, although he hardly monopolized their talents. In the *fabliaux*, for example, the bourgeois emerges with traits that have become traditional. He is prudent and thrifty, even avaricious, reluctant to bear arms and, though a strong family man, unable to keep a firm grip on the affections of a young and pretty wife. This medieval satire of the bourgeois, like that of the *vilain* and the clergy, is crude, mocking and disrespectful, but it is not intellectual, pessimistic or revolutionary. One finds in it scarcely a breath of true hostility, jealousy or scorn. It provides some of the armament for future attack, but little of the spirit.

The cessation of hostilities at the end of the Hundred Years War created vast opportunities for the expansion of commerce, and in the time of Louis XI the bourgeoisie began to acquire a new importance and wealth; soon it was launched on its irrepressible rise to power. Already during the fifteenth century there were attacks on bourgeois who seemed indecently rich. As early as 1422, in the famous *Quadriloque invectif*, the poet Alain Chartier associated the bourgeois primarily with their wealth. We readily recall the humiliation of Jacques Coeur, who had shocked public opinion by surpassing the highest nobility in wealth and princely magnificence. But in spite of his commercial gains and the purchase of titles and estates, the bourgeois continued to be satirized more in the role of the deceived husband than as a parvenu whose culture contrasted grotesquely with the fortune he devoted his life to accumulating. Renaissance collections of stories, such as the *Quinze Joyes de mariage* and the *Cent Nouvelles nouvelles*, are full of ribald, mocking tales in the fashion of Boccaccio, but, like Rabelais's great works, are malicious rather than hostile.

With the centralization of political power and responsibility in the monarchy after the time of Joan of Arc, Paris gradually became the undisputed center of the realm. More and more, fashion, taste and ideas emanated from the capital, and more and more the manners and language of Paris became a model for refinement and elegance. During the Renaissance the king's court acquired an unprecedented brilliance and importance, culminating in the splendor of Versailles. The early sixteenth century excursions into Italy and the spread of the Italian Renaissance into France had turned French kings into patrons of the arts and their aristocratic followers into courtiers. The salons of the *précieuses*, the love plays of Racine, d'Urfé's *Astrée* and the *romans-fleuves* of Mlle de Scudéry provided examples of gallant and tender behavior that the ladies and gentlemen of Versailles studied and imitated.

Deprived of many of its former functions, the fashionable Italianized "world" of the court taxed the industrious and increasingly important bourgeois with two complementary reproaches: When he sought to take the court as his model, he was a vain and ridiculous upstart; but, if his manners failed to reflect those of the court, he was vulgar, naïve and uncouth. Contemporary lexicographers were less cautious than the academicians of today, and did not wait for current usage to become past history. Oudin's *Curiositez françoises* (1640), a book designed to supply provincials and foreigners with the latest innovations in Parisian speech, defined "bourgeois" as *sot* and *niais* ("stupid" and "silly"). In 1680, Richelet defined some common expressions as follows: *"That is utterly bourgeois*, that is, lacking polish and elegance; *he looks bourgeois*, doesn't look like someone from the Court, isn't quite polite, is too familiar, and not respectful enough." On the other hand, Furetière, recalling Molière's treatment of a bourgeois who imitated the manners of the court, appended the following comment on *Le Bourgeois gentilhomme* to his article on "bourgeois" (1684): "This play makes fun of a bourgeois who tried to turn himself into a gentleman."

Molière has been rightly called a "bourgeois poet." The bourgeois characters most cruelly under attack in his theater—the Arnolphes, Harpagons and Dimanches—are few in comparison with the equally bourgeois *raisonneurs*, the men of good sense and moderation. Moreover, M. Jourdain, with all his pretensions, is not nearly so despicable as the aristocrat

Dorante and the comical, contemptible marquis of a number of other Molière comedies. Though the bourgeois was good for many laughs in the seventeenth century, he was not generally despised by men of letters. Most writers were themselves of bourgeois origin, and although they sometimes allied their fortunes with the pleasure of the king, they did not yet see good reason for hating their own class. Indeed, serious philosophical writers like Pascal and Descartes carried bourgeois culture to great heights without invading the fashionable world of Versailles. Nor was Paris totally neglected by the great dramatists in favor of the court. An intelligent and active bourgeois public filled the Paris theaters, a public Corneille is said to have preferred to all others.[15]

Bourgeois language and manners had not yet been released from the comic level. Heroes and style still were supposed to be "noble," and not until after the Revolution would a Victor Hugo assert, too boastfully, as usual, that he had freed "familiar" words from Vaugelas's emprisoning lexicon, words "Expressing only abject and familiar life, / Vile, degraded, blighted, bourgeois, good for Molière." Moreover, writers favored by the court were apt to be aware of the difference and inferiority of "the city." "The bourgeois," Scarron held, "is always a copier of the court." La Bruyère, always sensitive to social distinctions, remarked that Paris ordinarily "aped the court," although the imitation was not always successful.

For all these seventeenth century overtones, the word "bourgeois" was still far from its romantic and post-romantic equivalence with terms like *épicier, philistin* and *Béotien*. Yet nineteenth century vilifiers of the bourgeois could claim inheritance of a usage that excluded him, if not from the world of philosophical and scientific knowledge and eloquence, at least from all that was modish, elegant and courtly. The bourgeoisie of the century of Louis XIV included great men of ideas and of letters, jurists and parliamentarians. The king's great minister Colbert belonged to a family that had engaged in commerce for generations and was regarded by his contemporaries as bourgeois. Yet, even in his most varnished and respectable state, the bourgeois of the seventeenth century was but a successful imitation of his model, the *true* gentleman of quality, the aristocrat. Voltaire, cultivated son of a successful bureaucrat, but beaten by the lackeys of the Chevalier de Rohan, stated the matter very succinctly: "In a monarchical state, *a bourgeois* is a commoner."

This snobbish aristocratic understanding of the word "bourgeois" was inherited and exploited by future generations. Whatever other meanings the word may have kept or acquired, it would continue to suggest a man whose speech, manners, attire and whole way of life were inferior to the graceful and cultivated fashion of Versailles society or the *beau monde*. Thus, Leroux's *Dictionnaire comique* retained its original 1716 definition of the adjective as late as the edition of 1786: "Manner of speaking common to persons of quality in Paris, who say of everything that differs from the manner of the Court, '*that is bourgeois*,' and mean that it is inferior, stupid, naïve and artless." In the same year the Academy dictionary defined "having *a bourgeois look, bourgeois features, bourgeois manners*" as "having an undistinguished appearance, a vulgar countenance and manners different from those of high society people." Almost a century later, Littré still included one denigrating definition, "man lacking distinction"; he cited seventeenth century texts, but, interestingly enough, failed to label the meaning as archaic or obsolete.

Although the bourgeois of the nineteenth century continued to be vulnerable to ridicule based on reminiscences from the seventeenth century, he was no stranger to the royal court of the parliament-dominated monarchy of the citizen king. By 1830 the bourgeoisie was no longer an aggressively rising middle class; it had reached its apogee and was fairly secure from the attacks of the feebly resistant Carlists. The aristocracy had either been reduced to relative economic and political insignificance or had intermarried or identified its interests with the conservative element of the bourgeoisie. No doubt, some bourgeois found closed doors in the faubourg Saint-Germain, and others still bore their ancient stigma in the provinces; nevertheless, despite enduring nuances of social distinction, a moment had been reached at which there were no more important privileges to claim from above, but only those to protect from below. Thus arose the new opposition between bourgeois and proletarian, the importance of which was to surpass the residual opposition between the bourgeoisie and the nobility (as well as oppositions between the liberal bourgeoisie and authoritarian elements in the military and the clergy).

The concept of the bourgeois as an important and privileged person, socially superior to all others save the nobility and the clergy, can be traced to the Middle Ages. His privileges were implicit in the feudal expression *bourgeois du roi*, which denoted exemption by the king from normal feudal duties and services. In the late Middle Ages, the burghers of free towns won and maintained independence from the feudal system, patronized a vigorous art and literature and were, within the walls that protected their little worlds, free citizens of commonwealths in miniature. But when the monarchy acquired strength, centralized the government and began to regularize the national boundaries of France, the careers of many bourgeois families were radically altered. It was then that so many bourgeois bought titles, lands and privileges and sought, often with complete success, to be assimilated into the nobility. This process continued in the eighteenth century, despite a growing shortage of offices and military commissions, and despite the jealousy of the older *noblesse d'épée*.[16] Even later, the two Napoleons and the intervening kings swelled the ranks of the nobility with fresh batches of promising bourgeois.

What distinguishes the bourgeoisie of the eighteenth century, however, is not its social inferiority to the aristocracy, but a fresh consciousness of its intellectual superiority, its economic importance and its political progressiveness. As the French political scientist Charles Morazé says, the class now tries "to create a moral and economic doctrine which will constitute its theoretical basis and its intellectual justification, and which will effectively assure its spiritual unity." [17] The successful bourgeois of the Enlightenment is less ashamed of his class than his grandfather was in the age of Louis XIV. He is hungry for knowledge, eager to dispel the foggy mysteries of religion, curious, argumentative and aggressive, and has a dream of peace, prosperity and progress. He founds academies and concert societies, and gathers with his friends in salons and masonic lodges. Later, his eighteenth century conquests will bring him reproaches. Men will attack the fences he has built around his property, the capital he will make out of the Revolution and his exploitation of industrial workers, but without his leadership, there would have been no Age of Reason, no Revolution and probably no romanticism in France.

The eighteenth century model of humanity, as Paul Hazard puts it, was the bourgeois *philosophe*, who replaced the older ideal of the *honnête homme*.[18] These were both gentlemanly ideals. To the new concept of the *philosophe*, however, we might add that of the *citizen*, equally new, equally bourgeois, but more aggressive and more self-interested.

The *Encyclopédie*, among other texts, related the bourgeoisie to the exercise of civil rights and duties: "The *citizen* is a bourgeois considered in relation to the society of which he is a member" (Bellin, article on "Bourgeois"). The Revolution, it will be recalled, declared not only the rights of man, but also those of the citizen. Interest in citizenship was not a wholly new phenomenon, but, although concern for civil rights and duties had been strong among the burghers of medieval free towns and parliaments, the idea of national citizenship resisted development in France until the eighteenth century, when the bourgeoisie began to raise strenuous objections to internal tariffs, toll roads and other impediments to commerce and industry.

Arguments in favor of civic responsibility, however, were largely proposed by bourgeois and for bourgeois. As in England and in the United States, it was understood that only propertied individuals could run a government responsibly. Such arguments did not necessarily imply any desire for revolt against the throne, violent attack on the nobility, or the establishment of a republic. But they did sponsor the feeling that property was a primary determinant of political as well as economic injustice.

Before the Revolution, one important voice identified the origin of social inequality with the private possession of property. It is Rousseau who, in his *Discours sur l'origine de l'inégalité parmi les hommes*, leads us directly to Gracchus Babeuf and through him to socialistic and egalitarian thought of the nineteenth century. Babeuf was perhaps the first Frenchman to draw the attention of the lower classes to the fact that political liberty is not totally dissociated from economic independence. In the famous *Manifeste des égaux* the Babeuf group protested vigorously against the restriction of voting rights to the rich. Thus the new combat between rich and poor was not purely a question of property for property's sake. The nonimitative, nonassimilative bourgeois of whom Morazé speaks, sought political equality in the eighteenth century and secured it by the Revolution. From then on, all Frenchmen were declared equal before the law. But, like Orwell's animals, some got to be more equal than others. It was not until 1848 that all Frenchmen acquired the right to vote and hold office, regardless of how much they paid in taxes.

The constitution of 1794 did not immediately inspire hostility toward the bourgeoisie, as such, although there was agitation against the "gilded million" or, as Frenchmen say today, the "two hundred families." Even later, during the Restoration, Saint-Simon and Fourier did not clearly define an antagonism between the poor and the bourgeoisie. Saint-Simon, it is true, divided society into the slothful and the productive (*oisifs et travailleurs*), but there is no correspondence at all between his conception of these two groups and the Marxist opposition of capitalist and proletarian. In fact, Saint-Simon, like Proudhon, felt that even bankers might play a very important role in the redistribution of funds and the organization of a new society.

The year 1830 was in this connection as in many others the pivotal date. Only after the July Revolution did France become clearly aware of the existence of a proletariat, and only then did the proletariat and its sympathizers attribute its misery to the bourgeoisie. Enfantin, one of the Saint-Simonian leaders, observed in August 1830: . . . "It is no longer a question of priests and nobility, as it was in 1789, or even in 1829, but rather an opposition between the people and the bourgeois, or, better, between *working people* and the leisure class." [19] On March 21, 1831, at the beginning of a six-month period of uninterrupted rioting in Paris, the Saint-Simonian *Globe* repeated Enfantin's formulation, but in more detailed and hostile language:

It would be a mistake to believe that the most important fact of the Restoration was the reappearance of Jesuitism and the old nobility. The fundamental character of the period is marked by the triumph of the Bourgeoisie. . . . Now, the *bourgeois, in his role of bourgeois*, produces nothing, teaches nothing and has no other care than for himself . . . his loftiest ideas in politics can scarcely rise higher than the *conservation* of the present situation, the *status quo*, the *"juste milieu."* But what we have in the present situation is a slothful class living in the midst of a hard-working society.[20]

Much more incisive and interesting are the remarks of the Saint-Simonian, Jean Reynaud, who was perhaps the first to unite the scattered threads of anti-bourgeois, anti-property and republican sentiment into a new understanding of the word "bourgeois." For Reynaud, a reinstatement of the ideals of the Revolution (those, that is, that compose its most appealing slogan—liberty, equality and fraternity) required two major reforms, both of which were denied the workers until 1848. These were the right to organize and to be represented in the parliament. He pleaded eloquently for these reforms in two notable pieces of writing: an article in the *Revue encyclopédique* of April 1832, "De la Necessité d'une représentation spéciale pour les prolétaires," and the article entitled "Bourgeoisie" published in 1840 in the third volume of the *Encyclopédie nouvelle*.

"I hold," wrote Reynaud in the first of these articles, "that the population is composed of two classes, with a different station in life and with different interests. These are the proletarians and the bourgeois." Now, as early as 1680, Richelet had recorded in his dictionary that workers called the man who hired and paid them "le bourgeois." Yet, although the conflict may then have already been potential, Reynaud's thesis would have been impossible before 1830. Such a formulation had to await the creation of an industrial proletariat, employed irregularly and often not at all, ill-fed and ill-housed, discontent and ready at moments of crisis to take arms and barricade the streets. A difference of situation between employer and worker had existed for centuries, but in this new era both workers and bourgeois recognized a concomitant difference of interests, productive of mutual hostility and of a struggle for power for the bourgeois and liberty for the worker.

Men of letters were well aware of this new national problem, and it was inevitably to affect their assessment of the bourgeois, however conservative their own political views might be. In 1832, for example, Vigny wrote in his *Journal:* "The whole political issue today is the improvement of the condition of the most numerous class and agreement between property-owners with their inherited wealth and proletarians with the productive capacity of their labor." Both Stendhal and Balzac recognized the existence of a class struggle, although they described it in the older terms of "have versus have-not." Stendhal's banker Leuwen reads in Louis-Philippe's face the intention "to frighten the property-owners and persuade them that this is a war waged by those who have nothing against those who have something." [21] The words of Balzac's usurer-philosopher Gobseck express almost exactly the same idea: "Everywhere the struggle between rich and poor has set in, everywhere it is inevitable." [22]

The signal fact of this era was that political power, personal liberty and the pursuit of happiness were intimately associated with wealth, property and income. At the core of Reynaud's analysis of contemporary society is his choice of production as the primary criterion of the proletarian and income as that of the bourgeois:

> I call proletarians those men who produce the wealth of the nation, who possess only the daily pay for their work, which in turn depends on circumstances over which they have no control, and who derive each day from the fruit of their labor only a small portion which is itself always being reduced by their need to compete for it.

> I call bourgeois those men to whose destiny the fate of the proletarians is submitted and fettered, the owners of capital, who live from the annual income it brings them and keep industry in their pay.[23]

It is very likely that this manner of opposing the two groups was derived from Reynaud by Louis Blanc, when he wrote a decade later: "By *bourgeoisie* I mean all those citizens who, in possession of capital or the instruments of labor, work with resources that belong to them and depend on others only to a limited extent. The *common people* are those citizens who, owning no capital, depend entirely on others as far as the prime necessities of life are concerned." [24]

Liberty, Reynaud maintained, is essential to bourgeois status. But when he names as "bourgeois" "every citizen who is personally free," this definition depends on the following concept of the free man: "He whose sole engagement in society is that of a reciprocal contract, who is obligated only insofar as he also obligates others, and who works, but with the opportunity of controlling his work." Those whose situation does not satisfy these conditions can exist only by relinquishing their liberty. The proletarians, who must compete with each other for each day's insufficient pay, cannot enjoy real liberty. Too weak individually to demand a "reciprocal contract," they are legally forbidden to organize for their economic advantage and, voteless, cannot elect a parliament that would grant them the right to do so.[25]

Since the exercise of civil rights, from voting and holding office to service in the National Guard, depended on the possession of wealth and property, it is hardly surprising that the July Monarchy was attacked on moral as well as economic and political grounds. Wealth and property were denounced, not only as the appurtenances of a new bourgeois "aristocracy," but also as the chief values of a materialistic society that, if it was not entirely bourgeois, had been invaded from top to bottom by a corrosive hunger for money and material advancement. Saint-Simon had once predicted the morbidity of any society dominated by the passion for money. With the July Revolution many contemporaries felt that such a society had become a reality and that the bourgeois monarchy of Louis-Philippe had indeed made money its god and was worshiping above all other values the safe investment yielding a sure 5 per cent. To vote, to be a citizen, to have a voice in the government, there was but one official bourgeois formula: "Get rich!" Guizot himself had said it. According to one caustic journalist, Hippolyte Castille, the majority of bourgeois adolescents in school under the reign of Louis-Philippe were calculating and ambitious, morally unprepared to govern responsibly, their education distorted by the inordinate importance society was teaching them to attach to money.[26]

At the same time, it must be admitted that the vices of the bourgeois monarchy were recognized, proclaimed and condemned by bourgeois moralists. If the bourgeoisie of the nineteenth century failed to satisfy the demands of its new social authority, it was at least not so monolithic as to be incapable of providing some of its own sons to lead movements of reaction, revolt and protest.

Although the word bourgeois seemed often the equivalent of wealth, comfort, social leadership and political power, it also retained a "middle-class" meaning. Cognizant of the existence of a new society, a contemporary encyclopedia, *Le Dictionnaire de la conversation et de la lecture* (Paris, 1833), defined the bourgeoisie as follows: "[It] constitutes that middle class which is equally distant from the wealth of high finance and the misery of the common people: Viewed this way, the bourgeoisie is today the second order of the state, since, as things are now, the financiers seem destined always to be in the first rank."

It was indeed commonly asserted that the world of banking and high finance constituted a new aristocracy. Paul Thureau-Dangin, the historian of the July Monarchy, said in his discussion of the "omnipotence" of the bourgeoisie after 1830: "It was asserted that the reign of that class tended to establish a new feudalism, 'financial feudalism,' or, to use Proudhon's language, the aristocracy was replaced by the 'Bankocracy.' " [27]

Though it was not a novelty for *la haute banque* to occupy the top drawer of the bourgeoisie, its new, undisputed position suggested that money was the chief determinant of social rank. The bank did not enjoy an unmixed prestige; it never had. Financiers like Law and Bernard in the eighteenth century had excited a hatred and distrust for banking and speculation. Those feelings persisted, but bankers were both more respectable and more formidable in a society in which "king, legislator and merchant," in Baudelaire's words, were all bourgeois.[28]

Beneath the level of high finance, the bourgeoisie descended gradually, according to power, property, education and manners. It included all degrees of industrial, commercial and professional people. At its lowest, among the small shopkeepers and minor functionaries, it was not always clearly distinguishable from the lower classes. It was a group in constant flux. On the upper fringe, there was a considerable amount of brisk trading for the still highly esteemed aristocratic titles, involving, it is true, some sacrifice of status for those aristocratic families that married their children for bourgeois gold. From the class below, energetic and fortunate workers and peasants passed into the petty bourgeoisie and enabled their offspring to climb still higher, while, conversely, the poorer bourgeois lived in constant danger of the dreaded descent into the lower depths of the common people.

Yet the bulk of those within the indefinite confines of the bourgeoisie recognized what had become almost a national ideal. This was the status of the *bon bourgeois,* the *rentier.* It was founded on money, and for it the security of an income was essential. Whether that income was derived from the investment of inherited wealth, huge commercial or speculative profits, or the savings of a lifetime of thrift, the man who could live on it without working had achieved a solid bourgeois status.

The *rentier* ideal evoked scorn from many, but envy often accompanied it, as in Henry Monnier's satirical portrait:

> As for the Bourgeois, in the strict sense of the word, according to the grammar of the National Guard, he is represented by a man with an income of a good three or four thousand pounds, in debt to no one, eating well and drifting comfortably down the stream of life with cozy feet, cotton in his ears and a cane in his hand. . . . There is not a single little merchant, be he a haberdasher, a seller of hardware or toys, or even a grocer, who does not dream for the closing years of his life of this happy and trouble-free existence of the Bourgeois.[29]

Money was the key to this paradise, just as it was the requisite for voting, public office and all manner of success, liberty and happiness. It was no wonder then that all, save the most hopelessly poor and miserable, recognized the pressing need to achieve or maintain the comfortable, though sometimes despised, status of the bourgeois.

The New Situation of the Writer

The novelist or poet of the July Monarchy was not a detached observer of a society in which he had no personal involvement. His hostility, resentment, loneliness or discomfort was not simply the product of a clearly defined conflict between him or his profession and the ideals of bourgeois society. He often felt at least partly estranged from his own family, divided within himself, tempted by success and subject to outside pressure. He might even be uncertain about his place in the literary profession, especially if he saw it as a cog in the bourgeois machine and began to worry about his own complicity and the falsification of his personal situation. His feelings about the bourgeois and the role and character he assigned to a bourgeois hero in his novel depended not only on his perspicacity as an observer and critic of society but also on his personal security and sensitivity, his reasons for becoming a writer, his family's attitude toward his career and a great many other individual circumstances.

The writer· was almost certainly a bourgeois himself. He usually could not feel entirely bourgeois, though. This was partly, as Sartre has said, because writers had been so dependent on the nobility in the seventeenth and eighteenth centuries. They had been adopted by the aristocracy, "had been washed clean of the traces of their humble background," and had been allowed to feel at home among their betters. In a society run by bourgeois, writers felt they had been left dangling, considered themselves *déclassés*.[30] Also, even though the profession of letters required an education of a sort that only the son of a bourgeois was likely to get, writing was an abnormal bourgeois career in 1830. It was hardly the kind of breadwinning occupation for which one might purposefully prepare and train oneself in bourgeois institutions of learning. It did not promise the kind of life one could plan out carefully in advance. To many parents, it seemed a queer notion to try to earn one's living solely by writing books, instead of finding a comfortable and time-tested place in one of the regular bourgeois professions.

The general tenor of bourgeois life suggested that a son either continue his father's work or enter an occupation of at least equal social status and financial promise. Indeed, the very estimable ideals of progress and self-improvement led parents to hope that the boy's talent, intelligence and education, aided by family resources and a good marriage, might carry him to a higher level. Higher education was not expected to awaken dreams of a literary career, but rather to lead to law, civil service, medicine or, at the very least, to a notary's office. Such an attitude, wise and solicitous as it might be, could cause a young man ambitious for a literary career to resent family opposition and to strain at the bonds attaching him to the bourgeoisie.

"Painting and poetry, equally abominable in the eyes of one's family," said Gautier, remembering his own youth.[31] The examples of family opposition are legion. Gautier's father could really have been much more difficult. Although he opposed Théophile's becoming a painter and a poet, and urged him constantly to study law, he seems to have done so primarily because of the financial hazards of a life in art, and it must be said in his favor that the Abbé de Montesquiou's interventions finally won his consent. Among the more comfortably situated bourgeois, this was not an uncommon response. Victor Hugo's mother was much more amenable, but she too wanted a demonstration of talent before according her whole-hearted approval. Balzac's family gave him a trial in Paris, stipulating that if he produced nothing that would impress a competent judge of their choice, he should abandon his hopes. Flaubert's father seems to have talked him into his law studies, and it took the old man's death and a crucial attack of the famous "malady" to launch the author of *Madame Bovary* on a literary career. Others met even more resistance at home. Gérard de Nerval's father first wanted him to become a diplomat and, that failing, tried to shunt him into medicine. Arsène Houssaye, Nerval's friend and the editor of *L'Artiste*, tells the story that Dr. Labrunie once burned a sheaf of Gérard's poems in a fit of anger, "saying many nasty things about all poets." [32] Baudelaire's mother and stepfather did their best to discourage the poet from undertaking a literary career, even sending him off on a long sea voyage, as if to break up a love affair that threatened to end disastrously in marriage.

These incidents do not prove that bourgeois families were necessarily hostile toward art and literature. It is clear, however, that the profession of letters imposed financial risks and a way of life that did not meet bourgeois standards of comfort and security. Many bourgeois parents' objections, far from being spiteful and repressive, were inspired by a genuine concern for the future happiness of their children; and although happiness and security seem seldom to have been favorable conditions for the production of great works of art, they are not necessarily mean and despicable values. The eighteenth century had demonstrated that imaginative writing (chiefly novels and the theater) could be moral, respectable and even profitable. But only a handful of writers were able to amass even small fortunes. If only bourgeois parents could have been assured that their sons' books would sell like *Manon Lescaut* or *La Nouvelle Héloïse*, many of them might have gladly fostered their children's talents; but the sad destinies of Gilbert and Chatterton, as well as the less spectacular misery of a host of other writers, were as conspicuous in the home as in literary circles and in the pages of Vigny's *Stello*.

The question of a career was not of course the only source of family disagreement. Conflicts between fathers and sons do not usually wait for the ambitions of late adolescence. Though these may cause great irritation, a *violent* reaction on either side often stems from earlier sources of opposition. An obvious example is that of Stendhal, who detested his father long before he thought of writing a novel. Baudelaire, too, rejected his stepfather independently of the quarrels over his career. One might even go so far as to wonder whether a youth who is happily integrated into the life of his family can be moved to sever the bonds of common interest and love and enter a life foreign to all he knew and was content with in childhood. Perhaps an unhappy childhood is not, as Cyril Connolly says, an essential ingredient of "the one golden recipe for Art," [33] but there are few who have managed to do without it.

The details about family strife and an unhappy childhood, however important to the understanding of the course of an individual writer's life, do not really answer the very large question: Why, at this moment in history, did so many children of the bourgeoisie dream of abandoning the ideals and careers of the class of their origin in favor of a life in art?

The surge of young hopefuls into the world of arts and letters was not, to be sure, quite like the sudden, unannounced opening of a floodgate. The enormous intellectual development of the bourgeoisie in the century of Voltaire and Diderot and the creation of what the sociologist Karl Mannheim calls a bourgeoisie of *Bildung* [34] (as opposed to one founded purely on property) had measurably raised the social status of writers and encouraged the publication of books before the Revolution. Writers were lionized in the bourgeois salons of Mme Geoffrin and Mme Necker, sought after by aristocratic ladies, and asked to grace the courts of powerful foreign monarchs like Frederick the Great and Catherine of Russia. The vogue of tears and sentiment loosened the purse strings of ladies all over France and started the demand for popular novels of a kind that was to turn publishing into an "industry" in the 1820's and 1830's.

Quantitatively, the great expansion of the profession of letters (and of artists too) seems to have taken place after

1815, perhaps mostly during the July Monarchy. It is then that one begins to encounter complaints about competition and the debasement and commercialization of literature. Everyone wants to become a writer now,[35] observed Sainte-Beuve in 1839. Never, according to Hippolyte Castille, was so much printed as in the reign of Louis-Philippe.[36] Speaking of the novel, the publisher Werdet declared: "This new literary genre began so to expand at the end of 1830 that all France seemed to have become an immense reading room where everyone was impatiently awaiting his turn to devour each freshly hatched work." [37]

As these observations may suggest, it is almost impossible to isolate three interlocked phenomena from one another: the increase in the number of writers, the expansion of publishing and bookselling and the development of the public. Unfortunately, although the existence and growth of a larger and hungrier public offered some encouragement to would-be writers of all kinds, the level of its literacy was disappointing. A vast and new body of readers had been added to the book-buying public between the Revolution and 1830, but many of the most sensitive and gifted writing pens in France were alienated from it and were quick to denounce its bourgeois quality and taste.

Ironically enough, despite the "abnormality" of art or literature as bourgeois professions, and despite the bourgeois family's horror of the poverty and immorality of the artist's life, the increase in the number of writers was causally related to the circumstances under which the bourgeoisie achieved its triumph. Romanticism, as Arnold Hauser reminds us, was, in its origins, "an essentially middle-class movement." [38] We can go beyond this. Not only did the sentimentality, the moralism and the individualism of pre-Revolutionary bourgeois France and its literature help create romanticism as a literary phenomenon, but they also had much to do with the formation of attitudes that could only promote hostility toward the money-oriented, opportunistic bourgeoisie of the nineteenth century. And romanticism and the industrial revolution, with their moral implications, caused a proliferation of writers in the July Monarchy and aggravated the confusion and ambiguity of the feelings of sensitive writers toward their families, the bourgeois and sub-bourgeois public and all contemporary society.

The very ambition to be a writer can be and has been a phase of bourgeois development, even when that ambition was abandoned at the age of reason and sobriety. Both Jérôme Paturot and Joseph Prudhomme, in the long seriocomic histories of their careers, passed through Jeune-France-like stages in their youth. Oscar Wilde once remarked that whereas in England, every artist wants to be a bourgeois, in France, every bourgeois wants to be an artist. The joke has its limitations, but hits its mark among some of the art-crazed bourgeois youths of the second romantic generation. The standard type of middle-class subscriber to the *Constitutionnel* or the *Débats* (whose *qualité moyenne*, one contemporary nastily remarked, was admirably suited to the *classes moyennes*), who found his diversion in a novel by Paul de Kock and in singing Béranger's songs after dinner, had its counterpart in the sighing bourgeois adolescent who imitated Hugo and Lamartine and recognized his destiny in the suicide of Vigny's Chatterton.

There is considerable irony in the fact that late romanticism, like the pre-romanticism of the eighteenth century, had many elements in common with bourgeois taste. Just as the *bohême* is an excrescence of bourgeois culture, the taste and passions of many immature enthusiasts cannot be completely detached from the themes that charmed and entertained a large segment of the vulgar novel-reading public. Romantic themes, the sepulchral, the sentimental and the exotic, became immensely successful among the bourgeois and semiliterate popular public. In literature as in art, and even home furnishings and architecture, the bourgeois participated in the common rage for the satanic and the medieval. A shopkeeper, a petty government functionary or businessman (and, even more, his wife and daughters) might savor the exotic charms of American redskinned savages, of Turkish odalisques and African pashas, as well as the sex problems of impotent and transvestite lovers. Although those serious men who prudently cherished a more familiar or morally uplifting kind of entertainment might eschew the rasher new pleasures, the petty bourgeoisie and even chambermaids and concierges had become the clientele of a sub-romantic literary industry that cynically exploited the same themes that excited the self-styled individualists, culture aristocrats and Bohemian fanatics of the Impasse du Doyenné.

A passion for gaudy and sentimental romantic themes did not, of course, unite Pétrus Borel, poet of *Rhapsodies*, and these few bourgeois who read his novel *Madame Putiphar*. There were deeper and more important elements of the nineteenth century writer's bourgeois heritage that conspired to prevent his total alienation from contemporary society, while at the same time they conditioned him to feel isolated, superior, defiant and distrustful. In the immediate foreground, of course, was the series of quarrels between romantics and classicists. The second romantic generation had been schoolboys during the polemical 1820's. Attracted by the glamor of romanticism and excited to violent partisan passion, they accepted Victor Hugo as their god and the preface to *Cromwell* as their bible. The young writers of 1830 revered Hugo's *Orientales* primarily for the exotic coloration of their imagery, and as a bible of Art. Their enthusiasm, however, was not entirely inspired by literary romanticism. Sympathy for the Greek struggle for liberation was strong among all elements of the population during the last years of the reign of Charles X. The bourgeois, too, dreamed easily of exotic voyages, of melancholy love and military action, and regretted the glory of the Napoleonic era, especially in comparison with the exploits of Louis-Philippe's National Guard. Byron, who died heroically, if in bed, for the independence of the Greeks, was not only a mythical hero of poetry for the artist but also a hero of action and adventure.

At home the bourgeois lived tepidly, fearing democracy and permitting the troops of Louis-Philippe to fire on discontented textile workers. But the Greek war of independence had shown that the ideals of the Revolution were still strong when unopposed by economic interest. Frenchmen sympathized with the Greeks not only because of a sense of kinship with coreligionists oppressed by the heathen Turk but also because of a strong sentiment favoring nationalism, individual liberty and representative goverment. Even the most royalist romantics felt some solidarity with the bourgeois on these matters.

More important even than romanticism and the Revolution was the influence of the pre-romantic novel. Rousseau, Diderot and Bernardin de Saint-Pierre were sentimentalists and moralists. Like the *drame bourgeois,* their novels and their successes cannot be dissociated from the rising bourgeois culture of the eighteenth century. Rousseau, though, was set apart from the contemporary French middle classes by being a Protestant and a foreigner. He was also, as Joseph Aynard has said, the enemy of much that the bourgeoisie loved and lived for: "luxury and thrift, family authority and class superiority, property, profit, spending." [39]

Rousseau, like other pre-romantic writers, examined the sentiments of his heroes in such a way that the reader was tempted to identify himself with the writer (or a Saint-Preux) and with him to sense an opposition between himself and the external world. In the pre-romantic novel, the analysis of the human heart was individualized, and the hero was made the joining link in a chain of personal identity between writer and reader. Readers of *Manon Lescaut, Pamela, La Nouvelle Héloïse, Les Confessions* and *Werther*, although not prepared to condemn their fellow bourgeois for materialism, pursuit of money and interest, or ignorance of Art, would be inclined to recognize the superiority and sad isolation of the rare, sensitive, sympathetic, *feeling* soul adrift in an indifferent, if not hostile, world. Such novels establish between author and public bonds not of the intellect but of sentiment. By recruiting his potential sympathetic public among the *âmes sensibles* and by seeking rapport between the isolated unsocial hero and readers capable of sharing his passion, the romantic writer found and also created a new self-styled elite, instead of addressing a well-defined element of a stable and hierarchically constituted society. He did not please by appealing to conventional taste or convince by the logic of his argument, but blindly sent his book out on a sort of mystical journey toward soul mates everywhere (without irony, his *semblables* and his *frères*).

It is likely too that as Rousseauistic sentimentalists conditioned later generations of writers to accept the idea of a numerically limited elite, who would like themselves be superior to their contemporaries and isolated, even outcast from society, so also the philosophical critics of the *ancien régime* conditioned them to an enduring state of political discontent. The majority of political writers, like Helvétius, d'Holbach, Condorcet and even Rousseau, did not oppose the bourgeoisie. But in salon conversation, as well as in their writings, they created an intellectual atmosphere in which some degree of opposition to authority and to accepted ideas was constant, along with a spirit or feeling of moral superiority to the vulgar masses and to the court and the aristocracy. This atmosphere and this feeling were inherited by the romantics, who saw the bourgeois as a new kind of aristocracy and a new kind of vulgar majority group rolled together.

It is thus clear that although the literary generations of 1800 and 1810 did not find their anti-bourgeois sentiment among the dominant themes of the books of the preceding century—and in this respect they differ from those who followed them, for the latter, Flaubert's and Baudelaire's generation, were directly inspired and subverted by their elders—they were nevertheless prepared to sympathize with lonely victims of a cruel fate and armed to recognize the shortcomings of the bourgeois era. Anyone who had taken bourgeois political thought of the eighteenth century seriously was bound to be disappointed with the aftermath of the July Revolution. And anyone who had felt close to the victims of fate, like the Chevalier des Grieux, Saint-Preux and René, might feel himself the victim of society (and particularly bourgeois society) in 1830, like Chatterton or Dumas' Antony.

Publication and the Bourgeois Public

The relations between writers and their publics and publishers were often very bad after 1830. Some of the early publishers for romantics, like Renduel, Gosselin and Ladvocat, had won the esteem and friendship of the men who supplied them with manuscripts, but, as time went on, business principles tended to outweigh friendship and generosity, and competition for the favor of the bourgeois public imposed commercial standards on a profession that was most unused to them. Writers insulted their public in prefaces. The practices of publishers, editors and booksellers were "exposed" and attacked in letters, little reviews and books like Balzac's *Illusions perdues*.

Like the rest of society, the reading public had changed greatly since the Revolution. The new situation required adjustment on the part of writers and their intermediaries, and offered great opportunities for the exploitation of a vast new market. Where there were grounds for complaint, the villain was easily identified as the bourgeois, whether he was a reader, editor, publisher or fellow writer. Unsuccessful or petulant writers looked back with envy at rosy images they had built up of life under the *ancien régime* and at the very favorable conditions the early romantics had enjoyed during the Restoration. Young writers of the thirties went to see Vigny's *Chatterton*, the sad drama of a poet crushed by bourgeois society, and, identifying their fate with his, considered and even committed suicide. Perhaps Pierre Moreau accorded this work a little too much importance when he wrote that it was particularly from this play "that the young men of the second romantic generation who began their career toward the end of Louis-Philippe's reign derived their pessimism and their aversion for the bourgeois." [40] Hostility toward the bourgeois was already growing in strength before 1835, when the play was first performed, and there were enough important factors contributing to pessimism and anti-bourgeois sentiment to assure the growth of these feelings even if *Chatterton* had never appeared. It cannot be denied, however, that the play supplied a symbolic hero to the literary youth of the July Monarchy.

The new public was not entirely bourgeois. A large lower-class public was also in existence, swelling gradually during the course of the century. There were still a great many illiterates in France. Primary education was not universal before 1830. Nevertheless, illiteracy diminished considerably between 1829 (when 55 per cent of the military conscripts were illiterate) and 1847 (when the proportion had been reduced to 36 per cent).[41]

The enlargement of the public to include an increasing number of partly educated people encouraged many efforts to undertake the conquest of a mass public. Among workingmen, for example, were autodidacts who in the 1840's were devouring a literature of protest, writings that Heine, among others, saw being read and handed about in the workshops of the faubourg Saint-Marceau. To the extent that the *feuilleton* installments of the *Mystères de Paris* can be considered a work of social thought, such readers were also immersed in what Sainte-Beuve called "industrial literature." But the books Heine saw were of a grimmer stamp: speeches of Robespierre and Marat's pamphlets, Cabet's history of the Revolution and expositions of the doctrine of Babeuf, "writings that had, as it were, the smell of blood." [42]

These, however, were neither the writings nor the public that excited the anger or contempt of the anti-bourgeois writer. His hostility was directed principally against the newspaper *feuilleton* and cheap octavo novels and the easy successes of *amuseurs* in the theater, for it was in these regions of literature that contemporary "bourgeois" taste was formed and pleased and that names and fortunes were made. This was the sort of writing that could please both a true bourgeois and a sub-bourgeois public and unite them to form a huge, profitable mass public. The importance of such a public was recognized throughout the century and credit given to the low forms of literature that nourished it. As early as 1830, Henry Monnier, in his artlessly realistic *Scènes populaires*, described the efforts of a Paris concierge to spell out to her friends the text of a romantic novel. Champfleury maintained in 1857 that the true public was that of the penny dreadful (*le livre à vingt sous*).[43] A generation later, Zola, admitting

that most *feuilletons* were not true literature, still granted
them some literary value, because, as he said, the *feuilletonis-
tes* had created a new public among those who were incapable
of reading anything else.[44]

The *feuilleton* probably circulated more widely than any
other form of literature. That was because installments came
out in daily and weekly newspapers and because, with the
establishment of Emile de Girardin's famous *Presse* in 1836,
the newspaper became at last a medium of mass communication.

Probably no commercial development, not even the cheap
rental of books in *cabinets de lecture*, produced so sensational
an effect on the development of the public as the decision to
allow advertisements rather than subscription prices pay the
costs of publishing a newspaper. A newspaper of wide circulation (like *La Presse* or *Le Siècle*) could not interest its
readers with political articles and book reviews alone. Hence
the editors introduced the *roman-feuilleton*, which, together
with all sorts of premiums, served as bait to lure the public into
buying the paper and reading the advertisements, without
which publication was impossible. For that matter, the readers
of such papers were not limited to the subscribers. The *Revue
des deux mondes* or *l'Artiste* remained closed worlds to the
half-literate, but *La Presse, Le Siècle* or even the *Débats* could
be passed along to wife, children, neighbors and servants.
Chambermaids read the *feuilletons* after their mistresses, cooks
kept them handy among their pots and pans, and, torn and
grease-spotted, they descended at last to the concierge's lodge
for a final and painful reading.

Among the manufactures of the *feuilletons* were writers
whose own mentality corresponded to that of their readers
and who were condemned as "mediocrities" by their assailants.
Others were capable of better things but deliberately pro-

duced reading matter tailored to fit what they assumed to be the vulgar taste of a public they despised; these, in the nomenclature of their detractors, were the "prostitutes." These men, and the shrewd publishers and editors who employed them, bore much more of the brunt of serious writers' complaints than did the new mass public that had not quite got across the threshold of literacy.

Actually the years immediately following 1830 were still good for the trade in novels. Bookselling had undergone a sort of renaissance under the Restoration. From 1830 to 1840, according to the publisher Werdet, sales continued to boom. "These were the good days, the golden age for men of letters." Booksellers begged popular novelists for their latest pages. It is noteworthy, however, that those novelists whom Werdet lists as being most in demand were also those who had most conspicuously sought to please the general public: Dumas, Sue, Soulié, Kock, Karr and even Balzac.[45]

Poets, of course, had a different tale to tell. Even the great Hugo complained, in the preface of *Les Feuilles d'automne* (1831): "Unquestionably, even at the most critical moment of a political crisis, a pure work of art can appear on the horizon; but will not the passions, the attention and the intelligence of everyone be too absorbed by the social task?" Gautier, still very young and having more reason to feel neglected than Victor Hugo, exclaimed in one of his early poems (dated September 1831):

Oh, mon Jean Duseigneur, que le siècle où nous sommes
Est mauvais pour nous tous, oseurs et jeunes hommes!

* * *

L'art et les dieux s'en vont.—La jeune poésie
Fait de la terre au ciel voler sa fantaisie
Et plie à tous les tons sa pure et chaste voix,
On ne l'écoute pas . . .[46]

There were other troubling signs. Ladvocat, the celebrated publisher of many romantics, among them Hugo and Byron, was reduced to poverty in 1831. Royal censorship, at first removed, was reimposed. Later, in 1839, Sainte-Beuve began his famous article "De la Littérature industrielle" with a recital of the misfortunes that attended the sale of books of high literary quality after 1830. He was doubtless thinking mostly of his own, though, and may not be the most trustworthy witness.

Werdet, who had spoken in such glowing terms of the sale of novels before 1840, admitted that a turning point was reached that year. From then on to 1860 (when his own book *De la Librairie française* was published), he felt the fever was subsiding. Only a few of the *cabinets de lecture* survived the debacle; only rare privileged authors continued to dictate terms to their publishers.[47]

Between moments of great confidence, Balzac also was critical of his public in the middle thirties. In 1834 he wrote optimistically to his future wife, Mme Hanska: "We have reached *the era of intelligence*. Brute force and rulers of material things are on their way out. There are intellectual worlds where one may find Pizarros, Corteses and Columbuses. There will be sovereigns of the universal realm of thought." [48] But in another letter, written just two years later, his tone is radically different: "See how all society conspires to isolate superior men, how it hounds them up onto the heights. . . . No one comes to our aid. The masses do not understand us; superior people do not have the time to read us and to defend us." [49]

As a representative of the serious artistic or thinking writer, Balzac reproached the middle and upper levels of the bourgeoisie for failing to take him seriously, to consider imaginative writing as a vehicle for important ideas, and art as the highest achievement of human culture. His reproaches do not seem to have been wholly unfounded. In an important study of the literary situation of this period, Jules Marsan describes the main functions attributed to works of art by the bourgeois as follows: "The triumphant bourgeoisie wanted an art that suited it: vulgar, prudent, concerned with morality and principles, capable on occasion of bringing a tear to the eye and of dispensing healthy good cheer. Above all, it had to be an art without extravagant pretensions and was not supposed to exceed its natural functions: to entertain the respectable citizen and give him rest from graver cares." [50]

Edmond Goblot, who has treated the question of the French bourgeois in a perceptive and diverting book, agreed that on the whole the bourgeoisie of the middle nineteenth century had no great love for the arts. A doctor's study was furnished with medical books, a jurist had his tomes on law, but apart from these and a collection of dusty classics, the books in the average bourgeois household were likely to be in the ladies' bedrooms and boudoirs, for only they were thought to have the time and the mentality necessary for reading poems and novels and other useless frivolities.[51] At his socialistic worst, the artist was a menace, at his artistic best an innocuous fool, at least until toward the end of the century, when at last it became fashionable again for men of weight and substance to cultivate the artist and when writers were once more the lions of salons and high society.

Marsan's formula explains, indeed it is derived from, the success of the *amuseurs* in the theater—Scribe, Augier, Labiche, men who specialized in poking fun at the bourgeois, but very carefully and very inoffensively. It was the theater, contemporaries acknowledge, that offered the richest rewards. Most dramatic authors, said Heine in 1840, are getting rich and living in luxury, while the greatest French novelists and poets, ruined by Belgian pirated editions (that sold cheap and paid no royalties) and by the miserable state of bookselling, languish in poverty.[52]

Most writers were reluctant to admit that art required no vulgar monetary compensation. Sainte-Beuve's approval of the financially disinterested writer was partly the result of his own failure to please profitably and a matter of sour grapes. But even he cited Boileau's acknowledgement of Racine's right to be paid in money.

> Je sais qu'un noble esprit peut, sans honte et sans crime,
> Tirer de son travail un tribut légitime.

There was inevitably some envy and jealousy in the outpouring of contempt for the successful mass-public writer. Even serious and "artistic" writers were well aware that literature, like everything else, had turned into a commercial product and that success, influence and importance, as well as income, were coming to be related to sales. Balzac summarized the feelings of many writers much less successful than himself when he wrote Mme Hanska in 1835: "A fine thing indeed to hear stupid compliments on works written with our blood and which don't sell, when M. Paul de Kock has a circulation of three thousand copies and *Le Magasin pittoresque* has sixty thousand." [53]

There were indeed many brutal things said about the popular writer, prospering unduly at the expense of better men, robbing them of their money, their glory and their public. "If there is anything a thousand times more dangerous than the bourgeois," wrote Baudelaire in 1846, "it is *the bourgeois artist*, who has been created to be interposed between true genius and the public." [54] Flaubert is full of hatred when he speaks of Eugène Sue:

> At Smyrna, during some rainy weather that prevented us from going out, I got Eugène Sue's *Arthur* from a lending library.

It's enough to make one vomit; there's no name fit for it. You have to read that sort of thing to realize how pitiful money, success and the public are. Literature has got consumptive. It spits, it drools. It covers its pustules with pomaded taffeta and has brushed its head so much that all its hair has fallen out. To cure this leper we need Christs in Art.[55]

Elsewhere he has poured out his accumulated rage on Béranger ("that dirty bourgeois who has versified easy love encounters and threadbare clothing"), Feuillet ("a pure zero"), Scribe, Delavigne and Paul de Kock.[56] Kock was of course a favorite whipping boy of the commercially less successful writers. The best word about him is Gautier's, who said maliciously but with some justice that he had the advantage of being exactly like his readers.[57]

In the protests against the success of the Paul de Kocks and Octave Feuillets, there is true concern for artistic integrity, disgust with inferior writing and impatience with the injustice of public esteem. There is also implicit in these protests a discontent with the turn that the economic situation of writers and publishers had taken. Commercialism had become an element in all writers' conduct of their profession. Except for small, privately printed editions, literature reached the public, as it does today, by passing through the hands of commercial intermediaries. These men kept themselves and their businesses alive by profiting from sales. Whether he liked the idea or not, a writer who expected to get his work into print at another's cost—not to speak of profiting from it financially—was dependent on the taste and pleasure of the public. This in itself was no novelty in 1830; what was new was rather that the public had changed, had incorporated new elements and constituted part of a new society, and that the mode of publication had adapted itself to the change. By 1830 private patronage was practically a thing of the past. Even private subscriptions accounted for the publication of very few imaginative writings. The so-called *belles-lettres*—novels, poetry, plays, essays—required for their acceptance some assurance of the sale of a profitable number of copies.

Even relatively intransigent writers had to recognize the grim reality of this situation and were not always above taking a commercial hand in transactions that might assure their fame and fortune. Baudelaire, for example, would write to his publisher: "My name is getting forgotten! And the *Fleurs du Mal*, which, ably handled, could in the past nine years have had two editions a year. . . . We must think of billboards, of publicity and advertising. If you feel I am asking too much, I shall put in some of my own money." [58]

Although Flaubert was sincerely unwilling to publish an imperfect book and genuinely disdainful of the public and success, he was not entirely honest in asserting that he felt neither the need nor the desire to see his work in print. He *did* publish, and apparently spent a fair amount of time securing for himself advantageous financial arrangements with Lévy (whom he usually called "the son of Israel"). Publication is unimportant, he declared, shortly before submitting the manuscript of *Salammbô* (1862); but a few days later another letter revealed that he was shrewdly calculating the most opportune moment for the book to appear.[59]

To see Balzac immersed in the economics of publishing is much less surprising, although he too found himself in an ambiguous situation. This is evident when one compares his fulminations against Paul de Kock with words like the following: "I have a deal with the *Débats* to give them all my prose at a franc a line. That should fetch a howl from M. Seidlitz, the German poet, who is also a baron and a landowner, and was so scandalized . . . to hear me talk about literary 'produce.'" [60]

The existence of a large bourgeois public (apart from the

semiliterate masses) and the development of an economics of publishing that tempted the writer with a dream of wealth, comfort and bourgeois success placed him in an ironic situation. Like his fellow bourgeois in other professions, he was in the position of having a product to sell and customers to please. The esteem and power attached to commercial success made failures of those who did not achieve it. However proud he might say he was of his small sales and his limited and esoteric public, the writer who failed to please widely felt neglected and unsuccessful. It was almost inevitable that he should feel so, being exposed to the constant pressure of the new public values established under the bourgeois monarchy. Hostile toward the bourgeoisie, the writer felt himself maneuvered by history into a situation in which he could with difficulty avoid assuming a bourgeois pose himself. If we add the awareness of this problem to some of the other causes of ambiguity (family opposition, the disappointments of the July Revolution, nostalgia for the Napoleonic era and the vanished culture—both bourgeois and aristocratic—of the *ancien régime*), it is no surprise that almost every nineteenth century writer confessed in some way or other with Gérard de Nerval: "Je sens deux hommes en moi."

The Unheroic Bourgeois Hero

In 1838 Heine, a foreigner but no stranger to French literary circles, made the following analysis of the plight of the literary hero in France:

The tragic poet needs to believe in heroism, but that is entirely impossible in a country dominated by a free press, representative government and the bourgeoisie. . . . The diminution of all greatness, the radical annihilation of heroism, these things are above all the work of that bourgeoisie that came into power in France through the fall of the aristocracy of birth. In all spheres of life that bourgeoisie has caused its narrow and cold shopkeeper's ideas to triumph. It will not be long before every heroic sentiment and idea will get to be ridiculous in France, if indeed they do not perish completely.[61]

This is passionate and partisan exaggeration; yet Heine summarizes exceedingly well an idea and an attitude that are common to the three very different novelists whose heroes will be examined here. What sort of hero could be found and imitated with honesty and conviction in the France of Louis-Philippe? An old-time classic hero or a romantic one, in the style of the early years of the century, would have seemed like a modern Don Quixote, grotesquely out of place in a world from which storybook purity seemed to have vanished. Unlike Cervantes, the late romantic writer did not aim at "destroying the authority and acceptance the books of chivalry have had in the world" (if these words from the preface of *Don Quixote* really represent the author's purpose). Such authority and acceptance had already disappeared, and no small part of the anti-bourgeois sentiment was due to the romantic writer's resentment of their departure.

There were of course many kinds of representation of the bourgeois, some undertaken by writers and artists with whom we have no direct concern in these pages. The July Monarchy witnessed what might be called a flowering of caricature. One of the richest of all subjects for this caricature was the bourgeois. He was treated lightly and comically or sometimes attacked with savage and righteous anger by the creators of Joseph Prudhomme and Robert-Macaire. He also found his place readily as the central character of the comedies of Scribe, Augier and Labiche, competent, workmanlike jobs, but totally unrelated to the problems that concern us here. At another level, almost beneath literary consideration, is the popular "realistic" novel of Pigault-Lebrun, Ducray-Duminil and Paul de Kock. The last of these, who rivaled Eugène Sue and Octave Feuillet in popularity, had almost no trouble or misgivings in producing bourgeois heroes. He wrote unabashedly for the philistine public. "What my readers want," he wrote in one of his prefaces, "is a work which pleases them and which is natural enough for them to be able to identify themselves with the characters." [62]

There is doubtless much to be learned about the bourgeois from a study of the works produced to please him. In these pages, however, attention will be centered on novels of more enduring importance, for we are concerned not so much with anti-bourgeois sentiment for its own sake as with the role it has played in the creation and complication of the novel and its hero in modern times. Stendhal, Balzac and Flaubert were neither representative nor typical writers of their times. What brings them together here is that they were all responsible for novels that are sincere works of art in which the bourgeois is the hero. As artists, Stendhal, Balzac and Flaubert were all troubled and engaged by the problem—and indeed the challenge—implicit in Heine's complaint.

In art there is no single right and scientific solution. And so, there can be no question of proving that the bourgeois was or was not capable of heroic status in the nineteenth century novel. It is equally futile to ask whether the novelist's conception of his hero is right or wrong. Like all broad literary terms, the word "hero" loses all meaning if one tries to pin it down and define it in any absolute way. Such words have their own histories, and every man is entitled to his own conception of what a hero should be. For that matter, at any given time factors that determine his conception are different.

The chief question posed here can be stated briefly: From a combination of the novelist's awareness of the past literary and social status of the bourgeois, his awareness of the changes in society and of his own personal and professional situation, and his feelings about all of this, what sort of character emerges as the hero of a novel about modern bourgeois life? The naturalistic trend in the evolution of the novel and its growing importance as an art form impelled Stendhal, Balzac and Flaubert to consider their novels of modern life as much the future monuments to their talent as any tragedy would have been in the seventeenth century. Despite their varying degrees of hostility toward their century, they could not exclude the portrayal of contemporary society from their novels; they were, on the contrary, very much drawn toward it. One of the avowed purposes of Stendhal's writing *Lucien Leuwen* was the analysis of the structure of French society; the subtitle of *Le Rouge et le noir* was *Chronique de 1830*. Balzac conceived his *Comédie humaine* as a vast epic of modern humanity. Flaubert composed in his *Education sentimentale* what he called a "moral history" of his generation. Nor were these rare and unusual efforts. Comparable projects occupied George Sand, Victor Hugo, Lamartine, Vigny and many lesser writers, all of whom acknowledged some social consciousness, if they were not necessarily prepared to agree with Sainte-Beuve that "the human epic" was "the mission and task of art to-day." [63]

The novels of Stendhal, Balzac and Flaubert are neither pure documentary "novels of manners" nor pure psychological analyses of lovelorn characters unencumbered by a complex social setting. In them we can discover the secret ideal heroism the novelist cherishes, and understand how his reluctant choice of a contemporary bourgeois hero hinders and masks the kind of heroism for which Heine was so nostalgic. The writer's own ambivalent feelings about his age are revealed not only in background commentary but also in the action of the hero and in the warmth, irony and distaste the language describing that action communicates. Such heroes as Julien Sorel, Lucien Leuwen, César Birotteau, Lucien de Rubempré and Frédéric Moreau both represent and betray their creators, though in very different ways. Directly and indirectly, they expose not just the writer's enthusiasms and sympathies, but also his reserves and antipathies. All creatures of a bourgeois age, these heroes are expressions of the growing sentiment among anti-bourgeois writers that they could feel more sympathetic toward a solitary, sensitive and inactive hero than toward one who had innocently and whole-heartedly made his pact with contemporary society.

It is not going too far back to begin with Stendhal. His intellectual and sentimental formation belong to the eighteenth century, the Revolution and the Empire; but he was a true romantic, writing in the manner of a gentleman who had lived beyond his time into a new crude age of materialism, hypocrisy and social degradation. Better than anyone else, Stendhal can usher us into the bourgeois nineteenth century. His heroes are closer to us than Chateaubriand's René, Byron's Manfred and even Musset's *"enfant."*

Balzac was to some extent Stendhal's literary contemporary, but the fictional world he created was that of another generation, a full-blown bourgeois world of which Stendhal's was only anticipatory. Balzac was a loyal citizen of that new era, although even in his acceptance, there was an element of protest and compromise. His *César Birotteau* is significant for its failure to represent a "heroic" and truly "bourgeois" bourgeois hero, as opposed to Stendhal's success in creating an "unheroic" and "unbourgeois" hero in *Lucien Leuwen.*

Flaubert, an adolescent during the July Monarchy, lived to bear witness, not so much to the crude vigor of that aggressive era, but to the later shame and moral decadence of the bourgeoisie under the Second Empire.

The sequence of the works of these three men is no strict chronicle of the progressive alienation of the kind of modern artist who has been forced to the margin of society, if not into permanent exile. But each can cast some light on the emergence in the twentieth century of what Wallace Fowlie has called "the modern hero of inaction." [64] In the great French novels of the bourgeois nineteenth century were born the prototypes of Swann, Bloom and all those introspective twentieth century heroes who can reconcile their personal feelings and worldly success only with a sense of compromise and loss.

II · Stendhal—The Bridge and the Gap Between Two Centuries

Bas, ridicule, bourgeois en un mot.

STENDHAL

Stendhal was only fifteen years younger than Chateaubriand, a scant generation behind those "precursors" of romanticism who flourished during the Empire. But unlike Chateaubriand and Mme de Staël, whose work has retreated to the ghostly though respectable limbo reserved for so many important landmarks of literary history, Stendhal has acquired an ever-increasing freshness and contemporaneity since the time of Taine. That he outlived his century is partly because he was never comfortably at home in it. Attached by reason and sentiment to the eighteenth century, Stendhal was never entirely happy with his situation in post-Revolutionary France, and it is the very quality of his dismay and its literary expression that makes him akin to the writers of our century.

Jokingly, Julien Sorel once said to himself: "In truth, man has two selves within him." [1] These words might be taken as the motif of the great nineteenth century bourgeois writers, whose subtle minds were always prey to ambiguous feelings and contradictory impulses. Stendhal himself was doubly heir to the eighteenth century's sceptical disillusionment and its romantic sensibility and dreams of progress and perfectibility. Diverse influences were at work on him from childhood on, from the time when he was most attached to his rakish uncle Romain and his "Spanish" great-aunt Elizabeth, and when his favorite bedside books were *Les Liaisons dangereuses* and *La Nouvelle Héloïse* ("I who thought I was at one and the same time a Saint-Preux and a Valmont" [2]). Among the contradictory, though not mutually exclusive, elements of the adult Stendhal's character we must begin with a recognition of his allegiance to disparate elements of the century in which he was born.

The novelties born of political change affected him early. Although his father's family had been in the lower ranks of the seventeenth century *noblesse de robe*, and in his own lifetime Beyles and Gagnons alike were all well-to-do gentlemen of the high bourgeoisie of the *ancien régime*, Henri Beyle's formal education began in 1796 in one of the new Revolutionary Ecoles centrales—an abrupt step from an old world into a new one. After this untraditional schooling, the stages of his career correspond roughly with the succession of early nineteenth century governments: He was a soldier under the Consulate, a bureaucrat during the Empire, journalist and man of letters for most of the Restoration and finished off his life in the consular service under the July Monarchy. It was a life filled with rude shocks, unrealized hopes and disabused ambitions. Younger men, the generations of Vigny and Musset, were to suffer from a sort of second-hand nostalgia for a past they knew only by hearsay, and to feel compelled to declare the inferiority of the present. Stendhal, at least, had known something at first-hand of what Vigny called the "ancien bon ton du monde" and, though no fighting man, had participated in the Napoleonic adventure.

Throughout his life, Stendhal disapproved and felt estranged from many persons and places in the world he was compelled to inhabit. He professed hatred of his father, of Grenoble, of the bourgeoisie, of the aristocracy, indeed, at moments, of all France. One aspect of this general attitude merits particular attention here—his hatred of his own time or, more specifically, of the post-Napoleonic era. It was always his habit to dissociate himself from the present and to disavow sentiments of loyalty or attachment to the political regimes that succeeded Napoleon's downfall. Although his education and military career situated him inevitably in the nineteenth century, he set himself apart from contemporary society, condemning it for the disappointing changes it had undergone since the Revolution. *Le Rouge et le noir* could not have been written before the Revolution or even before Waterloo, but it is not an expression of solidarity with the new era. Instead, it is filled with regret and nostalgia for the world that the new century had demolished.

In the project for an article on *Le Rouge* that Stendhal sent to Count Salvagnoli in 1832, his criticism of the manners of the Restoration—"such are the manners that the government of Louis XVIII and Charles X has given to provincial life in France"—expresses the judgment of a historian who is sentimentally attached to the past and estranged by the present. Stendhal's condemnation of the new age is pronounced in the manner of a survivor from the eighteenth century whose taste is offended by what he considers a degeneration of his childhood world.

> Everything, but everything, is completely changed in France. . . . The *moral* side of France is unknown in other countries. That is why, before getting to M. de S's novel, I have had to say that there is nothing less like the gay, amusing and somewhat libertine France that was a model for all Europe from 1715 to 1789 than the grave, moral and morose France that we have inherited from the Jesuits, the *congrégations* and the Bourbon government of 1814 to 1830.[3]

Even though expressed indirectly (since they were destined to reach an Italian public under a name other than Stendhal's own), these reproaches constitute only a limited and narrow attack on modern France. They are specifically an indictment of the new, cautious manners of the aristocracy, rather than those of the bourgeoisie. The proletarian-oriented Saint-Simonians were abandoning attacks on the Jesuits and the nobility in 1832 and centering their fire on the bourgeoisie. But Stendhal was not a socialist, although he approved of republicanism in theory. He seems chiefly to regret the disappearance of wit, grace and elegance under the Restoration. His unfavorable comparison of the present in which his life was engaged, with a past of which he had only childhood memories culminates in a rejection of the new era that is neither political nor economic, but rather moral and esthetic: "this so moral, so hypocritical and consequently so boring century." [4] His ennui is not quite the later sentiment of a Baudelaire or even that of the young Gautier; it is largely the boredom of a cultivated gentleman of wit and intellect who misses the freedom and refinements of a time when conversation was less timid and inhibited and when society, for all its iniquities and faults, seemed likely to maintain a stable structure indefinitely, while even undergoing gradual progress.

Only those who lived during the last years of the eighteenth century, Talleyrand once said, knew that *douceur de vivre* for which Stendhal was so nostalgic. It was a time, the Comte de Ségur recalled, when "institutions were monarchical and manners were republican." It was also a time highly propitious for men of letters: "On many occasions, literary rank was even preferred to that of the nobility. Nor were men of genius the only ones to enjoy those tokens of respect that caused all traces of inferiority to disappear for them. For one often saw second- and third-rate men of letters received and treated in society with a respect that was not accorded to the provincial nobility." [5]

George Sand's grandmother's recollection of the world of her youth suggests strongly Stendhal's own feelings about the pursuit of happiness:

> Was one ever old in those times! It was the Revolution that brought old age into the world. Your grandfather, my daughter, was handsome, elegant, well-groomed, perfumed, cheerful, amiable, affectionate and well-tempered up to the day of his death. People knew how to live then, and how to die. . . . They felt it was better to die at a ball or a comedy than in a bed surrounded by four candles and ugly black men. . . . They enjoyed life, and when the time came to surrender it, they didn't try to spoil other people's taste for living.[6]

An admirer of those final gracious and philosophic years of the *ancien régime* might feel that when cruelly frank remarks were suppressed in those days, it was because of the dominion of good taste, tact, manners and politeness. The hypocrisy that Stendhal and Balzac, among others, found prevalent in nineteenth century society, both aristocratic and bourgeois, was considered the product of timidity and calculation, the fear of offending one's superiors, mingled with the ambition to rise to their level.

This was doubtless a result of living in a competitive, dynamic society, in which the increasing mobility of the individual was not unrelated to the advances of the bourgeoisie. Doubtless, too, the weakening of religion and the entire complex of bourgeois philosophizing that accompanied the rise of the bourgeoisie in earlier centuries had something to do with the many eighteenth century analyses of human conduct and character. The furthering of ambition through calculation and hypocrisy was studied by *philosophes* and *idéologues* before Stendhal ever laid a pen to *Le Rouge et le noir*.

Stendhal's triple condemnation of his time—moral, hypocritical and boring—is also the judgment of his most sympathetic heroes: young men sentimentally oriented to an earlier
time, solitary exiles in an age of vulgarized manners and crude
aggressiveness among the lower elements of society, and pallid
insipidness among the sons and daughters of the aristocracy
and upper bourgeoisie. His portraits of the contemporary
scene are always mirrors reflecting a degenerate image of a
more refined, more vigorous and more civilized era, of which
sometimes the Renaissance, but more often the last decades of
the eighteenth century, were the authentic but vanished model.

Yet Stendhal's distaste, boredom, disillusionment and
estrangement did not entirely disengage his interest in modern
French society, which, on the contrary, inspired several of
his greatest novels. Although none of them can be called a
"social novel," Stendhal by no means evaded and repressed
the unpleasant realities of the world about him. True, he was
not a social visionary, and did not seek to further any program
of social or political action through his writings. Detached and
critical as he was, his reproaches always have a personal bias,
for they are inspired by what offended his own sensibilities.
But he was still not the man to maintain, as Gautier did, that
revolution would affect him only when bullets broke the win-
dows of his study.

Stendhal's role of displeased spectator and his participation
in the almost universal concern of French writers of the 1830's
with the state of contemporary bourgeois society are most
directly and most interestingly evident in *Lucien Leuwen*.
Lucien Leuwen is quite literally a bourgeois, and, certainly,
even if his "heroism" requires definition, he is much more than
a neutrally observed central character. He is, however, a very
special kind of bourgeois, so special in fact that he is practically
déclassé, being dissociated both from the sort of bourgeoisie
his family represents and from the vulgar new kinds he en-

counters in what one might call his pilgrimage through life. He is also a special kind of hero, directly identifiable neither with the author (although there are close sentimental bonds) nor with the ideals of contemporary society, as Stendhal conceived them.

These ambivalences of Lucien's status in the author's esteem are best illustrated by direct allusion to the text. As in other novels of Stendhal's, there is in *Lucien Leuwen* a very remarkable scene of humiliation, in which the hero is subjected to physical indignity and a loss of moral dignity. Such moments are always curious, for they reveal simultaneously Stendhal's closeness to his heroes and his efforts to dissociate himself from them, the duality of Stendhal's own judgment of others and of his representation of himself. They are also far more revelatory of the impact of the nineteenth century bourgeois world on Stendhal's art than any direct attack on a unidimensional character could be.

Lucien at Blois—A Moral Comedy[7]

In October 1835 the Comte de Vaize, Minister of the Interior for Louis-Philippe, sends Lucien, then his confidential assistant, on a delicate and important political mission. In two localities in which the government's candidates for the Chamber of Deputies are weak, Lucien is expected to assure the defeat of the opposition by whatever tactics he sees fit to use. On the way to the first of the threatened areas Lucien and his helper, Coffe, stop at Blois for dinner. Having left a carriage-load of defamatory pamphlets outside the inn, they are peacefully seated at table when they hear the sounds of a mob assembling in the street. Their frightened host enters to tell them that their carriage is being pillaged. At the door, Lucien is greeted by a deafening shout: "Down with the spy! Down with the police official!"

Although aware that the activity in which he is engaged is not regarded with universal approval, Lucien's first reaction is neither fear nor dismay, but a shocked and outraged feeling of indignation: "Red as a rooster, he did not deign to reply and tried to get to his carriage. The crowd separated a bit. As he opened the carriage door, an enormous shovelful of mud fell on his face and then down on his neckerchief. As he was speaking to M. Coffe just then, some of the mud even got into his mouth." To cap this humiliation, so precisely and objectively narrated, a tall, red-whiskered clerk, observing the mud on Lucien's face, cries out to the crowd: "See how dirty he is; you have put his soul upon his face." This is indeed the cruelest blow of all. (Conceivably, Stendhal meant to recall Mme de Merteuil's physical punishment for her moral crimes. It was said of her, after smallpox had disfigured her beauty at the end of the *Liaisons*, that "her disease had turned her inside out and now her soul was on her face.")

Lucien is clearly unprepared to meet this situation. He is sincerely indignant, tries to get his saber out of the carriage and would defy the crowd with military courage if Coffe, a cooler head, were not at hand to stifle his protests and hustle him out of town. Once they are on the highway, Coffe analyzes the episode for Lucien's benefit and offers him some observations that fill the young hero with rage and shame.

"Well," Coffe answered coldly, "the minister offers you his arm when you leave the Opera. Your fortune is envied by magistrates on duty at the State Council, by prefects on leave and deputies handling warehouses of tobacco. This is the other face of the coin. It's that simple."

"Your composure is enough to drive me mad," said Lucien, beside himself with rage. "These indignities! That atrocious remark: 'His soul is on his face'! That mud!"

"That mud is for us the noble stain of the field of honor. That public uproar will weigh in your favor. These are the shining deeds of the career you have chosen and into which my poverty and gratitude have moved me to follow you."

"You mean that you would not be here if you had an income of 1200 francs."

"If I had only three hundred, I should not be serving a minister who keeps thousands of poor devils locked up in the dungeons of Mont-Saint-Michel and Clairvaux."

There can be no doubt that Coffe's voice is Stendhal's own. In it are reflected the irony, bitterness and detachment that color not only the author's personal view of contemporary politics, but all the political incidents of *Lucien Leuwen*. This does not contradict the fact that Lucien is the "hero" of the novel and of this episode as well. It signifies rather that Stendhal has identified himself partially with two points of view, that of Lucien, the subjective or sentimental hero, and that of Coffe, the objective or rational observer or *raisonneur*.

The interest of the above text resides not so much in its exposure of the eternal techniques of scheming politicians, or the revelation of Stendhal's well-known estimation of certain ministers of the July Monarchy, as in the curious kind of comical humiliation to which the author has subjected his hero. Lucien, his face covered by "an enormous shovelful of mud," is in a mortifying situation that was, if not exactly dear to Stendhal, at least something of an obsession with him. He had long before used a similar incident to illustrate his definition of the comic in *Racine et Shakespeare*. An elegantly attired person, leaving his carriage, falls flat on his face in a puddle of mud. According to Stendhal's analysis, the comedy in this is not merely the result of the contrast between the *before* and the *after;* the spectator senses that the victim has put himself into an embarrassing and inferior position, feels a momentary superiority and cruelly laughs.[8]

Both this incident and the episode at Blois can of course be viewed in a number of different ways. There is the point of view of the spectator in the narration—crude, vulgar persons in both stories; there is the humiliated protagonist, sensitive to the laughter, inwardly sure of some kind of superiority, but furious that the tables have been turned; and, omitting the unknown quantity represented by the reader, there is the author himself, deliberately plotting his hero's discomfiture, ironically, perhaps even with some intention of tormenting himself and hoping that the sympathetic happy few will see through the jest.

Of the several other such incidents in Stendhal's writings, incorporating falls, mud-splattering, the laughter of onlookers and injured pride on the part of the subject, perhaps the cruelest and the most injurious to a character's self-esteem is the fall taken by Dr. Sansfin in *Lamiel*. His frightened horse rears and throws the little hunchback head first into half a foot of mud, in full view of a group of jeering washerwomen. When Sansfin raises his muddy face, he too confronts a chorus of vulgar laughter. He then leaps furiously back on his horse and gallops away. Some of these details were also put into the account of Lucien's fall from a horse in Nancy before the window of Mme de Chasteller. There, it is true, Lucien escaped a mud-bath. Not so with Julien Sorel, who early in his stay in Paris fell from a horse and "covered himself with mud." Stendhal himself confessed in the *Souvenirs d'égotisme* that he had spent his life falling from horses,[9] and in the *Vie de Henry Brulard* he tells how he was almost thrown into the

Lake of Geneva and barely escaped being humiliated before his groom.[10]

Surely, then, with all these examples from reality and fiction, this matter of humiliation, this horrible and cruel experience of having to present a mud-splattered face to a laughing crowd, was as much "pour Dominique" as the sagest reflections on love and courtship. One might say that this experience stamps Lucien unmistakably with the mark of the Stendhalian hero. Yet, at a moment when the hero threatens to merge with the writer, Stendhal retreats. He seeks partial refuge in Coffe's coolly analytical personality and at the same time maintains an aloof objectivity. Despite his sympathy for Lucien, Stendhal amusedly watches the young hero turning "red as a rooster" and finds a perverse and ironic intellectual pleasure in pricking Lucien's sensibility to the quick.

There is not a breath of overt anti-bourgeois sentiment in this episode, but it is nevertheless a sort of literary proof of Heine's thesis. In Lucien we have a man who might have behaved "heroically" in another age, under another government or even, for that matter, under Louis-Philippe, if the ambitions proper to his class, his education and his family had not led him into a situation where heroism was absurd. Lucien's role is falsified from the start of this electoral adventure. He may behave intelligently, competently, courageously; but heroism is impossible. Once again, we might think of Don Quixote, especially as Arnold Hauser describes him, that is as a seriocomic combination of saint and fool, humorous in a new ironic way because of his ambiguity.[11] But this temptation should be resisted. Stendhal's writing is not "manneristic." He was too seriously sad and too personally involved with his age and his hero to be capable of the decorative, theatrical and sophisticated baroque irony. There was plenty of irony, to be sure; Stendhal was outstandingly ironic, but romantically, passionately, sentimentally, even bitterly so.

The deeper moral comedy implicit in the Blois episode is confirmed and defined in two almost identical marginal comments Stendhal jotted down in the manuscript. The first is opposite the beginning of the episode: "Source of the comic, the following absurdity: Lucien wants to combine the profits from his ministerial position and the fine sensibility of a man of honor." A bit below, the comment is expanded as follows: "GENERAL PLAN.—I am constructing the backbone around which the animal will be built. The laughter will come when I get to the outermost layer of the skin. *Source of humor.*— Lucien is playing a role that covers him with contempt and doesn't know how to swallow it. He wants to combine the profits of his ministerial role and the sickly sensibility of the perfect man of honor. *Good.*" [12]

Stendhal seems to have thought so highly of this observation that, as was sometimes his habit with such notes, he incorporated it into the text several pages later, in the form of a reflection of Coffe's (which he discreetly refrains from communicating to Lucien): "See how he suffers from his absurdity. He thinks he can combine ministerial profit with the delicate sensibility of a man of honor. Is there anything sillier!"

Now, at the moment at which these events took place, Lucien was not an altogether innocent young man. He had served long enough in the Army to take the measure of its men, and, both in the employ of the Comte de Vaize and in his father's salon, had witnessed and served as a subaltern in some of the political intrigues of the time. When asked to undertake the electoral mission, he had accepted only when assured the action would be bloodless. He is thus well aware that his role is not, at least according to his own standards, an entirely honorable one. But when surprised, as he is at Blois, he reverts to a "natural" and undissimulated display of sincere feelings of anger and shame. His imperfectly fitted mask slips, revealing ideals of honor and gentlemanly conduct that are incongruous with his situation and with his role. It is this incongruity that Stendhal labels "comic."

The narrative details of this incident are less important than the sentimental reaction they elicit from Lucien, the evidence of his sensibility. Stendhal in his notes stresses heavily the word "sensibility," qualifying it successively as "fine," "sickly" and "delicate." Let us not be misled, however, by the apparently pejorative sense that Stendhal gives to this word "sensibility" in a spirit of *sécheresse*. Lucien's sensibility makes him vulnerable to mockery, but it is also his true strength and virtue. And it is because this incident touches on Lucien's live *feelings* that it is significant. The factual historical information in Stendhal's novels has no value for the modern historian, Léon Blum has observed; whatever truth his work has lies in what he *felt*, "in what could stir or hurt his feelings." [13] Indeed, Stendhal himself asserted that he only wrote truthfully when his feelings were involved.[14] In this episode, the kind of humiliation Lucien endures is akin to feelings Stendhal himself knew very well. When he mocks Lucien, he is to some extent his own willing victim. But Lucien's story is not pure confession or self-analysis. It is the result of a problem Stendhal set himself in the representation of contemporary reality. Stendhal's elaborated conception of Lucien is meaningful only against the background of contemporary society as he saw it. It is only by sharing Stendhal's view of that society that we can understand his investing Lucien with a kind of "heroism" that depends partly on his failure to succeed in that society and on his lack of the kind of hypocrisy Stendhal felt was necessary for success in that sort of society.

A Problem in the Representation of Reality

Like all of Stendhal's heroes, Lucien Leuwen is disoriented and unattached, a stranger in the fictional world in which he moves. His sentimental isolation, however, is opposed to his bourgeois status, for Lucien is a scion of the new aristocracy of the July Monarchy. "Since July," his father tells him, "bankers have been at the head of the State. The bourgeoisie has replaced the faubourg Saint-Germain, and bankers are the nobility of the bourgeois class." [15]

Thus, unlike Julien Sorel, the hero of this novel is confronted by no important social barriers. This does not mean that in real life a banker's son would find no doors closed to him in all France. Within the novel, however, Lucien is rebuffed nowhere because of his origin. He is, in fact, much sought after by provincial aristocratic hostesses and is a highly privileged person. The *walls* of Verrières, which Mr. Turnell finds so conspicuously symbolic in *Le Rouge*, have no counterpart here.[16] Lucien has never had occasion to feel the savage isolation of "the unhappy man at war with all society." He has all a young man eager to be accepted by contemporary society could wish: wit, charm, beauty, intelligence, and the wealth and social position of his father.

Both Lucien's social origin and personal qualities vastly overqualify him for the bourgeoisie, as Stendhal understands the word when he expresses his horror of bourgeois pettiness and baseness and his distaste for "merchant grocers and the people with money." The loathed type of wealthy, powerful, rising bourgeois is better represented in this novel by Grandet, "the enriched ginger merchant who wants to get to be a duke," than by Lucien's cultivated, witty father, who is closer to the *haute bourgeoisie* or the enlightened aristocracy of the *ancien régime* or even of the Empire.

The moral death of the aristocracy in the nineteenth century is a constant theme in the writings of Stendhal. In his opinion, the *émigré* nobility, sobered by the Revolution and uneasy despite the Restoration, lacked the courage to be witty and the energy to be passionate—a judgment that is manifest in the early pages of the *Souvenirs d'égotisme* and in the second part of *Le Rouge*, when he had occasion to speak of the young noblemen of the time. "Good God!" he once exclaimed in the heat of his contempt. "How is it possible to be so insignificant! How can one depict such young men! These were questions I thought of in the winter of 1830, when I was studying these young men." [17]

The problem of representing young Restoration aristocrats like Caylus and Croisenois, so despised by Mathilde de la Mole, came up again in the process of the creation of Lucien Leuwen, aristocrat of the July Monarchy bourgeoisie. The reader will recall that crucial moment when, from behind the half-opened shutters of her window, Mme de Chasteller saw Lucien fall from his horse. Commenting on the incident, Stendhal entered the following note on his manuscript: "No sudden passion, only pricked vanity. He knows that he sits a horse very well, and is irritated that this pretty woman should have seen him fall. The rich young Frenchman: (1) does not think of matters of love—his century indeed discourages him from being in love; (2) lacks the courage to love. Leuwen, the type of rich young Parisian.—No, that won't do—too stupid." [18] A firm decision, but as late as January 1835, when he was close to the end of the second part of the novel, Stendhal still betrayed uncertainty about Lucien's character. "What is Lucien's character like? Certainly not

Julien's energy and originality. That is impossible in the world
(of 1835 and of 80,000 francs income). To suppose so is
clearly unrealistic." [19]

In these irritated comments Stendhal reveals his distaste for
the contemporary reality he feels he must portray. More than
that, he sees his task impaling him on the horns of a dilemma.
It would be "too stupid" to make a hero out of an average rich
young Parisian; but it would also be "impossible" to endow
any rich young man of 1835 with the qualities of a Julien
Sorel. Stendhal has a fixed conception (whether it is right or
not is irrelevant) of the character of a particular social or age
group at a chosen historical moment: A rich young man of
the July Monarchy is dissuaded from love by his *century*. In
Lucien's social and historical situation, Julien Sorel's energy
and originality are as impossible as Mme de Rênal's character
would have been "impossible in the midst of the gay life that
prevailed in France from 1715 to 1790." [20] (On the other
hand, in Mathilde de la Mole, Stendhal did manage to create a
character who, he said, *was* impossible "in our century"—
although Henri Martineau suggests that this remark was intended to protect Marie de Neuville, one of the models for
the character.) [21]

Stendhal, of course, had no interest at all in creating a vul-
garly "ideal" type of hero or of indulging in the escapism of
a daydream kind of novel. In his estimation the always perfect
and ravishingly handsome hero was fit only for the taste of
chambermaids, a taste he cannot be accused of having pleased.
He warned the reader of *Lucien Leuwen* to close the book,
if he were "bored, sad, consumptive, too noble or too rich."
Although the marginal notes reveal timidity before the public
and a tactful reluctance to speak in undisguised language,
Stendhal claimed dispensation from the care of pleasing the
general public, "which will consider these pages coarse and
insufficiently noble." [22]

It is, therefore, reasonably clear that Lucien's ambiguous status as a hero can be partly explained by the conflict between Stendhal's wish to make his central character a person who would be "possible" in the upper bourgeoisie and in the time of Louis-Philippe and his conviction that such a hero, if faithfully mirrored, would not correspond to his own ideals of courage, originality and vigor. This conflict led him to create a hero who, although a member and product of bourgeois society, is not comfortable in it and is "maladjusted" and discontent in the role assigned to him by the time and place of his birth. Although in principle Stendhal sought to achieve "realism" in his novels, he toyed with the idea that Lucien must be something of an anachronism. "He is not made for his century," says M. Leuwen. No Manfred, René or Chatterton, the more subtly drawn Lucien is by virtue of his sensibility and kinship with Stendhal a solitary romantic hero lost in a world to which he does not belong. This does not really make Lucien "impossible." Lucien *feels* foreign to his surroundings, but his character and behavior depend on them nonetheless. Heine maintained, we recall, that the truly "tragic poet" with his innocent belief in heroism had become an impossible anachronism, implying perhaps that "heroes" of the bourgeois present and future could be conceived only in a spirit of irony and with limited and confused sympathy. His thesis is exemplified by Stendhal's treatment of Lucien. Stendhal's narration of the action at Blois mocks Lucien's innocence and seems to turn him momentarily into a comic character. But Lucien's inability to play his part with consummate hypocrisy is funny only on one level; on another it is a betrayal of his heroic and tragic quality. Stendhal is a romantic ironist who laughs bitterly at what he respects most.

In a recent book on the theater P.-A. Touchard formulated the following difference between comedy and tragedy: "The relation between the image presented by the mirror and the spectator can be understood only within these two limiting cases: The spectator recognizes himself completely, and identifies himself with the image—or on the contrary he declines to establish this identity, denying any resemblance, any point in common. In the first case is born the tragic atmosphere; in the second, the comic. One implies participation, involvement, identification; the other, liberation, rupture, deliverance.[23] This distinction is not far from an epigram of Aldous Huxley's, "We participate in a tragedy; at a comedy we only look" [24]— which is in turn reminiscent of Walpole's famous quip, "Life is a comedy to the man who thinks and a tragedy to the man who feels."

For those who are sensitive to what Jean-Pierre Richard calls the two essential Stendhalian climates of *sécheresse* and *tendresse*,[25] *Lucien Leuwen* is simultaneously a comedy and a tragedy. In a formula Stendhal himself used in one of the prefaces he wrote for this novel, he seems to imply that he wrote a comic work with a tragic hero: *"Except for the hero's passion, a novel must be a mirror."* [26] Lucien is not entirely tragic, however. Although the participation of the reader (Stendhal) and his identification with his hero are intense, in some situations, among them the scene at Blois, the reader is also very much a spectator, and his participation is diluted, weakened or relieved by his apparent withdrawal and his refusal to "establish identity." There is a double process: maintenance of the tension of participation and temptation to be delivered of it. The result might be described, not as spontaneous and uncontrolled laughter, but as a wry, ironic smile. At such moments, Stendhal's style is richest and reaches its most appealing heights, mingling the passion, sympathy and violence of the romantic writer with the cool, remote intelligence of the enlightened analyst.

The Duplicity of the Stendhalian Hero

Lucien Leuwen is not a story of simple and open conflict between an individualistic hero and society. Lucien undertook his electoral mission unenthusiastically, as part of a job he did not want but had accepted because it fitted the role his father wanted him to play in society. This role is illustrative of the uneasy marriage of Lucien's sentiments and his conduct, a duality that is an aspect of what we might call his "duplicity" (since hypocrisy may be too harsh a word). This duplicity is inseparable from the question of the Stendhalian hero's engagement in society and from the quality of his heroism.

Lucien, I have said, does not disengage himself so absolutely from society as some of the more extreme romantic heroes, Schiller's Karl Moor, for example, or Byron's Manfred or Balzac's Vautrin. He is constantly making half-hearted efforts to engage himself and to do what is expected of him. With no need to rise in society, Lucien's only strong personal ambition is the pursuit of happiness. It is neither necessary nor possible for him to behave with bourgeois prudence or to display the driving courage of a Julien Sorel. His search for a career is motivated only by his awareness that society expects him to "succeed." To please his father and in response to the challenge offered him by his cousin Ernest, Lucien undertakes, though with lukewarm enthusiasm, the task of integrating himself into a society from which he is profoundly alienated. Ernest, the successful academic bourgeois, deplores Lucien's lack of gravity, his failure to assume an air of importance and substance. "Be serious," he advises his cousin, "assume the role of a grave and earnest man." But for Lucien the role Ernest wants him to play is rather that of *un homme triste*, and, worse, he fears that once he has mastered the role, it will become a reality. Nevertheless, he accepts one part after another, in the army, in the offices of the ministry of the interior, during the electoral campaign and in the courtship of Mme Grandet. All these roles he accepts out of a sense of duty, because they are what is expected of him.

The idea of action undertaken not for pleasure or intrinsic value, but as a response to duty, had been exposed earlier in *Le Rouge*. There the major steps toward the seduction of Mme de Rênal and Mathilde de la Mole are described as acts of courage, dutifully performed but accompanied by no thrill of pleasure. Julien's enterprises, indeed, seem much more than Lucien's the calculated gestures of a role, because the hero of *Le Rouge* is socially more insecure and more susceptible to ridicule and the fear of humiliation. Julien plots the conquest of his employer's wife so that he may not be mocked for failure to do what others might expect of him. The role *does* later turn into reality, perhaps even according to Stendhal's complicated formula for the development of love; nevertheless, even at the moment when Julien invades Mme de Rênal's bedroom, the idea of *duty* (Stendhal himself underlined the word) never ceases to be present in his mind. "Did I play my part well?" is the essential question he asks himself after the victory.

This "inauthenticity," as we might call it, is only one of the many aspects of Stendhalian duplicity: masks, roles, poses, diplomacy, discretion, timidity, charlatanry and hypocrisy, as well as the corollary attributes of sincerity and *le naturel*. All these aspects are of importance in relation to the problem of the Stendhalian hero's situation in contemporary society. They also are an expression of the author's own personal insecurity and timidity. In the marginal notes of *Lucien Leuwen* one often finds the treatment of a problem in the text compared with something similar in the life of Dominique. For that matter, Stendhal's fondness for pseudonyms, anagrams and code names (like Clara and Zotgui), and his frequent denial of personal responsibility for the statements of obviously sympathetic characters, add another dimension to the question of duplicity in his work. Moreover, we should remember that although Stendhal respected sincerity and naturalness, he was also contemptuous of naïve and blundering frankness, courageously forthright though it might be.

Stendhal felt that the exercise of hypocrisy and other modes of duplicity was a function of life in the bourgeois nineteenth century. Stendhal said once that the hypocritical Don Juan, in all his authentic vigor, was possible only in the Italy of the Renaissance. Nonetheless he called the nineteenth century "a hypocritical century" and declared the necessity of charlatanism in the degenerate time of the Restoration. "The more public opinion becomes queen in France, the more hypocrisy and *cant* there will be; that is one of the disadvantages of liberty." [27] It is evident that a contemporary hero incapable of some kind of duplicity would be defenseless, according to Stendhal. Disagreeable though the connotations of the word may be, duplicity is a means Stendhal allows the man of sensibility for coming to terms (or perhaps evading having to come to terms) with a world in which he feels apart and different.

This is also much the same conclusion reached by Victor Brombert, who, in a delicate and illuminating study of the "obliqueness" of Stendhal's style and of the oblique way in which he reveals his heroes, finds a relationship between Stendhal's own fear of the reader and Lucien's father's concern for public opinion:

Stendhal's fear of the reader is expressed in the character of Lucien's father by his constant concern for the impression

Lucien makes on social opinion. He never ceases to repeat to his son that he must learn to play a role and carefully hide his own true self. However secretly charmed he may be by Lucien's naïveté and by his "extravagances," he is afraid of unveiling his true feelings, but fears even more that Lucien will seem ridiculous in the eyes of others. Doubly vulnerable through Lucien, he instills in him the need for wearing a mask. Is not hypocrisy the only way of keeping one's independence in a hostile world? [28]

Lucien Leuwen does not have the kind of courage that has made other men shake their fist at the universe and defy their adversaries. He fits a series of masks to his face and flees into exile at the end. Already at Blois, he has a sense of being trapped by his own life. "I've done things wrongly all my life," he keeps repeating to Coffe, "I'm in a mudhole and there's no way out." But even Julien Sorel, with all his aggressiveness and calculation, is not capable of defining his situation honestly and lucidly until after he has been condemned to death. Then, at last, like the present-day hero of Camus's *L'Etranger*, he asserts openly his final and absolute opposition to a world in which he does not belong.[29]

Julien is in a special situation, different from that of either Stendhal or Lucien. He is constantly on the defensive, in fear of the reprisals that revelation of his true sentiments might provoke. He learned the use of hypocrisy as a weapon of defense early in his childhood, to combat the ridicule, abuse and brutal blows of his father and his elder brothers. Julien's rise from his peasant origins was at each step an assault upon a new bastion of society. In his subordinate position, at the Rênals' in Verrières, in the seminary at Besançon and in the Hôtel de la Mole, he was at all times susceptible to hidden and sometimes nonexistent affronts; he imagined that those around him, jealous of their superior position, were constantly plotting to humiliate him and keep him in his place. Julien's hypocrisy is therefore doubly inspired: It is an attack, calculated to further his aggressive movement toward worldly success; but it is also a protective mechanism, the product of fear and insecurity.

Yet, sometimes the mask slips and uncovers the "natural" Julien beneath it. He is "himself" when he complains to the Abbé Pirard of his boredom at the dinner table in the Hôtel de la Mole [30] and when he speaks with Altamira at the Duc de Retz's ball. On both occasions (and this by Stendhal's careful design, as he charts the course of Mathilde's passion), he is overheard by Mathilde. Both times, Julien's value rises in her esteem. To Mathilde, who, like Stendhal, despises the men of her time and class and judges Julien by standards she has derived from history, his secret character, proud, passionate and uncompromising, is a revelation of his true superiority.

Julien keeps his true thoughts and feelings secret from his father and brothers. Among them he is, as Dr. Sansfin says to the young Lamiel, "surrounded by coarse creatures to whom one must always lie in order not to be the victim of the brutal force they have at their command." He must make use of hypocrisy and charlatanism to succeed among the calculating bourgeois and timid aristocrats of the Restoration. His "real" qualities, those Stendhal himself admires, win the love of Mathilde, who, the author declares, is "impossible" in the nineteenth century. But, ironically, Julien does not dare to be sincere with her. Although she is won by his courage, his pride and his passion—qualities that must remain hidden to the world—Mathilde would be intolerant of his timidity, his fears and his anxiety. He is capable of pleasing Mathilde *naturally* when he does not know she is observing him, but alone with her, he must counterfeit a temperament that is not his own in order to please her special taste for being dominated and humiliated by her lover.

Julien is only really liberated from the practice of hypocrisy when he has nothing more to gain and nothing more to lose. In the courtroom at Besançon, before a jury of "indignant bourgeois," who he thinks will surely condemn him, he attacks their *caste* and denounces the suppression of the poor. In his cell he reaches the conclusion—Stendhal's own—that in his time almost everyone is and must be a hypocrite. What he had earlier taken for a particular he now recognizes as a universal. Even Napoleon, he decides, was a charlatan. " 'I have loved truth. . . . Where is it? . . . Everywhere there is hypocrisy or at least charlatanism, even among the most virtuous, even among the greatest.' His lips curled with disgust. . . . 'No! Man cannot put his trust in man.' "

The shadings of Lucien Leuwen's character are subtler and more delicate. Julien Sorel had been conditioned to be aware of his duplicity and had consciously (though unhappily) embraced hypocrisy as the only means suited both to his ends and to his situation. Lucien's comfortably secure place in society, on the contrary, did not require a posture of defense. Launched upon his career, Lucien is surprised and disgusted to discover that his new roles put him into ambiguous situations to which his childhood and adolescence had not accustomed him. It is important to recognize that he is not *naturally* a hypocrite and that duplicity is not such an ingrained habit that it has become an essential part of his character. Comparing Lucien with her circle of friends in Nancy, Mme de Chasteller realizes that, like herself, he is tender, sincere and ardent. This is Stendhal's own judgment: "She knows Leuwen and perceives *that he is not a hypocrite*." [31]

Stendhal is very careful to limit Lucien's exercise of hypocrisy in love. The young hero's courtship of Mme Grandet is a calculated act, but undertaken reluctantly and abandoned when Lucien is at the very threshold of victory. He toys with the affections of Mme d'Hocquincourt, but is determined not to let her become his mistress. "He does everything needed for her to adore him. He forces himself to play this comedy, but swears never to possess her. One day, tempted after a very emotional scene, he runs away. Lucien plays at *rouerie;* it is his only pastime." [32]

There is admittedly a complication introduced by the charlatanism Lucien practices when he pretends to a piety and to political beliefs that are abhorrent to him. He does this to obtain admission to the society of Mme de Chasteller. But this is not part of a Don Juanish seduction. It is love and not merely the desire for physical conquest that motivates his hypocrisy. He knows that Wertheresque love may be impotent if Don Juanish techniques are not employed to insure its success. Yet, Lucien can not play the part of a Don Juan. He lacks the talent. He is embarrassed and awkward in Mme de Chasteller's presence and incapable of abusing the advantages he has secured by his entrance into Nancy society under false pretenses.

Stendhal himself, we know, had complicated feelings about the great European myth of Don Juan. He was obsessed by the concept of the Don Juan type of character and found a troubling correlation between Don Juan's success in love and his cynical, polished hypocrisy. Stendhal admired Don Juan as an embodiment of some traits of his personal image of the Renaissance man, bold, vigorous and cunning; but he also despised him for his insincerity and was jealous of his success. In Stendhal (and in Lucien Leuwen) the sensibility and the virtue of Werther are dominant traits. Don Juan's libertine competence and success were impossible for Dominique and his hero, whose delicacy, timidity and authenticity reward them simultaneously with a feeling of superiority and with frustration and regret. Like Valéry's Narcissus, Stendhal might well have said of his *"inépuisable moi"*: "J'y trouve un tel trésor d'impuissance et d'orgueil. . . ."

"Le Naturel"

Let us now turn up the other face of the coin. Opposed to hypocrisy and its allied manifestations (charlatanism, artificiality and "bourgeois prudence and calculation") is the hidden figure of the "natural man." *Le naturel* is an individual virtue, obscured and suppressed by the social vice of hypocrisy. It is part of the tragedy in the lives of Stendhal's heroes that their better selves should be seen only through the chinks of the armor of hypocrisy that nineteenth century society compels them to wear. Such men are not wholly free. Their passions and energy are leashed, and the suppression of these qualities has become so habitual that they are in danger of disappearing from the character. Julien Sorel and Lucien are men capable of passion, but whereas that passion would be free and active in the Renaissance or in contemporary Italy, it is stifled and inhibited in the France of the Restoration and of Louis-Philippe, among men "who love money above everything else and scarcely ever sin because of hatred or love." [33]

Stendhal was not alone in his appreciation of *le naturel*, nor the only one to lament its general disappearance and glorify its survival in the characters of his heroes. Most of the romantics shared his taste for it in one way or another. Heroes from Chactas to Jean Valjean reveal symptoms of natural, untutored goodness. The charm of Sylvie is her unspoiled rustic innocence. (How disappointed her city lover is to learn that she is reading books and has learned to *phrase*!)

The idea that what is natural is good or at least untainted and unspoiled was part of Stendhal's inheritance from the eighteenth century. The essence of the idea represents a denial of original sin and a departure from the belief (still strong in the seventeenth century) in the need for mortifying the natural man. Baudelaire, who had his own complex notions about the relation betwen nature and sin (on the esthetic as well as the moral level), was of course ready to identify admiration of the natural with the secular thought of the eighteenth century: "Most errors about the beautiful arise from the eighteenth century's false conception of morality. At that time, nature was taken to be the source, the basis and model of every possible good and every possible beauty. The negation of original sin did not count for little in the general blindness of the era." [34] In some writers, like Chateaubriand and Wordsworth, it is ironic that religious beliefs should be buttressed by the secular bourgeois restoration of innocence to the natural man; in Stendhal, whose grandfather had made a pilgrimage to Ferney to see Voltaire, and who blamed Rousseau (if at all) only for his obsequiousness, the affiliation is more direct.

The Stendhal who prefers the sentimental virtue of Werther to the refined vices of Don Juan is not really anti-bourgeois, in an absolute sense of the word. It was primarily the bourgeois who, in reaction to the debauchery and libertinism of the Regency, and also in the interest of a stable government and economy, fostered the creation of a moral atmosphere in France. Rousseau's insistence on the corruption of dramatic entertainment and the immorality of novels, his unfavorable comparison of civilization with the purity of rustic and simple life, his moralism and austere virtuousness, the importance he granted to *feelings*—these were individual manifestations of a phenomenon that was widespread among the bourgeois of the eighteenth century.

The sentimental novels and *drames bourgeois* of the eighteenth century were often vehicles for the effusion of sincerely felt emotions, favored simplicity of character and an almost Protestant *examen de conscience*, and were lacking in ostentation and formality. The simple affections and rude honesty of middle-class family life were favorably contrasted with courtly frivolity, artificiality and immorality. For that matter, sentimentality and the love of nature and the natural were not confined to these genres. The pastoral had been newly reborn in lyric poetry—"l'idylle antique—traduite une seconde fois d'après Gessner"; Watteau had been followed by Chardin, Boucher and Greuze; Marie-Antoinette preferred her Petit Trianon with its milch cows and English park to the formal French gardens of Le Nôtre. Such flights from classic artifice and such mannered cultivation of the natural were as much a part of the background of Stendhal's intellectual and sentimental formation as the sophisticated correspondence of Valmont and Mme de Merteuil.

Moreover, naturalness is not merely an attribute of appearance or of manners; it is not merely a question of *dandysme* or of *maquillage*. It is also related to the idea of equality and the concept of an elite of merit, as opposed to the older elites of blood and property. "The great dispute that troubles the nineteenth century," says Stendhal in *Lucien Leuwen*, "is the wrath of rank versus merit." This was a new secular development of the old Christian idea that the gentility of the soul is independent of earthly station. When François Villon mingled the bones of kings and beggars, he meant no disrespect to the living monarch. But when Rousseau drew a distinction between *natural* and *political* inequality (defining the natural differences as those of age, health, physical strength and—more significantly—qualities of the mind or of the soul), his words had the effect of an attack on the elites of blood and property and a defense of the elite of merit.

It was only because of the success of the idea of natural or personal merit, the idea that a peasant or an untutored savage may be the intellectual or moral equal of an aristocrat or propertied bourgeois, that Stendhal could write the kind of novel he did about a man of Julien Sorel's origin. Nor could he expect a public, however small, to sympathize with his hero, either the poor Julien or the rich Lucien, without the ideological preparation of the social thought of the preceding century and its condensation in the ideals of the French Revolution.[35]

Much the same might be said of George Sand's proletarian heroes, of Hugo's Ruy Blas and Jean Valjean. But none of Stendhal's novels is really a moralistic tale, and even Julien Sorel is not a simple popular or proletarian hero. Stendhal was not wholeheartedly devoted to simplicity. He was impatient with vulgarity and unsophistication, as well as "moroseness" and puritanical morality (witness his many gibes at contemporary manners in the United States). The artificiality of the early eighteenth century court was also the expression of a kind of moral freedom, and certainly courtly manners were no more a repressive mask of the *naturel* than the tight, narrow and often hypocritical code that Shaw called "middle-class morality." Indebted though Stendhal was to the bourgeois heritage of the previous century, he still regretted the France that was "gay, amusing and somewhat libertine" and complained of the moral, hypocritical and boring present. He was touchily aware that while modern morality might extoll the virtues and merits of simplicity, directness and naturalness, Christian teaching still required the repression of the excesses and appetites of the (pejoratively defined) natural man, and imposed an arduous morality so difficult that many might be tempted to preach hypocritically in its favor, while secretly following their personal interests. Like other rebels against the tyranny of social and political institutions, Stendhal detested puritanism for its repression of the individual and for the desiccating effect it had upon the sensibility.

Thus, although Stendhal was attached to a bourgeois tradition that had extolled sentimentality and had helped to discredit courtly libertinism and immorality, he detested the hypocrisy that, he contended, accompanied the hypertrophy of puritanical bourgeois morality, and reproached the faubourg Saint-Germain for its timidity, its fear of losing still more property and its domination by the *congrégation*. He resented the way he and the heroes of his novels were involved in this sort of hypocrisy and were obliged to mask their true qualities, expressing them only indirectly.

Mixed Feelings about Money

For an indication of the way regret for the past and involvement in the present are mixed in both Stendhal's life and the conduct of his heroes, there can hardly be a better touchstone than the question of money. To be sure, neither Stendhal's own career nor his novels reveal anything like Balzac's all-pervading obsession with the ups and downs of business life. Financial dealings constitute a very minor theme in Stendhal's work, but what does appear betrays a mixture of sincere disdain for money and an acknowledgement of its importance.

From the first, Julien Sorel is distinguished by his rejection of the money-grubbing ways of his family. "Mme de Rênal believed all men were like her husband until after six months she began to see that this pale-faced little abbé, seated at the lower end of the table, beside the children, did not adore money more than anything else. And yet he was so poor!"

Julien is incapable of bargaining with his employer. He is not interested in an increase of his pay, but in the defense of his dignity. He is bored by his father's negotiations for his wages. His real concern is exposed when he declares he does not want to be a servant and asks: "But in whose company shall I take my meals?" When Mme de Rênal secretly offers him a present of money, he replies angrily: "I am still short, madame, but I am not low." When M. de Rênal raises his salary, in answer to the offended Julien's threat to leave, he succeeds only in increasing Julien's contempt for him. "I didn't despise the animal enough," he thought. "That is doubtless the most that so base a soul can do by way of apology."

Yet, inevitably, Julien is aware of the importance of money. Horrified by the destitution of the Abbé Chélan, he writes a letter to his friend Fouquet, designed to leave the door open to commercial success if prospects in the Church become too bleak or, as he puts it, "if cheerless prudence should outweigh heroism." Julien is determined to succeed and reach a higher station in society, so determined that he is even willing to consider the possibility of selling wood for a living. It is important to note that Stendhal views an action undertaken purely to avoid poverty as a compromise and a departure from "heroism." But it is equally significant that Julien should be unwilling to push heroism so far as to live in the abject poverty to which the Abbé Chélan seems condemned.

We might recall some scattered details of Julien's life: He keeps a careful account of his expenses at the Rênals; at the Hôtel de la Mole he devises a new accounting system for the Marquis's affairs. Are these merely acts of self-defense, meant to protect Julien against future accusations of dishonesty, or are they evidence of the seepage of bourgeois habits into his character? Readers of Gérard de Nerval's letters to his father know how much of this correspondence is filled with lists of petty expenses of the day. This may have been about all

Gérard felt like communicating to his father, but does not the fact that he had to be constantly alert to note these expenses suggest the strong influence his bourgeois origin exerted on him?

The bourgeois Lucien Leuwen is obviously in a much better position than Julien to be completely indifferent to money. His father has ten millions, but, remarks Stendhal, nothing in Lucien's manner shows it. Lucien despises the money-minded Carlist aristocrats whom he cultivates in the salon of Mme d'Hocquincourt in Nancy in order to further his acquaintance with Mme de Chasteller.

> "Good God! Into what flat company chance has thrown me! How stupid these people are—though if they only had the wit for it, they might be even more spiteful. How can one be stupider and more pettily bourgeois? What a fierce concern for the slightest matter involving money! And to think that these are the descendants of Charles the Bold!"

The language of this series of exclamations, including the oath that begins it, is plainly Stendhal's own; like many of Lucien's *sotto voce* comments, it is reminiscent of the style of Stendhal's autobiographical writings. The voices of the hero and the novelist merge here in contempt and tension, the tension of an estranged individual in an unpleasant world he refuses to recognize as his own. Once more, too, the reader is aware of Stendhal's way of juxtaposing the present and the historical past, invariably to the discredit of the present.

Like Julien, however, Lucien cannot tolerate the prospect of poverty. When his father dies, he leaves his family almost penniless. Lucien, unwilling to hear of using a bankruptcy petition to profit at the expense of his creditors, immediately seeks a position with the government. He admits he is unqualified for the post of first secretary to an embassy, but feels that an attaché's pay will be insufficient for him. "Attaché is too little: I have an income of twelve hundred francs." We are again reminded that there is an economic floor below which the Stendhalian hero is extremely reluctant to descend. He is a bourgeois, as Stendhal was. To be unduly concerned with money is in poor taste; to seek one's happiness in it is un-heroic. But heroism is not worth the price of poverty.

Stendhal's personal repugnance toward a world in which the importance of money was so overtly stressed appears also in numerous passages of his intimate writings. This delicacy dates from his early childhood, for even in the household of his despised bourgeois father, the discussion of money matters was taboo. "In my family any attention paid to money matters was considered vile and base in the supreme degree. It was in a way indecent to speak of money, which was a sort of sad necessity of life, regrettably indispensable, like toilets, but never to be mentioned." [36] This attitude is perfectly in keeping with the manners of the old established bourgeoisie of the eighteenth century, who maintained the traditional aloofness of aristocrats from commercial and financial dealings. "Under the *ancien régime*," observes Henri Martineau, "one never spoke of money or people's fortunes in good society. These questions were left to one's steward, one's notary and to the lawyers and merchants." [37] And, as Stendhal himself informs us, he was born "of a good bourgeois family which aspired to nobility, and nine years later in 1792 there were no prouder aristocrats than they." [38]

Indeed, despite Chérubin Beyle's reluctance to discuss money matters in domestic situations or in the salon, he was of course always engaged in speculative enterprises. Stendhal's father's acquisitive personality would later cost the son his inheritance, but apart from the personal loss, Stendhal found this a character defect. His father was, he said, "an extremely unlikable man, always reflecting on acquisitions and sales of property, excessively shrewd. . . . Nothing could be less Spanish and less extravagantly noble than the soul of that man." [39]

Paul Hazard, in constructing his argument for the new bourgeois ideal of the *philosophe* in the eighteenth century, cited the following definition from the 1694 edition of the Academy dictionary: "One gives the name of *philosopher* to a wise man who leads a tranquil and secluded life, *apart from the entanglements of business.*" [40] It is evident that this sort of life depends on an income. A *philosophe* so defined may avoid the market place for his peace of mind or for snobbish reasons, but if he is to serve as a model for bourgeois, his independence from the pursuit of money must be bolstered by a supply of money trickling in from somewhere, no matter how invisible or unmentionable it may be.

This concept was very important for Stendhal. Money, he acknowledges, is a "sad necessity of life." Without a fixed minimum amount of it, independence and the pursuit of happiness are almost impossible. His feeling is substantially that of Chateaubriand: "O Money that I have despised and cannot love! Whatever I do, I am still forced to admit your merit. You are the source of our liberty and settle a thousand discomforts in our existence, where all is difficult without you." [41]

Baudelaire spoke approvingly of this attitude toward money and said Delacroix felt the same way: "I can affirm that Delacroix shared completely Stendhal's opinion about money and economy, an opinion that is a harmonious blend of greatness and prudence. 'The man of wit,' Stendhal used to say, 'must apply himself to acquiring what is strictly necessary for him to depend on no one (in Stendhal's time, that was an income of 6,000 francs); but if having obtained this security, he wastes his time increasing his fortune, then he is a wretch.' " [42]

In money matters, therefore, Stendhal was no sentimentalist. He would have found Murger's Bohême intolerable. For all his romantic impetuosity and sensibility, his character was marked by a strong strain of bourgeois prudence, which he transmitted intact to the heroes of his novels. This is entirely in keeping with the character of a rationalist who valued independence and praised the pursuit of happiness. The Saint-Simonian Reynaud, we have seen, found that only the bourgeois was free and independent in nineteenth century France. The very idea that the pursuit of happiness on earth is possible and desirable (an anti-Pascalian idea and a denial of the older Christian conviction that this earth is a vale of tears) is a product of the same secular middle-class philosophy that produced the American Declaration of Independence. Stendhal is not a proletarian, a socialist, a capitalist or a "boss." Stendhal detests the new bourgeoisie of the Restoration and July Monarchy for its greed, its vulgarity, its hypocrisy and its "dryness." But he remains a bourgeois, jealous of bourgeois independence and cherishing an older bourgeois culture's ideal of the pursuit of happiness.

Stendhal and the Profession of Letters

An important element of Stendhal's alienation from society and the ambiguity of his heroes may be traced to the collapse of the Empire. The disappointments were great and numerous, not only for him but also for many of Napoleon's officers and bureaucrats, as well as for the youth of Vigny's generation, who came to military age too late to participate in the great events that had shaken their childhood. An era of national adventure and glory had departed, leaving in its wake nostalgia and regret, chauvinism and a bitter resentment of the drab and discreet foreign policy of Napoleon's successors. These were the feelings that—intensified by fifty years' dedication to the Napoleonic myth—were to permit the emperor's nephew another great national folly, even more damaging perhaps than the Hundred Days. Moreover, although some lamented only the victories and the conquest of Europe, others felt, and to some extent justly, that Napoleon had been the final heir to the principles of the Revolution, abandoned with the return of the Bourbons and betrayed by the ministers of Louis-Philippe.

Stendhal regretted the change for two main reasons. As a republican, in sentiment at least, he resented the restoration of the monarchy. Personally, he witnessed the demolition of his career and the end of a securely comfortable way of life. From 1815 to 1830, his only certain income was the 1,600 francs he got annually from his mother's estate, plus his army retirement pay of 900 francs, reduced by half in 1828. Chérubin Beyle's death in 1819 ended whatever dreams Stendhal may have had of an inheritance. His father's estate was encumbered by so many debts that almost nothing remained to divide among his children. Whatever else Stendhal was to spend had to come from his books and journalistic work. "It was as much the return of the Bourbons as his own taste that made him a writer." [43]

We know a good deal about Stendhal's finances during the Restoration. Things were not bad at all during the Milan years (1814-1821). In 1823 and 1824, Martineau estimates, Stendhal had a total income of 5,000 to 7,000 francs, and 8,000 to 10,000 in 1825 and 1826. This was a budget of abundance, as much as Stendhal himself thought necessary for a life of independence. In 1827, however, Colburn, his intermediary for money matters in London, stopped sending him payments, and a year later the *demi-solde* was halved.[44] On the other hand, even during these later leaner years, Stendhal was never really in dire poverty. Factory workers of the time earned only two francs a day, and skilled workmen got four or five.[45] Even if Stendhal had done nothing at all and lived only on his little *rente viagère* and the reduced *demi-solde*, his income would have been equivalent to a skilled artisan's full-time pay. But Stendhal was accustomed to a comfortable bourgeois standard of living, and according to that standard, he was poor after 1827.

Stendhal found little satisfaction in his career of professional writing. He often said he wrote only for his own pleasure, but much of what he produced during the Restoration was also intended to bring him a financial return and raise his small fixed income to a bearable minimum. But he did not relish the idea of pleasing the "parterre." And he did not. The sale of his books was spectacularly unsuccessful.

It was not lack of success alone, however, that made Stendhal critical of the profession of letters. In a letter written on the 1st of December of 1817, in which he reiterated his intention to write for his own pleasure and not that of the general public, Stendhal affirmed that he found the writer's trade degrading or, rather, degraded—"le métier d'auteur . . . semble avilissant ou, mieux dire, avili." [46] Stendhal needed money and hoped to get some from what he wrote, but he could not sell himself like the popular writer who sees in the production of literature only a special kind of commercial enterprise. As a "trade," writing is *degrading* because of the effect it has on those who practice it, and *degraded* because of what the industrialists of literature have done to it.

As with so many other questions, Stendhal judged the writing profession from a historical perspective. Like Sainte-Beuve's, his conception of the past status of the writer was somewhat rose-tinted. His norm was the disinterested man of quality, the writer of means, the Montesquieu, Voltaire or Laclos, who could write and publish his books without caring how many people bought and read them. The independence of such men did not depend on the approval of a mass public. This is indeed a fundamental ingredient of Stendhal's resentment of his century: the fact that during the Restoration (which displeased him for so many other reasons) his independence hinged on the pleasure of the vulgar new public.

In the discussion of the *Rouge* that Stendhal sent Count Salvagnoli, he made a rough and brief analysis of the contemporary public. It is fairly evident that by the provincial chambermaid, whom he contrasts with the more sophisticated Parisian reader, Stendhal meant all the readers taken in by commercial novels. And, like Balzac and Flaubert, he expresses freely his contempt for the purveyors of "industrial" literature. He attacks La Mothe-Langon, Ducange and Paul de Kock and the bookseller Pigoreau, and contrasts the novels manufactured for export to the provinces with those published by Lavavasseur and Gosselin, whose authors "seek literary merit." [47] In *De l'Amour* Stendhal accorded Ducray-Duminil the dubious honor of being the novelist whose work would constitute in two thousand years the most authentic record of contemporary manners.[48] From a romantic this was most damning praise. It is reminiscent of an incident related by Baudelaire: "One day I reproached some Germans for their taste for Scribe and Horace Vernet, and they replied: 'We admire Horace Vernet profoundly as the most complete representative of his century.' " [49] Vernet, needless to say, was admired by the bourgeois and scorned by artists, much as Scribe and Paul de Kock were by men of letters. "Horace Vernet," wrote Heine in 1843, "is regarded by the multitude as the greatest painter in France." [50]

Just as Stendhal admired the Don Juan in Valmont for his

success, while despising his lack of sensibility, is he not as envious of a Paul de Kock's success as he is contemptuous of his lack of merit? Stendhal's envoi addressed to the "happy few" is an ironic prediction of his book's commercial failure. It was not a sentiment of satisfaction that dictated such words as the following: "I wanted a small number of readers and have had my wish completely fulfilled." [51] The hundred readers Stendhal said he wrote for were not really enough for him. He protected himself with a mask of irony, but without fully concealing some disappointment and bitterness.

Despite his high bourgeois origin, the author of the *Vie de Rossini* and of *Promenades dans Rome* was not a man of great means and he wanted money from his books. He knew that there was a large new public ready to pay that money and enrich the literary man as few writers were enriched before the Revolution. He had been ambitious in his youth and planned and studied the ways of pleasing a theater audience. Let us be just. These hopes were accompanied by the firm resolve to write with integrity, and Stendhal's early ambition to please the public did not mean a total sacrifice of the idea that he would also write to please himself. But, though disappointment and retirement came quickly, Stendhal tried to make a small bid for commercial success. His superiority to most of those who triumphed then in the bookstores is obvious today, but he was in many ways a timid man, sensitive to rebuff and to his failure to please. The very way he left *Lucien Leuwen*, unfinished and unpublished, with its hero's brief and fragmentary voyage to a new life of exile in Italy, is symbolic of Stendhal's own adieu to a literary career in France in 1830.

For all Stendhal's hatred of the bourgeois and his constant use of the word as an epithet of disdain and contempt in such expressions as "bourgeois pettiness" and "bourgeois baseness," he did not, as an artist, single out that class as the sole object of his hostility. He had none of Balzac's snobbish admiration of the aristocracy, nor did he profess a sentimental attachment to the vulgar masses. He did not join with other resentful artists to snipe at the *épicier* or the philistine, for he did not want to be classed as a professional writer, but rather as a gentleman who wrote. His alienation from contemporary society was more general. He was dedicated to ideals that he felt were no longer realizable in the passionless, hypocritical, morose and boring country that France had turned into after 1789. On the other hand, he might have been less bitter if he had not lost his good job with the fall of the Empire or if he had been left a decent income by his father. His commercial failure in writing might have been less painful too if he had not hoped to be able to supplement his income.

Stendhal's feelings, therefore, constitute a sort of bridge between the eighteenth century writer's attitude toward his elite public and society as a whole and the intransigent hostility of those writers of later generations who identified both public and society with the bourgeois and, in varying degrees of complicity and alienation, opened the gap that so widely separated a Baudelaire or a Flaubert from the general reading public of his time. Stendhal's hatred of his time, his resentment of the role, even of the hypocrisy, he felt was required for the man of sensibility to get along in society, his contempt for the uncultivated and unsophisticated elements of the new general public and for the writers who stooped to conquer it, and, finally, his attachment to the semi-aristocratic *rentier* ideal inculcated in him by his eighteenth century bourgeois origin: All these factors, in some shape or other, were to contribute to later writers' hostility toward the bourgeois and their inability to make a strong positive hero of him in the novel.

III · Balzac
the Great Compromiser

Ce je ne sais quoi de cossu qui donne aux
masses bourgeoises un aspect commun.

BALZAC

Balzac and the Profession of Letters

Balzac was only a child when Stendhal made his first trips
abroad in the service of the Consulate and the Empire. The
two men were sixteen years apart in age. In the early decades
of the century, that difference was equivalent to thirty or
forty years a half-century before or after. When Balzac began
his literary apprenticeship in the 1820's, Stendhal had already
witnessed social changes that the younger man could only
imagine, had built a career and seen it crumble with Napoleon's fall, while Balzac was still a schoolboy at Tours and
preparing for his baccalaureate in Paris.

Although the publication of both men's first great novels
began around 1830, the differences between their literary
experiences under the Restoration were immense. Early in
this period, the author of *Wann-Chlore* and *Argow le pirate*
had, with the aid and guidance of Le Poitevin d'Egreville,
mastered the art of composing salable *romans noirs* and created
for himself a modest but respected place among the manu-
facturers of commercial literature. Moreover, the young Balzac had not been squeamish about even more frankly com-

mercial and industrial enterprises, although his publishing house and type foundry were a failure and rewarded him only with the first of the heavy debts that were to pursue him for the remainder of his life.

Balzac's passion for devising fresh projects and his tireless capacity for making and spending money and digging himself out of financial holes are in strong contrast with Stendhal's limited interest in money. Stendhal solved his money problems by abandoning his unsuccessful literary career and accepting in its place the relative security of a government post in exile. Balzac, on the other hand, might never have risen to the heights of the *Comédie humaine* if his financial misfortunes had not stimulated and required feverish production and complete twenty-four-hour-a-day engagement in the profession of letters.

The difference is of course not purely due to age or situation, but is also a matter of temperament. Balzac had none of Stendhal's timidity; he was a man of tremendous energy, enormously self-confident and capable of a sometimes naïve enthusiasm that would have been impossible for the subtler, more analytical Stendhal. In this connection, credit, if not complete acceptance, should be given to Pierre Abraham's physiological explanation of Balzac's character. His construction is ingenious and even plausible. The three major elements Abraham distinguishes in Balzac's personality—imaginative forces, derived from Balzac's capacity for "lying," social mimesis, derived from "servility," and unifying or synthesizing forces, derived from "appetite"—were all weaker in Stendhal and probably go a long way toward explaining their difference.[1] Balzac also had what might be called a spirit of compromise, represented in literary terms by the famous question in the *Avant-propos* of the *Comédie humaine*: "How is it possible to please simultaneously the poet, the philosopher and the masses, who want their poetry and their philosophy set in thrilling images?" [2] Balzac accepted his time; he sought to please his public and to enrich himself. But he also recognized the fact that the public was multilayered and that there was some conflict between the taste of an "intellectual" (poet, philosopher) and that of the "bourgeois masses."

Notwithstanding Balzac's intense engagement in his work, his profession and contemporary society, he was by no means content with his age or ready to identify himself with the bourgeoisie. He had complicated feelings about the profession of letters and the way he had to practice it. Even in the creation of his greatest novels he was unquestionably a professional and commercial writer, interested simultaneously in the payment of his debts, in the maintenance of a luxurious and wasteful standard of living, and in the construction of a durable literary monument filled, he thought, with important ideas that would some day reach the intellectual and political elite of the country. He was, on the one hand, jealous of the greater success of a Paul de Kock and an Eugène Sue,[3] but, on the other, professed to look forward, perhaps a little too sanguinely, to a time when extended literacy and the commercialization of literature would justify themselves, ennobling the writer of the future and his new public.[4] At the same time, he was affected by the contemporary fashion among artists to consider themselves solitary, unappreciated geniuses, thwarted by the vile bourgeois public and even more so by scheming petty publishers and editors.

Balzac's troubles with his publishers are legendary, as are his feuds with assorted journalists and editors. He liked, in his letters to Mme Hanska, to attack the "pitiless" booksellers and compared poor Werdet with Prometheus' vulture.[5] His great public attack against both booksellers and the press was launched in the second part of *Illusions perdues,* of which he wrote in the braggadocian style that characterizes so much of his correspondence with Mme Hanska: "But this work will be especially deserving of the attention of foreigners because of its audacious depiction of the inner workings of Parisian journalism—a depiction that is frighteningly exact. I alone was in a position to tell our journalists the truth and wage total war on them." [6]

Though, thanks to his fame, Balzac's difficulties and protests are better known to us than those of many others, and though he doubtless sinned as much as he was sinned against, his complaints were by no means solitary or unusual. The July Monarchy was both a boom time and a hard time for the press and for publishers, despite, and perhaps because of, the expansion of the public and the industry. Success was for the shrewdest and the hardest, and there was a wealth of protest against venality and commercialism. Emile de Girardin, the director of *La Presse*, was despised and hated in many quarters, as was Dr. Louis Véron of the *Revue de Paris*, who never lost an opportunity to flaunt his medical degree and who, in Hippolyte Castille's words, had stolen his character from Molière.[7] These were big, important names of the day. Between 1830 and 1850, Philarète Chasles recalled with some bitterness, there was no one so important as the men who ran newspapers.[8]

Many of the attacks on the venality of the press were made, partly at least, in the name of art. In fact, Gautier's celebrated preface to *Mademoiselle de Maupin* is notable for attributing sincere motives to its victims. Louis Reybaud's caricatural hero Jerôme Paturot, who tried out almost every profession and career, ran his own unsuccessful paper, *L'Aspic*, and wrote *feuilletons* for a more important organ. His first interview with the editor of that paper does away with his innocent artistic notions:

"Just stop right there, sir, if you please," he said, interrupting me. "What you call the question of art can only be of secondary importance when you are addressing a large public. Let's not get away from reality. What goes to make up the bulk of newspaper readers? Landowners, merchants, industrialists and a sprinkling of magistrates and aristocrats. Those are in fact the most enlightened ones. Well now, what would you say is the average intelligence of this clientele? Do you think these people are interested in your theories on art, that they will find them important or even understand them? When you address the man in the street, you have to use his own language. . . . We are living in a bourgeois century." [9]

To address the man in the street, to speak to everyone and, in so doing, to reduce language to its lowest common denominator—this was the aim of the big business newspapers. Balzac too wanted everyone to hear his voice. For France the July Monarchy was a time of bigness, of expansion. Balzac recognized the quality of the situation and tried to exploit it, as Stendhal did not.

It is one thing, however, to see a challenge in an expanded mass audience, and another to define that challenge uniquely as an opportunity to make money. But who is to blame for the development of a sub-literary industry dominated by the profit motive? Is this entirely a "revolt of the masses"? "Cheap art or, rather, that horrible product, vulgar art," Joseph Aynard has said, "is perhaps created for the people, but not by the people." [10] Paturot's cynically realistic editor justifies his paper's contents in terms of the supposed taste or intelligence of the public, but what he wants to print is likely to change that public for the worse.

Henry Monnier carries the matter to its logical extreme. His caricatural hero Joseph Prudhomme also enters journalism, toward the end of a long and varied career. At a meeting of stockholders, he hears the following advice on how to run his paper:

"A newspaper is above all a commercial enterprise, like an alcohol distillery, a refinery of beet sugar or a bone-black factory. You keep it prosperous in the same way, by producing a cheap, uniform and quality product. . . . I have been noticing that our maid, who used to devour the serial novels in our paper passionately, no longer reads them these days. That proves that the merchandise we are offering leaves something to be desired with respect to its quality. Let's try then to spice our novels up. If the subscriber isn't content with four or five bonus books, give him another or even two if necessary. That's all there is to it." [11]

Now, Balzac himself was actively concerned with the economic aspects of authorship. He was president of the *Société des gens de lettres* and, like Beaumarchais, tried to secure for authors a juster share of the profits from the literary property they create. But he could not assume a businessman's attitude toward literature, whether it was printed in newspapers or books. In the *Comédie humaine*, his treatment of business, commerce, banking and money in general is often more sinister than exuberant. One feels indeed that the sordid details of banking and commerce, the horrors of poverty, indebtedness, foreclosure and bankruptcy, have been obsessively scrutinized under a magnifying glass in those many novels of Balzac's in which the hero comes to financial ruin.

Balzac was not a withdrawn or objective philosopher, but an involved and active *arriviste*, like other bourgeois of his time. Simultaneously, however, he had a dark and vivid vision of the new bourgeois culture and was aware that he too had been caught up in the general craze for wealth and success. Time and again he denounced the importance money had acquired during the reign of Louis-Philippe and the corrupting and demoralizing effect on youth and particularly on young writers and artists. The great hero-villain Vautrin was surely speaking for Balzac when he reached the following climax of a long and unfavorable judgment of post-Napoleonic France: "Your Society no longer worships the true God, but the Golden Calf! That is the religion of your Charter, which bases politics on property only. Isn't that as much as to say to the subjects of your king: try to get rich?" [12]

Representation of the Bourgeois

The quest for wealth and the satisfaction of ambition are major themes in Balzac's *Bildungsromane*, the novels that trace the careers of handsome, charming young semi-aristocrats like Lucien de Rubempré, Eugène de Rastignac and Félix de Vandenesse. These are the heroes who come closest to resembling Lucien Leuwen, Julien Sorel and Fabrice del Dongo. But just as failure is a sort of justification and even a triumph for the Stendhalian hero, the success of Balzac's young men is accompanied by corruption and compromise. In their stories Balzac mingles his loyalty to the bourgeoisie with a harsh condemnation of the bourgeois era. The ambitious Lucien de Rubempré leaves his provincial home, the "pure, hard-working and bourgeois" life of his youth, gradually abandons his honor, his decency, his morality, among corrupt cynics and vile plotters in the capital. For life in the Paris of the *Comédie humaine* is a constant temptation to debauchery and degradation.

In the lives of these heroes, Balzac betrays his true respect for the so-called bourgeois virtues: thrift, modesty, industry and perseverance. For him, it is one of the ironies of the triumph of the bourgeoisie that the morality of that very class should be subverted. There are rare examples of resistance to the common trend. Joseph Bridau and Daniel d'Arthez represent an ideal for artists and poets. Devoted to their work, they work for long hours alone in their shabby rented rooms, avoiding the company of their idle and cynical friends. Balzac's introduction of such characters into the *Comédie humaine* is indeed, as Albert Cassagne has said, proof of his romanticism. Although he himself did not live as they do, he suggests nevertheless that the true artist flourishes most nobly in poverty and solitude. Cassagne cites the example of the Polish sculptor Steinbock, in *La Cousine Bette*, who produces works of genuine merit while he is poor, but is spoiled by success. Delivered to worldly temptations, the artist's imagination is sterilized, and "because he has mingled in bourgeois society, he becomes a bourgeois." [13] But, while he becomes one kind of bourgeois, he ceases to be the kind of bourgeois he was before; artists like Bridau and d'Arthez, for all their disdain of profit and their unique concern for an art that the philistine bourgeois cannot understand, are men of bourgeois character and of careful, prudent and sober bourgeois habits.

There is thus a double value that Balzac attaches to the word "bourgeois." The traditional traits of the bourgeois are respectable and admirable and particularly necessary in the character of a sincere artist; but Balzac also saw around him a changing new world, expanding, unstable and populated by a new, crude and mercenary bourgeoisie.

César Birotteau

The range of Balzac's attitudes toward the bourgeois is immense. He is fond, respectful, patronizing, contemptuous and full of hate. For an analysis of the complexities and ambiguities of his feelings, as revealed in the literary representation of a bourgeois hero, one is embarrassed only by the wealth of examples in the *Comédie humaine*. *César Birotteau* is of special interest because in this novel Balzac seems to have made a sincere effort to give heroic stature to the generally despised shopkeeper type of bourgeois. The portrait is sympathetically drawn and even has some points of contact with Balzac's own history and personality.[14] Yet, the novelist also betrays snobbish feelings of superiority to his hero, an inability to accept his kind of bourgeois as a serious candidate for sympathetic Rousseauistic representation. This is not entirely the result of Balzac's being caught in the tide of anti-bourgeois sentiment. Deep-seated conservative class feelings and misgivings about the downward expansion of the bourgeoisie appear not only in this novel, but throughout Balzac's later work. Although heroes like Rubempré, Rastignac and Louis Lambert may be more nearly parallel to Stendhal's young heroes, César Birotteau comes closer to summing up Balzac's feelings about the nascent problem of the vulgarization of nineteenth century bourgeois culture.

According to Balzac, *César Birotteau* was conceived about six years before publication.[15] Apparently, however, he wrote a good part of it in less than two months of feverish work at the end of 1837. The reason for this sudden spurt of concentrated energy, he said (in a letter written to Zulma Carraud, 22 November 1837), was that the *Figaro* had promised him twenty thousand francs if he could finish *César* in December.[16] This he did, and the book appeared in December 1837. Both the *Figaro* and the *Estafette* offered it as a premium to their subscribers.[17] Thus, the birth of this work of art, like that of many other novels Balzac wrote, was amply commercial. It would almost certainly not have been finished when it was, if at all, had not the *Figaro* galvanized Balzac's creative energies by dangling its twenty thousand franc offer and forcing him to accept a deadline. It was bought and printed, moreover, to help increase the circulation of a newspaper.

This novel had a dual importance for Balzac. Although he finished it for money, he had conceived it more idealistically. There is, in fact, an ironical incongruity between Balzac's original ambitious conception of this work and the hurried way he wound it up to meet a payment deadline, an incongruity that would seem to be matched by the evolution of Balzac's attitude toward César and the way he finally worked out the structure of the novel.

The very title suggests a condensation of the novel's major ambiguity: *Histoire de la grandeur et de la décadence de César Birotteau, marchand parfumeur, adjoint au maire du deuxième arrondissement de Paris, Chevalier de la Légion d'Honneur, etc.* The first element of the title, inflated by the reminiscence of Montesquieu's classic work of a hundred years before, loses all dignity as it dissolves comically into the list of pretentious bourgeois titles. Even the hero's name suggests an ironic contrast between the noble heroic past and the vulgar bourgeois present.

Irony, to be sure, is not necessarily ambiguity. The ambiguity of the title, and also of the work, resides in the fact that *César Birotteau* is not really a farce or a satire. Balzac

meant the novel seriously, wanted it to serve as an illustration
of his own deep thought on the subject of the decline of
individuals and nations from former greatness. But as he wrote,
he seems to have found that his feelings toward the hero were
mixed, in a way that corresponds with the disparity between
the stately beginning and the comic end of the title. There is
evidence to confirm this, both within and outside the text.
Let us first examine the external circumstances.

According to Lovenjoul, *César Birotteau* was originally
supposed to follow *La Peau de chagrin* in the series of *Etudes
philosophiques*, although when it entered the *Comédie humaine* in 1844, it found its place among the *Scènes de la Vie
parisienne*.[18] Somewhere between the moment of conception
and the time the novel assumed its definitive shape, Balzac
apparently decided it was better classified as a study of manners than as a philosophical work. This is a distinction of some
importance, for it suggests that *César* turned out to be different from the kind of novel Balzac had wanted it to be. In
the vast history of contemporary society that was to be the
Comédie humaine, Balzac intended his novels of manners to
have the primary function of recording social phenomena,
while the philosophic (and analytic) novels were to analyze
their causes and principles. He also extended this difference to
the conception of fictional characters that would appear in the
two categories of novels. In a well-known letter to Mme
Hanska (26 October 1834), Balzac treated this question in
detail. The characters of the novels of manners were supposed to be "individus typisés," that is, portraits drawn after
nature and used to represent social groups; on the other hand,
characters in the philosophic studies were to be "types indi-
vidualisés," or, in other words, created from the imagination
so as to incarnate philosophical ideas or principles.[19] If we
provisorily assume consistent obedience to this scheme, we
may tentatively conclude that the shift from one category to

the other signifies that Balzac had ceased to regard César primarily as an example of "grandeur et décadence," illustrative of the causes of a broad historical phenomenon, and judged him better suited to represent an element of the contemporary bourgeoisie.

More important, however, than these always doubtful arguments derived from letters and other external sources, is the evidence provided by the text itself. After having plunged the reader *in medias res,* as was his custom, Balzac interrupts the action in order to review the past life of his hero. This characteristic exposition section, inserted to delay development close to the crucial moments of the action, is followed by a long and earnest dissertation on the rise and fall of men and nations.

Every existence has its apogee, a period during which causes are active and in exact relationship with results. This noonday time of life, when live forces are in equilibrium and exert themselves in all their brilliance, is not only common to organized beings, but also to cities, nations, ideas, institutions, commerce and enterprises, which, like noble races and dynasties, are born, rise and fall. Whence comes the rigor with which this theme of growth and shrinkage is applied to all organized things on this earth? . . . History, by relating the grandeur and decline of everything that ever was on earth, could warn man of the moment when he must interrupt the exercise of all his faculties. But neither conquerors nor actors, neither women nor authors, hear this salutary voice. César Birotteau, who should have realized he was at the pinnacle of his fortunes, took this stopping-point rather as a new point of departure. He did not know . . . the cause of those reversals with which History is pregnant, and of which so many royal and commercial houses offer such illustrious examples . . . that principle which must govern the policy of nations as well as that of individuals: *When the effect produced is no longer in direct relationship or in equal proportion with its cause, then disorganization sets in.*[20]

This text is proof enough, it would seem, of Balzac's intention to make *César Birotteau* a philosophic study, with all the dignity and seriousness of literary level that category implied for him. The central idea resembles the major theme of *La Peau de chagrin*, namely the cyclic rhythm of life forces, surging to an apogee and then declining to extinction. It is entirely plausible that Balzac should have wanted to put the two works side by side. His thesis is hardly original, and his prose is inflated with emphasis, but the theme is noble, provocative in his time as in our own. It awakens thoughts of the fall of Rome, of the Revolution and the dead civilizations of ancient cities buried in time, all richly productive of speculation, not only on the part of eighteenth century men, like Montesquieu, Gibbon, Vico and Volney, but also on the part of Balzac's contemporaries, like Ballanche and Quinet, and of moderns, like Spengler and Toynbee.

In this context, however, it is hardly important to hunt for sources or parallels of Balzac's philosophy of history. Our curiosity should be excited rather by the fact that Balzac chose the career of a little Parisian manufacturer and vendor of cosmetics to represent so lofty an idea, with such vast historical resonances. A personage like Raphaël, who is a sort of cross between Louis Lambert and Eugène de Rastignac, filled such a role more gratefully. But César Birotteau hardly seems the sort of man to star in the philosophic sequel of *La Peau de chagrin*.

The shopkeeper hero of this novel was chosen with a purpose. *César Birotteau* was to be a sort of modern middle-class epic, a bourgeois *Iliad*. The bourgeoisie, Balzac argues (in the second chapter of the novel), *seems* an unfitting source of persons and actions of magnitude, but in reality its griefs and

vicissitudes are immense, and, though no one has thought of
them before in this way, he, Balzac, will dare to initiate a
new kind of epic poem, the epic of bourgeois humanity.

This is not such an innovation as Balzac would have his
reader believe. *César Birotteau* follows a general trend toward
the liberation of vulgar and middle-class persons, action and
language from the comic level in literature. It is in the lineage
of Diderot's and Beaumarchais's *drame bourgeois*, the novels
of Fielding and the early poetry of Wordsworth; it accom-
panies the humanitarian novels of Hugo and George Sand
and, like them, points toward the work of Emile Zola. Beaumarchais had been very much concerned with the misfortunes
of the middle class and, he once said, wrote his *Deux Amis*
"in honor of the businessman and, in general, to honor the
people of the third estate." [21] Still, it is probably fair to admit
that even at a moment when the prestige of the popular hero
was rising, when there was much talk of writing new epics of
modern humanity, Balzac exhibited some audacity in trying to
make a serious hero out of a Paris shopkeeper. In the literary
mind of 1837 it was not so much poverty or humble status
that disqualified a man from heroism. It was rather the act of
selling goods over a counter that seemed most incompatible
with high ideals, nobility of the soul or poetic sensibility.

But, as things turned out, *César Birotteau* did not get to be
an entirely philosophical novel. In the novel of manners that
it turned into, the whole philosophical prologue seems reduced
to an almost superfluous digression and seems like a relic of
the early days of composition. Doubtless, one reason for this
is the haste in which Balzac completed the novel. Another
reason, perhaps more important, involved his complex and
ambiguous feelings about the kind of bourgeois that César
Birotteau comes to represent. After his initial excitement,
Balzac seems to have found himself in an awkward situation,

which he himself described some years later in a letter to Hippolyte Castille:

> I kept *César Birotteau* for six years in the form of a first draft, despairing of ever being able to interest anyone in a rather stupid and mediocre shopkeeper whose fortunes are vulgar and symbolize something of which we all make a good deal of fun, *small business in Paris.* Well, sir, at a happy moment, I said to myself: "I must transform him by making him the image of *probity!*" And it seemed possible.[22]

It is significant that Balzac stresses the importance of pleasing his public and that he assumes his public will share his own estimation of the Paris shopkeeper. But it is of more immediate concern to us that Balzac's earlier, ebullient eagerness to write a "bourgeois epic" is totally absent from the note to Castille and from the state of mind it recalls.

Such retrospective remarks, even when pronounced in complete sincerity, do not always describe accurately the sentiments of the author at the time of composition. But apart from the bare external fact that the novel was transferred from the *Etudes philosophiques* to the *Etudes de moeurs*, the very structure of the novel corroborates Balzac's later statement. Both the title of *César Birotteau* and the long philosophical dissertation suggest a bipartite work, with the stress to be laid on the causes of César's decline. In reality, however, the novel is not limited to César's initial rise and decline; it also deals with his agonizing and truly mortal struggle to pay his creditors and regain his honor and reputation for probity. In other words, Balzac added a third part that does not seem essential to his original conception of the novel.

The early part of *César* conforms to Balzac's enunciation of the principle governing the rise and fall of men and nations. Céasar's failure is due to his inability to perceive that he has exhausted his capacity to rise. Without knowing it, he has reached his apogee. To this extent, his story is commensurate with the philosophic idea it was intended to illustrate. One might indeed make a modest case for César as the tragic hero, seeing in his obstinate determination to speculate on the property around the Madeleine, to enlarge his shop, beautify his home and invite his friends to an extravagantly expensive ball, a modern bourgeois manifestation of the Greek *hubris*. In fact, Plato's definition of the tragic hero's major flaw coincides with Balzac's analysis of the cause of César's failure. "If one sins against the laws of proportion and gives something too big to something too small to carry it—too big sails to too small a ship, too big meals to too small a body, too big powers to too small a soul—the result is bound to be a complete upset." [23]

Apparently, however, this aspect of César's behavior later impressed Balzac less as heroic intemperance than as commonplace stupidity. As the novel progresses, the author dwells less and less on César's personal responsibility for his decline and more and more on the part others played in it. Before long, it is clear that César is the innocent victim of a conspiracy, entangled in the mesh of financial intrigue and villainy woven by Du Tillet, Keller and Gobseck. To preserve interest in the action and sympathy for the hero, the philosophic study becomes a *feuilleton* novel of suspense and sentimentality. The short-lived effort to analyze the causes of decline from greatness is minimized and suppressed, while interest is centered on César's virtue and his honorable retirement from the scene of action. Cleared of his debts after a heroic exercise of humble virtue, he dies—"a martyr of commercial probity." Balzac, overwhelmed by the beauty of the new turn his novel has taken, writes to Mme Hanska: "He is the *médecin de campagne*, only in Paris, a *stupid* Socrates drinking his hemlock drop by drop in the shadows, an angel trodden underfoot, an unrecognized *honnête homme*. Ah! it is a great picture. . . ." [24] (If, as Balzac said in his letter to Castille, *César* took six years to write, this panegyric was penned at the midpoint between conception and publication.)

César Birotteau—A "New" Bourgeois

We are now in a position to examine César Birotteau as the central character of a novel of manners and to attempt to define Balzac's sympathy for him. We are already aware of some ambiguity of sentiment: César is admirably honest, but Balzac has ironically qualified his probity with the adjective "commercial." César is "stupid," "mediocre" and, despite Balzac's original temptation to discover an epic quality in his misfortunes, his troubles are, after all, "vulgar." These judgments, however, indicate only the surface of Balzac's feelings toward his hero and the bourgeoisie. We must now ascertain more exactly just what sort of bourgeois César Birotteau really is.

The reader is first presented to César in an artfully contrived dramatic situation. The novel begins in César's bedroom, where his wife has just awakened from a terrifying dream. Old and wrinkled and in rags, she stood at the threshold of her own shop, begging alms, while behind the counter stood another, younger image of herself. Mme Birotteau's terror is renewed by the discovery that she is alone in her bed. And Balzac lists in the most meticulous detail all the symptoms of intense animal fear: César's wife lies petrified in her bed, in a cold sweat, hearing strange imagined sounds, her hair on end, unable to speak or even turn her head, her throat dry, her heart contracted and her eyes distended. It is a superb beginning for a popular novel and perhaps for any novel at all.

Mme Birotteau's terrorized heart beats are the thumpings of fate, for her nightmare is a prophecy of future poverty and ruin. Indeed, to heighten the dramatic quality of the moment, her dream takes place just when César, in an adjoining room, is calculating and planning the rash speculative enterprise that will bring about his downfall. From the first, Balzac establishes a dramatic or literary duality, a contrast between César and his wife. César, confident with success and excited by his ambition, has become impatient and is no longer content with the modest returns of his business or with his wife's hope to retire to a little country home. On the other hand, Mme Birotteau's prophetic dream and also her calm and cautious personality, her fixed conservative conception of the slow, careful and sure way in which security should be achieved, lead her to protest against her husband's plans—to speak, like Cassandra, the truth that will not be heard. This is, of course, the first chapter, in which Balzac's philosophic notion is still strong. He is using César's obstinacy in pursuing his foolish scheme as an example of the causes of decline from greatness. Mme Birotteau's voice is the voice of wisdom, and César's the voice of folly.

But perhaps these first scenes are not totally objective. The voice of Mme Birotteau may, as André Billy suggests, also be reminiscent of voices in the personal life of Balzac—those of Mme de Berny, Mme Carraud, his sister Laurence—all advising him against his own rash enterprises of the past.[25] Balzac almost certainly did not intend his reader to identify the novelist behind the figure of his hero, but it seems evident that there is a tenuous bond of sympathy between him and César—a sympathy dependent on their common folly and their common aggressiveness and ambition.

There is not only a dramatic but also a social contrast between César and his wife. In his youth he had been an agricultural laborer in the provinces and had arrived in Paris a poor boy, owning only the clothes on his back. He had served an apprenticeship in the perfume shop, saved money, invested it well, bought the shop and improved its business. He is a self-made man, a new bourgeois. His wife, on the other hand, is the daughter of shopkeepers. Her ambition is a careful and humble one, a vision of modest and unadventurous security, built out of patient and unenterprising work, in accordance with the traditional virtues of her class.

Mme Birotteau's qualities are those of her family and indeed of all the preceding generations of shopkeepers in the *Comédie humaine.* For Balzac's panoramic work embraces at least three successive generations of nineteenth century bourgeois. It was perhaps Brunetière who first suggested the affiliation of these generations, in which César occupies the middle place. "About twenty years older, César would no longer be César, but Ragon, his predecessor at the Reine des Roses; twenty years younger, he would be his own successor, the triumphant Crevel." [26] This is not quite exact, however; the difference between these three men is not simply chronological. They are men of different eras, but also of different origins and classes, with totally different ambitions and ideals. César Birotteau, the self-made man of the Restoration, lives in a different world from that of "le sieur Ragon," who was court perfumer to Marie-Antoinette and who, thirty years after the Revolution, still powders his hair and wears knee breeches, silk stockings and buckled shoes.

There are other differences between César and the previous generation; it is not merely a question of attire and a sentimental attachment to the graces of the *ancien régime*. César is an exemplar of a new, expanding bourgeois society, in which commerce and industry are being transformed. Two other critics have made brief comparisons between César and old Guillaume, the proprietor of the Maison du Chat-Qui-Pelote. Paul Louis describes César as "a Guillaume tormented by his need to invent and already affected by the mania for speculation." [27] A study undertaken by Emile Failletaz is lengthier and still more perceptive. Despite the chronology of the novel, the action of which is set in the Restoration, César, observes Failletaz, is in reality the type of the new July Monarchy shopkeeper; Failletaz finely analyzes the contrast between the conservative manners of a Guillaume and César's flair for new commercial techniques.[28]

César's new business spirit, animated by the desire for change and progress, is indeed particularly remarkable if one compares his plans for the new store near the Place Vendôme with the dingy store front of the Maison du Chat-Qui-Pelote, the gold "parsimoniously" applied to the letters of the old sign.

> I shall burn our sign REINE DES ROSES and erase the inscription CESAR BIROTTEAU, MARCHAND PARFUMEUR, SUCCESSEUR DE RAGON and simply put *Parfumeries* in big gold letters. . . . The workshop goes up into the attic! Passers-by shall no longer watch the labels being stuck on, bags being made up, bottles sorted and flasks being corked. That's all right for the rue Saint-Denis, but when it comes to the rue Saint-Honoré, it's a different story. Our store should be fixed up like a salon. After all, are we the only cosmeticians who are doing well? Aren't there vinegar-makers and mustard merchants commanding the National Guard and with influence at the Château? Let us imitate them, expand our business and get up into high society.[29]

These innovations are not only commercial, but social as well. It seems evident that Balzac was indeed thinking of the bourgeois monarchy of Louis-Philippe and in a spirit of mockery and resentment.

The fact that César is getting up in the world, is "upwardly mobile," as the sociologists say, underlines another very important difference between him and earlier generations of Paris shopkeepers. César is not a born bourgeois. He is unhampered by the traditions that fix the life and manners of the bourgeoisie of the rue Saint-Denis. Although not strong enough or clever enough to thwart his powerful enemies, he has the energy and aggressiveness of the man of the people. In fact, it is not really necessary to return to past generations in search of the traditional, cautious, conservative type of bourgeois. Mme Birotteau herself is almost instinctively opposed to all of César's larger, riskier and more extravagant gestures.

It would take a long stretch of the imagination to picture César Birotteau in the role of Werner Sombart's dynamic, adventurous, speculating bourgeois. He is drawn on too small a scale and is too vulnerable to Balzac's scorn for him to be identified with the type of capitalist bourgeois who, since the Renaissance, had gambled with immense fortunes—the sort of man who outfitted frail ships to carry precious cargoes from the Indies and set out to create and conquer vast markets and industries. Still, there was an element of adventure and risk in the financial turmoil of the mid-nineteenth century in France. Notwithstanding the search for investments that would pay a sure 5 per cent and the fear of conducting any business enterprise without the protection of a tariff barrier, this was also an era of wild and crooked ventures, of wildcat stock companies, exuberant speculation and gambling. Although handicapped by his innocence and honesty, César has his part in all this. He is not a timid conservative bourgeois, like his wife, but an advocate of change, of innovation and of risk.

Moreover, Balzac's sympathies are not with César's wife. He fully shared his hero's foolish ambition to climb up higher in society. He portrays César as an energetic, imaginative and inventive man. Balzac mocks César's new cosmetic creation, "cephalic oil," and the ridiculous scientist who endorses it (a forerunner of the men in white coats we see in cigarette and toothpaste advertisements today); but the sureness and agility with which César conceives and launches the new product are qualities the novelist describes with sympathy and approval. César's advertising copy, too, combines satire of a vulgar new merchandising technique with admiration for its effectiveness (in *Illusions perdues*, Balzac called Ladvocat's poster ads for books a "new and original creation" [30]).

Balzac gave César drive, ambition and the will to rise. It is likely that he attributed these qualities to his hero's humble origin. Like Stendhal and Hugo, he implied at times that the lower classes were the repository of a kind of raw, fresh energy and crude vigor that no other class possessed. He may even have felt some faint kinship between César and himself, for Balzac was only a few generations removed from his own peasant ancestry. But, at the same time, he wanted to leave no doubt that he, the author, was situated far above his peasant-shopkeeper hero. For Honoré de Balzac was a snob and had his own social ladder to climb. For that reason, snobbish condescension was as much an integral part of his characterization of César as his lyrical praise of his honesty and his indirect sympathy with his *arrivisme*.

Peasant Hands and Bourgeois Feet

A sure sign that Balzac let his class feelings filter into his art
is his identification of physical characteristics with the social
origin of his characters. This is due partly to his susceptibility
to the use of the literary cliché, but his particular choice of
clichés has something to do with his snobbish adulation of the
aristocracy and his confused feelings about other classes.

The question of Balzac's characterology has been treated in
one of the most curious and most interesting critical studies
of his art: Pierre Abraham's statistical analysis of the color of
Balzac's characters' hair and eyes. Although the statistical
method is woefully unsuited to most areas of literary criticism,
Abraham has handled his subject with great delicacy and
demonstrated fairly conclusively that the passionateness of the
characters of the *Comédie humaine* is rigorously proportionate
to the pigmentation of their hair and eyes.[31]

While Balzac's well-known interest in the writings of
Lavater and Gall may have had some effect on the construction of this "system," it is hardly certain. That particular influence is more easily perceptible in descriptions of the physical manifestations of the emotions. The description of Mme
Birotteau in a state of terror produced by her dream, for
example, is very similar to Lavater's descriptions of men and
animals paralyzed by fright. The notion that the highly
pigmented Latins are more volatile, more emotional, than
meditative and cooler-nerved, blue-eyed blond Nordics is a
part of popular mythology and has found its way into the
characterology of many other novelists.[32] Indeed, we cannot

say to what extent Balzac himself was aware of how consistently he related physiognomy with character, temperament and intellect.

On the other hand, Balzac decidedly seems well aware of his espousal of another popular notion, namely the idea that aristocratic bodies are shaped more delicately and pleasingly than those of peasants or bourgeois. In his novels, it is a rule that a bourgeois must not only act and speak his part: he must look it as well. And this does not work out to his advantage, as a few examples of Balzacian "social description" may show.

In the idiom of the *Comédie humaine*, a man's physiognomy *announces* his character and his features *attest* or *accuse* his origin. (This is, of course, no innovation in the storyteller's art; on the first page of *Candide*, Voltaire introduced his hero by saying "his physiognomy announced his soul.") Balzac finds the hands and the feet particularly reliable signs and symbols of social class. Of César Birotteau he wrote: "His origin would have been attested by his broad and hairy hands, by the fat joints of his creased fingers and their large square nails, if indeed vestiges of his birth had not been distributed throughout his body." [33] César's daughter is described somewhat more complexly, for her body must betray the alliance of two class strains, as well as the effects of a bourgeois environment.

> The beauty of this lovely girl was neither that of an English lady nor that of a French duchess, but the curvaceous and auburn beauty of Rubens' Flemish women. She had her father's snub nose . . . her mother's beautiful forehead. . . . Despite the delicacy of her figure, she was robustly built. Her two feet accused her father's peasant origin, for her beauty suffered from a hereditary defect and also perhaps from the redness of her hands, a sure proof of her purely bourgeois life.[34]

Part of this description is reminiscent of Eugénie Grandet, who "belonged to that type of robustly built child that we find among the petty bourgeois and whose beauties seem vulgar." [35] Like Césarine Birotteau, Céleste Colleville, a young lady in *Les Petits Bourgeois*, also advertises her family background whenever she displays her hands and feet: "One of her charms was her magnificent ash-colored hair; but the hands and the feet had a bourgeois origin." [36] In his portrait of Elizabeth Baudoyer, Balzac abandons all restraint, allowing no charm or beauty to temper an extreme image of bourgeois vulgarity. "Elizabeth Baudoyer, *née Saillard*, is one of those figures who defy the painter's brush by their very vulgarity. And yet they must be described somehow, for they typify the Parisian petty bourgeoisie, situated above the rich craftsman and below the upper class. Their virtues are almost vices, and their shortcomings inspire no sympathy. . . ." [37]

In this tight system, replete with stock phrases and pat ideas, even the exception may prove the rule. Augustine Guillaume, the daughter of the draper of the rue Saint-Denis, seemed like an evolutionary sport. In contrast to the unpleasant bourgeois faces of her parents, the grace and delicacy of her features so captivated the aristocratic painter, Théodore de Sommervieux that he not only painted but married her. Her non-bourgeois beauty, confessed Balzac, was inexplicable. "She was one of those girls," he said, "who because of the absence of any physical resemblance to their parents, lend credence to the prudish saying, 'children come from God.' " [38] (But Balzac had enough faith in the immiscibility of the two classes to require a future separation of the bourgeois Augustine and her frivolous, high-living husband.)

Balzac is equally consistent in the description of his aristocratic characters, who, both male and female of the species, are ever endowed with "noble" features. Mme de Mortsauf, for example, has fine hair, small ears, a Greek nose and "the feet of a woman of good breeding" ("les pieds d'une femme comme il faut").[39] The Duchess of Langeais has all the elements of Balzac's ideal image of the aristocratic woman: "The predominant feature of her physiognomy was an elegant nobility. Her face was a bit too long and had a grace, something fine and slender, that recalled the faces of the Middle Ages. Her complexion was pale, slightly rosy. Everything about her erred, so to speak, because of an excessive delicacy." [40]

There is in Balzac's description of the aristocratic face a vague and wordy insistence on "grace," "nobility," "delicacy" and "fineness," in addition to the more concrete attributes of pallor and slenderness. He seems to envy these qualities, but does not necessarily attribute a moral value to them. David Séchard, for example, is "a heavily-set Silenus," an image of rude, unadorned virtue.[41] But his character wins Balzac's approval. On the other hand, both the character and the aristocratic origin of Lucien de Rubempré combine to give his face a weak and effeminate grace. He might well have sat for the portrait of Dorian Gray.

> Lucien posed in the graceful stance that sculptors have devised for the Indian Bacchus. His face had the distinction of the lines of antique beauty. He had a Greek forehead and nose, the velvety whiteness of a woman's skin, eyes so blue they seemed black. . . . There was a divine sweetness in his gilded white temples, an incomparable nobility in his short chin. . . . He had the hands of the well-born man, elegant hands that women love to kiss. At a sign from those hands, men felt compelled to obey.[42]

This description of Lucien is ludicrous, but it is doubtful that Balzac felt the slightest twinge of irony as he wrote it. No further examples, I think, are needed to demonstrate Balzac's serious association of physiognomy with social class.

Nor is his "system" presented in a cool and objectively detached way. The physical traits that announce the aristocrat are graceful, delicate and refined, while peasants and bourgeois are betrayed by coarse, thick, gross, hairy and reddened features. Balzac will grant a pretty peasant or bourgeois girl the heavily filled curves of a Venus de Milo or the rosy, robust charms of Rubens' women, but the Greek noses, the delicate lines of "an antique statue," noble hands and aristocratic feet are all the hereditary property of the upper classes.

Social Change

By constantly correlating physical characteristics with class origin, manners and culture, Balzac reveals a strong attachment to the idea of a rigid—almost a racial—separation of classes. Nevertheless, his representation of contemporary society was not purely caricatural. Balzac was extraordinarily sensitive to the mechanics of social change. He recognized that the nineteenth century had not only brought about the triumph of the bourgeoisie, but had also created a new hierarchy that was more flexible and more dynamic than the old order of social classes under the *ancien régime*.

There is a curious sentence in the *Avant-propos*, mingling respect for the vitality of the bourgeois era with a snobbish nostalgia for the past. "If a few scientists still don't admit that an immense life current is bridging the gap between Animality and Humanity, it is certainly true that grocers are getting to be Peers and that noblemen descend sometimes to the lowest social levels." [43] Balzac was often contemptuous of the clambering, awkward rise of petty bourgeois characters, perhaps partly because he secretly had to admit he was like them himself—with his own hunger to associate with the aristocracy and his persistent courtship of the blue-blooded Mme Hanska. Yet he also had egalitarian feelings, fostered in him by the liberal republican family friends with whom he consorted during his youth. Bernard Guyon, who has examined this part of his background very thoroughly, finds that Balzac's scornful anti-bourgeois attitude, first adopted around 1830, is only a superficial rallying to a cause he did not really espouse. [44] This is partly true. Nevertheless, even Guyon is compelled to admit that, when Balzac was faced with the necessity of making a choice between a democratic and egalitarian ideal and an aristocratic and hierarchical ideal, he "immediately and spontaneously" chose the second. [45]

Certainly, there is great evidence of sympathy for the bourgeoisie in early treatments of the theme of intermarriage. From Balzac to Proust this theme has served to dramatize social change and decay. In the *Scènes de la vie privée*, written soon after the *Physiologie du mariage*, Balzac treated the question in several stories (*La Maison du Chat-Qui-Pelote, Le Bal de Sceaux, Une Double Famille*). He was openly sympathetic to the aspirations of the bourgeoisie and critical of the way aristocrats resented having to adjust to a new society. He mocks the arrogance of aristocrats confronted with new bourgeois wealth. There is only disapproval in the way he treats Emilie de Fontaine's refusal to marry the man she loves, just because he is a businessman. Indeed, there may well have been something personal in the severity of his portrayal of this woman. Emilie, he observed maliciously in the *Bal de Sceaux*, was astonished "to see people in percale having the same fun as those dressed in satin and to see the bourgeoisie dance as gracefully as the nobility and at times even better." [46] It is the same Emilie who, at the Birotteaus' ball, insults César's wife by expressing her astonishment that there should be an "odor of good taste" in the newly decorated apartment.[47]

Balzac was no democrat, however. He can take the part of hard-working, sincere, good-hearted, intelligent bourgeois, and castigate frivolous, arrogant and class-conscious aristocrats. But he too draws a line. He accords to the new bourgeois aristocracy of finance and government administration some of the physical and cultural graces of the old nobility and is suspicious of small shopkeepers and minor government functionaries. There is an opportunity for a significant contrast at César's sumptuous housewarming.

> With the exception of three women representing the Aristocracy, high Finance and Government, Mlle de Fontaine, Mme Jules and Mme Rabourdin, whose flashing beauty, costume and manners distinctly set them apart in this gathering, the women displayed in their attire a heaviness, a solidity, and had that indefinable monied, substantial air that gives the bourgeois masses a common look, and was so cruelly obvious in contrast with the lightness and grace of the first three.[48]

The key expression here is "bourgeois masses." These are not proletarians or peasants, but an element of the bourgeoisie which, profiting from social and political change and from the Revolutionary transfer of property, had been able to leave the ranks of the "people" during the Empire and Revolution. They are not necessarily poor, can even be well-to-do and rich, but they lack the polish, the social graces and the cultural refinements of the upper bourgeoisie. Even when they are morally admirable, like César Birotteau, they bear the physical marks of their lowly ancestry, are unused to the refinements of salon and boudoir and are strangers to the world of arts and letters.

This is the class for which the cheap press and vulgar novel were created. César himself has only a few fleeting moments of contact with art and literature. His daughter gets him a great many books to fill the shelves an architect has put into his newly decorated bedroom. They make up the sort of "well-rounded" set of classics a well-meaning person might suggest for a man who has never opened a book in his life: Bossuet, Racine, Voltaire, Fénelon, Pascal, Rousseau, and the like—all magnificently and expensively bound by Thouvenin—"in short," Balzac nastily remarks, "a commonplace assortment of books that you find everywhere and that her father would never read." [49]

Though César does not read books, and hence has no literary taste, good or bad, he does have a few words to say about artists. These come out in his conversation with the architect Grindot, who has come to redesign his living quarters. In a scene that might have been written by Henry Monnier, César uncovers his total ignorance of art and in his role of customer, treats Grindot with overbearing arrogance. In fact, Balzac shifts to a different style and permits himself a kind of caricatural humor that is incongruous with his characterization of César at more serious moments. On time for his engagement with César, the architect is greeted with an absurd line of chatter:

> "Contrary to the habit of talented men, you are on time, monsieur," said César, with a show of his most distinguished commercial graces. "If being on time—to quote the King, a man of wit as well as a great politician—is a royal form of politeness, it is also good business for us merchants. Time—time is money, especially for you artists. And architecture, if I may permit myself to say so, combines all the other arts."

These are indeed "commercial graces." The speaker is not the peasant-bourgeois Birotteau, the simple, honest man whom

Balzac describes elsewhere as a symbol of probity. This is rather the style of Joseph Prudhomme, or, to quote Balzac, "one of those bourgeois who are the constant butt of the artist's barbs and jokes, the eternal object of his contempt." [50]

This is assuredly only a superficial sortie of Balzac's, an example of his indulgence in the general anti-bourgeois fever that raged among contemporary artists and writers. But it is likely that at the moment Balzac composed this scene, he was feeling a sincere resentment toward his buying public, the ignorant pseudo-bourgeois masses on whom a good part of his livelihood depended. His hero doesn't read, but in this scene he represents part of the art market. Today he wants his house redecorated; tomorrow he may want a portrait or may even commission the writing of a book (like the collection of Napoleon's thoughts and maxims that Balzac once wrote and sold to a bonnet-maker who thought he might be awarded the cross of the Legion of Honor for it [51]).

Balzac's objection to this kind of bourgeois is real and strong. Despite his sympathy and perhaps even momentary self-identification with César, his admiration for his virtues and pity for his misfortunes, Balzac's conviction that the old social hierarchy was best does not allow him to accept without protest the way men like César—good men in their place—are subverting the values of a society built downward from the aristocracy.

Depuis 1830 . . .

In a vast number of digressions in the novels written after 1830, Balzac condemned manifestations of what he seems to have considered the spirit of a new age. In fact, the decadence of both individuals and society is one of the great and pervading themes of the *Comédie humaine*. Of course, the most frequent complaint is that money had acquired an exaggerated importance under the July Monarchy. The commercial bourgeois in these novels is usually willing to praise the king and identify him with the interests of the bourgeoisie and with the general adoration of the Golden Calf. "I adore Louis-Philippe [exclaims Achille Rivet, a bourgeois who has enriched himself by making gold braid for officers' uniforms]; he is my idol, the august and perfect representation of the class on which he has founded his dynasty. I shall never forget what he has done for the gold braid industry by re-establishing the National Guard." [52]

One might say that, for Balzac, 1830 assumed something of the same significance that 1789 had for Stendhal. In *Une Fille d'Eve*, he spoke of "the strange upsets that 1830 was to bring about in the politics, the fortunes and the morality of France." [53] In later writings, like *La Cousine Bette* and *Les Petits Bourgeois*, 1830 is often mentioned as a pivotal date that was followed by a bourgeois era of sham, hypocrisy and moral and physical decay. [54] Even the art of making love, he once declared, had been undermined by hypocrisy, "the dominant trait of our age." [55] He inveighs against the *embourgeoisement* and degradation of elegant and beautiful sections of Paris during the July Monarchy, sometimes because old buildings have sunk into a new misery and ugliness, but more often because new constructions seem to symbolize the hypocrisy and false pretensions of the new bourgeoisie. [56]

Gold and pleasure dominate the life of all the classes of Parisian society: Such is the gist of Balzac's introductory observations on the soul of the infernal city in *La Fille aux yeux d'or*. All the citizens of Paris breathe alike its fetid exhalations; all are corrupted and debased by it. Some day, perhaps, wrote Balzac, thinking doubtless of himself, this Hell will find its Dante. Worst of all and unhappiest of all, he felt, were the men of affairs, or of business, who swarmed in the Parisian belly, its notaries, lawyers, bankers, merchants, speculators and magistrates. "What soul," he asked, "can remain great, pure, moral and generous" in the debasing exercise of these cruel occupations? "Such men must hide their hearts . . . if they have any." Even the artist, who dwells in a higher sphere, is not immune to the corrosive bite of this competitive, money-oriented society. In vain he seeks to reconcile worldly success and glory, money and art. Those few who resist (the Joseph Bridaus, the Louis Lamberts, the Daniel D'Arthez') die young, unknown and misunderstood.[57]

These are Chattertonian sentiments. But though Balzac, like Vigny, attributed nobility to the solitary, poverty-stricken artist who refused to compromise with society, his policy was not a retiring one, either in life or in art. "Silence alone is great" was certainly not his motto. No doubt oppressed, or at least disturbed, "by the need to produce, overwhelmed by costly whims, fatigued by a rapacious genius and starved for pleasure" (his own words),[58] he pursued what he himself called a "sinuous" course betwen the Scylla of uncompromising, unrewarding artistic purity and the Charybdis of commercial venality. And it seems to have been one of his great literary preoccupations to portray the devious lives of heroes who sought to meet the challenge of this cruel, turbulent and dynamic society on its own terms, romanticizing and justifying his own life's struggle in the career of a Rastignac or even a Rubempré.

In a well-known passage of *Le Père Goriot*, Balzac suggests there is an esthetic factor in the crumbling morality of Eugène de Rastignac.

After a series of compromises, men reach the kind of relaxed morality that is professed in our time, when we encounter more rarely than ever before, those rectangular men, those fine men of strong will who never yield to evil. . . . Perhaps the study of the opposite would not be less beautiful or less dramatic—a depiction of the sinuous path along which a man of the world and of ambition leads his conscience, trying to skirt evil in order to achieve his ends, but still keeping up appearances.[59]

The dramatic and romantic qualities of Balzac's vision of a dark and sinister world in which virtue is always prey to corruption and destruction are a further reason for César Birotteau's failure to achieve heroic stature in the *Comédie humaine.* He is a good bourgeois as bourgeois go, but his virtues are too petty and too tame.

In a later work, Balzac put into the mouth of Bixiou an ironical and contemptuous definition of the pallid "commercial probity" that is César's chief qualification for heroism:

We are navigating in an essentially bourgeois era, in which honor, virtue, delicacy, talent, knowledge, in a word, genius, all consist in paying one's bills, owing nothing to anyone and minding one's own business. Be orderly and decent, have a wife and child, pay your rent and your taxes, take your turn at guard duty, be just like all the other fusiliers in your company, and your opportunities are unlimited—you may even get to be a minister of state.[60]

This is César Birotteau in a nutshell. His tragedy is bankruptcy, and his triumph is achieved when he pays off his creditors. Bixiou sneers at this sort of dull and unexciting bourgeois punctiliousness, and so, to some extent, does Balzac. There was some adventure in César's ambitious rise. But once risen, he is an ordinary bourgeois unable to cope with the powerful villains set against him and unable to compete with their esthetic charm.

Rather Vice than Bourgeois Virtue

Many of the most monumental characters of the *Comédie humaine* come to view their lives as a constant struggle in a social jungle where no holds are barred. The Rastignac of the closing pages of *Le Père Goriot* is a new type of romantic individualist hero, a Julien Sorel of the July Monarchy. In him Balzac studies the man who is determined to succeed, though with a full awareness of the moral price he must pay. But such novels are not merely a moral commentary on the times or a condemnation of the moral surrender of an impressionable young hero. In the *Comédie humaine* evil or vice takes on a positive beauty of its own, becomes an esthetic quality.

> If we compare society with a painting, must there not be shadows and chiaroscuro? What would things be like the day when there were only honest people in the world? . . . We should be bored to death; life would have lost its piquancy and we should put on mourning clothes the day we no longer needed locks on our doors. . . . As far as literature is concerned, the services rendered by thieves are even more eminent. . . . Men of letters owe them much. Thieves have entered the texture of a multitude of novels. They form an essential part of our melodramas, and it is only to these energetic collaborators that *Jean Sbogar, Les Deux Forçats*, and so on, have owed their success.[61]

Certainly, the *Comédie humaine* cannot be accused of erring in the direction of flat, monotonous reproduction of the everyday life of the honest bourgeois. Quite to the contrary, however vulgar and bourgeois the settings and characters of Balzac's novels may be, he manages to inject into them the sinister and foreboding atmosphere of a *roman noir*.

Essentially, *César Birotteau* is a horror story in which the protagonist's weakness and innocence and the strength and trickery of his enemies combine to drag him down to financial ruin. The chief villain is Du Tillet. When a clerk in César's shop, he had been caught pilfering the till and, enraged and afraid of possible later embarrassment, was determined to reduce his former employer to penury and insignificance. The course of his revenge assumes a pattern that appears frequently in the *Comédie humaine* and that was useful for creating suspense and horror. It is of course significant that the suspense and horror should develop so often, not in plots involving physical violence, but in the anticipation and the detailed description of financial ruin.

It is thus Du Tillet's plan for revenge that lends color and brings adventure into the career of the dull, flat, monotonous little bourgeois shopkeeper of the rue Saint-Honoré. As in so many other novels of Balzac's, an unscrupulous character, motivated by evident or obscure feelings of jealousy and hatred, patiently weaves a web of intrigue in which the victim, usually unaware of his precarious situation, is inevitably trapped. César's brother, the curé of Tours, is such a victim. So is David Séchard in *Les Souffrances de l'inventeur*. In *La Cousine Bette*, Mme Hulot is enmeshed in just such a long-nourished plot of revenge as Du Tillet's. In the second volume of *Illusions perdues*, Sixte du Châtelet, affronted and jealous, not only deprives Lucien de Rubempré of his mistress, but succeeds in humiliating the innocent young hero in the high Paris society Lucien had sought to enter. Generally, though not always, the denouement of these devious plots seems to affirm the inevitability of the defeat of innocence and virtue when they encounter evil.

Apart from the exceptional Vautrin, a remarkable number of the most sinister villains of the *Comédie humaine* are powerful bankers and usurers, with landlords and even publishers figuring among the minor ones. Balzac complains of the tameness and dullness of bourgeois virtue, but the evil of his bourgeois men of finance guarantees suspense and thrills at the humblest levels of business life. The harassed debtor, once his initial innocence has been dispelled, approaches the lairs of men like Nucingen, the Kellers, Cerizet and Gobseck with fear and horror, while the narrator reveals an underlying admiration of the immense power they wield and the sureness and cunning with which they trap their victims. Balzac even allows some of them (for example Gobseck) their own peculiar code of honor and a not altogether indefensible cynical philosophy. In short, if in this vast spider web of intrigue it is the fly that inspires our pity, the spider has greater dimensions and exerts a cruel fascination.

To be sure, the importance of the nonvirtuous characters and more or less unpalatable villains in the *Comédie humaine* is partly due to a naturalistic trend of the novel, which in the eighteenth century was already moving away from the unique description of love and pure paragons of virtue. In a significant passage of her *Essai sur les Fictions* (1795), Mme de Staël proposed the serious treatment of emotions usually considered base or comic. "People consider that novels are uniquely intended to portray love, the most violent, the most universal and the truest of all passions [but] ambition, pride, avarice and vanity could be the chief objects of novels containing fresher incidents and with situations as varied as those inspired by love." [62]

Realism alone, however, does not fully explain why César

Birotteau is a pygmy in the *Comédie humaine* and Vautrin a giant among hero-villains. The chiaroscuro effects Balzac sought in the *Comédie humaine* also derive from the immense craze for Satanism and Byronism that swept over Europe in the 1820's. His early novels, like *Argow le pirate* and *Jane la Pâle*, were composed in the style of the popular *roman frénétique* and catered to the romantic taste for tales of terror and strange adventure. There can be no doubt that what Mario Praz calls "the shadow of the divine Marquis" [63] hovered over Balzac and sharpened his perception of cruelty, horror and evil.

It would no doubt be stretching the point to associate Balzac's esthetics with that of Poe, Baudelaire or Huysmans, Moreau and Félicien Rops. The bloody, Lesbian cruelty of *La Fille aux yeux d'or* is unique in Balzac's novels. Here and there we find a suggestive word, as when Balzac says that Bixiou commits "evil for evil's sake." [64] It is certain, however, that like most of the romantics, Balzac wrote with the moral-esthetic conviction that if goodness is better than evil, evil is more exciting than goodness. And *César Birotteau*, like the other novels of the *Comédie humaine*, is not a reasonable apology for bourgeois virtue or a sober, objective, "realistic" document. Eighty years ago, Philarète Chasles perceived clearly what some critics still do not understand today: Balzac "was a *voyant*, not an observer." [65]

The bourgeois of the Balzacian novel is not a product of exhaustive, scientific study, but rather of the novelist's vision of society, and particularly of his vision of Paris. That vision was abetted, of course, by observation, and Balzac's grim moral judgment of his era is substantiated by denunciations from the pens of many other writers. He was himself obsessed by his personal struggle, by a sense of the inevitable triumph of evil and by a curious fascination for the processes of compromise, corruption, degradation and demoralization that are always operative to some extent in the soul of the ambitious and intelligent man.

The failure of César Birotteau to achieve real heroic stature is thus related in several ways to Balzac's vision of contemporary bourgeois society. He is too weak, too common, too peasant-bourgeois to resist the tide of contemporary forces. He participates in the gold rush, but commonly, mediocrely, boringly. The cruelty, cunning and hypocrisy needed to succeed in his time are denied him, and he cannot become a great figure of evil, an anti-hero, like Gobseck or Vautrin. He is too honest to pose for a fascinating portrait of moral decline and material success, like Eugène de Rastignac. And, finally, his virtue is unenlightened and instinctive and cannot be placed on the heights of Louis Lambert's and Daniel d'Arthez' intellectual and artistic integrity. In him, as in the other shopkeepers of the rue Saint-Denis and the petty government functionaries of *Les Employés* and *Les Petits Bourgeois*, Balzac sees the formation of a new class of "bourgeois masses," dedicated to material success and restrained only by their own personal limitations—rather than by respect for superior intelligence and talent or by a code of honor imposed from above.

To be sure, César is represented as a paragon of virtue, but his honesty is probably most significant for the amazement it creates among Cesar's contemporaries. In this respect alone, César clings to the ways of the pre-Revolutionary past when, as Balzac felt, a stratified society had kept all men's honor bright. Like his brother, the curé of Tours, César is at heart an innocent peasant, unable to cope with the hypocrisy and dishonesty that Balzac thought were gradually pervading bourgeois France after 1830.

IV · Gustavus Flaubertus Bourgeoisophobus

> *Le bourgeois (c'est-à-dire l'humanité en-*
> *tière maintenant, y compris le peuple)* . . .
>
> FLAUBERT

In all the nineteenth century there was probably no French writer who invested the word bourgeois with more savage contempt and bitter hatred than Gustave Flaubert. His hostility was not simply a hypertrophied romantic pose, a snobbish sense of identification with the nobility or an aggressive sympathy for the masses. Although Flaubert's romantic beginnings doubtless gave an important initial impetus to his feelings about the bourgeois, he later developed those feelings in an individual way that transformed the tradition that had transmitted them to him.

There is much about Flaubert, of course, that sets him apart from the tradition and from his own time. Perhaps the most estranging factor in his life was the still unsatisfactorily diagnosed "nervous" malady that dealt him such a heavy blow in his youth and was to haunt him for the remainder of his days.[1] Yet the picture of Flaubert living like a wounded hermit in total reclusion at Croisset is an exaggerated one; he lived in relative isolation, but not in an ivory tower. Flaubert was estranged and alienated from the bourgeois civilization and mass public of his time, but he was very knowledgeable about them. He did not participate in contemporary journalism or have much to do with the commercial side of literature, but he was by no means a stranger in Paris literary circles or even totally unconcerned about money matters. He judged his time harshly and perhaps even wrongly, but his judgment was not derived from ignorance.

Apart from his individual greatness, Flaubert is historically important for the influence he has wielded over the generations that followed him, an influence perhaps as considerable in its way as that of Mallarmé or Rimbaud. Moreover, his conception of style and art has been accompanied by a conception of the artist's relationship with the public and with society as a whole: The author of *Madame Bovary* diagnosed acutely the trend of separation between the democratized culture of the bourgeois masses and the art created by and for the modern intellectual elite. His estimation of the situation of the intellectual and artistic writer with respect to the mass public darkly complemented in a cultural way the Marxist prediction of the inevitable dictatorship of the proletariat.

Flaubert's "Vocation" for Art

There is an important difference between the manner of Flaubert's introduction to literature and the way in which most of the "realist" group became men of letters. The end of the July Monarchy and the early years of the Second Empire witnessed the rise of a generation composed not only of well-educated, literarily sophisticated writers like Flaubert, Baudelaire, Leconte de Lisle and Edmond de Goncourt, but also ill-educated men of petty bourgeois and even humbler origin, like Murger, the son of a tailor and concierge, and Champ-fleury, whose father was a provincial clerical worker. Their rise to literary and social respectability is symptomatic of a social change described more generally by Barrès and very specifically by Pierre Martino:

> Ambition mixed with romantic melancholy: that is what we keep encountering in this century, among thousands of young men—the Julien Sorels, the Rubemprés, the Amaurys—for whom the conquests of the bourgeoisie have burst open all social barriers and made everything possible.[2]

> In Paris, after the revolution of 1830, political and social changes that had been slowly at work for almost a century permitted a large number of young men from both the capital and the provinces, of humble birth and without much money, to embark on literary or artistic careers, which had been hitherto almost exclusively reserved for the Parisian bourgeoisie or the nobility. The dazzling triumphs of romanticism, the liberties allowed by the new regime, an active fermentation of social-istic ideas, a broader spread of secondary education and many other causes contributed to democratize the previously closed world of men of letters and shortly afterward literature itself.[3]

The 1850's, when both these widely different groups reached maturity, constituted a period in the history of French literature when the novel became in some hands a delicate, sophisticated and artistic form of expression, and in others a crude, "sincere" imitation of Bohemian and petty bourgeois life. These disparate kinds of literary effort were associated in their reception by contemporary critics and censors, were attacked as "immoral" and labeled as "realistic,"—judgments that time has not yet altogether erased. There are some com-mon denominators of the Champfleury kind of "realism" and that of Flaubert, but an initial and important distinction between the two men resides in the radically different origin, education and conception of art which separate Flaubert from the "intellectual proletariat."

The literary themes of Flaubert's early correspondence and of the posthumously published juvenile writings are not in the least indebted to Henry Monnier, Dickens and other presumable sources of the humbler "realistic" group. The youthful Flaubert shows no interest at all in the sincere, brutal and even ironic depiction of humble and petty bourgeois life in contemporary France. His major themes are rather those of the earlier *Bohême galante* and the Petit Cénacle of Gautier, Nerval, Borel and O'Neddy. He said in the preface he wrote for Louis Bouilhet's *Dernières Chansons:* "I do not know what schoolboys dream about now, but our dreams were superb in their extravagance. The last expanding developments of romanticism, reaching us and being cramped and squeezed in a provincial atmosphere, produced curious effervescences in our brains. . . . We were not only troubadours, insurrectionists and Orientals; we were, above all else, artists." [4] This recalls the florid aspirations of Philothée O'Neddy and Pétrus Borel, freshly out of school in the early thirties, when Flaubert and his friends were still dreaming in the classroom:

My soul soars piously upward only toward Poetry, that twin sister of God.[5]

And I swore by God a most lovely oath
To belong forever to art, and to it alone.[6]

Among all those who began around that time there was the same overflow of lyricism and quest for passion. To develop freely all the caprices of thought, even if they shocked taste, propriety and the rules; to hate and reject as much as possible what Horace called the *profanum vulgus* and what art students with their mustaches and long hair call green-grocers, philistines, or bourgeois; to extol love so hotly as to set fire to the paper, to proclaim it the sole end and means of happiness and to sanctify and deify Art as a second Creator: such were the basic ideas of the program that everyone tried to realize to the extent of his capabilities, the ideal and secret demands of romantic youth.[7]

Flaubert accepts the cult of Art (which he often capitalizes in the early letters); he is addicted to colorful and sensuous dreams of the Orient and of physical love. To the young Gustave, the profession of literature seems to signify dedication to an Art of which he is scarcely worthy, and not to the pursuit of a career, leading to fame and fortune or the services or implementation of a social ideal. The themes of his writing are personal, not the self-justifying confessional autobiography of a Rousseau, but the lyrically described imagery of passionate voyages and loves, derived from his romantic childhood readings. It is in the later introduction of such themes and such lyrical prose into the novels of modern French life (like *Madame Bovary* and the second *Education*) that critics like Faguet see the persistence of Flaubert's romanticism; [8] René Dumesnil, on the other hand, is convinced that the introduction was accomplished deliberately and that the romantic elements of these novels acquire a new and ironic meaning in their context.[9]

Despite his early enthusiasm for literature and the fact that the profession of a man of letters seemed to be his own vocation at the end of his college days, Flaubert's renunciation of a "normal" bourgeois career and decision to devote his life to art came neither soon nor directly. He seems in a mood to write purposely toward publication only after his return from the Orient, when he plunged into regular work on *Madame Bovary*. This hesitation was not because of any attraction, however weak, that the bourgeois professions held for him. It seems rather the result of an initial timidity, abetted by his father's insistence that he study law; the turning point, on the other hand, seems intimately connected with Flaubert's sudden physical collapse in 1843-44 and the death of his father in 1846—both events tending in different ways to make an "active" life less imperative, and both compelling and permitting the kind of life Flaubert would lead at Croisset, almost without interruption, from 1851 on.

Flaubert's vocation was not announced with confidence and in a spirit of aggressive ambitiousness. He was not the child to write, "Je veux être Chateaubriand ou rien," or the man to proclaim, as Balzac had, his intention of accomplishing with the pen what Napoleon had done with the sword. Flaubert's attitude toward Art is from the beginning one of humility and is marked by an almost exaggerated sense of insufficiency. In 1839 his future seemed to require some sort of decision. Writing to his friend, Chevalier, Flaubert confessed to a state of confusion. He will not become a writer, he declares, but will find his place in one of the banally bourgeois professions. Which one he does not know, for all repel him equally. "As for writing, I have renounced it completely and am sure my name will never be seen in print. I no longer have the strength for it and no longer feel capable of it. That is the sad or perhaps the happy truth. . . . I shall be like any other, as I must, like everyone, a lawyer, a doctor, a sub-prefect, a notary, an attorney, a *judge*, as judges go, a stupidity like all stupidities, mingling in society or shut up in a study. This last would be even sillier, though, for you really have to be in this all the way; there is no middle ground." [10] As a tentative decision that decides nothing, he has agreed to study law in Paris ("which, instead of leading to everything, leads to nothing"). He will thus spend three years there ("to get the 'syph' and then what next?"), but, he concludes, all he would really like to do would be to spend the rest of his life in an old ruined castle by the seashore.

The feelings of the family toward the possibility of a literary career are discreetly left to Chevalier's imagination in this interesting letter. However, we have some indirect testimony on the subject. Flaubert's niece, Mme Commanville, recalled that Flaubert's father was opposed to the idea and that it was primarily at his urging that Gustave enrolled at the Faculty of Law in Paris.

> His only vocation was for literature. But "literature" isn't a career; it doesn't lead to a "position." My grandfather would have wanted his son to be a scientist or a practitioner. To dedicate oneself solely and exclusively to the quest of the beautiful and of form seemed madness to him. He was a man of very austere character and very active habits and found it difficult to understand the nervous and somewhat feminine character of the artistic temperament. Had there only been his mother to consult, my uncle would have got more encouragement, but she insisted he obey his father, and it was decided that Gustave should study law in Paris.[11]

This is, on Dr. Flaubert's part, the perfectly normal and predictable bourgeois attitude toward a life in art. If there is any surprising element of the situation, it is the apparent total absence of protest and hostility from Flaubert himself. This is only partially explained by the enormous respect he had for his father (whom he later incarnated as the competent and respected Dr. Larivière of *Madame Bovary*).

Achille-Clophas Flaubert was not the caricatural money-grubbing type of provincial bourgeois. His family had for generations been veterinarians in Champagne, and he was the first of his line to reach the elevated position of chief surgeon in an important hospital. Others have depicted him as a man devoted to science and healing, respected and even venerated by his students, a great man in Rouen—"Nous sommes à Rouen ce qui s'appelle une famille." His death was an occasion for public mourning, and workers on the quays sought the honor of bearing his coffin to the cemetery.

Money could not have been the most important factor in whatever opposition such a man presented to his son's apparent vocation. The older Flaubert was too dedicated to his life's work to care for social climbing or self-enrichment. Moreover, there seems to have been little need to insure a profitable career for Gustave. Later, when Flaubert failed his second law examination in Paris and suffered his great "nervous crisis," and after his father's death, these events, though unsettling and even crucially important, had no immediate pronounced effect on the financial status of the family. Shortly after his father's death, Gustave moved with his mother into the recently acquired house at Croisset, and with the exception of his trips abroad and fairly frequent visits to Paris, he remained there for the rest of his life. After 1843 there seemed to be no pressure at all on the young man to resume his studies or seek any sort of position in the outside world. Mme Flaubert caused her son no difficulties when he set about writing the version of the *Tentation* that Bouilhet and Du Camp advised him to burn. There were no acute money problems and would be none in Flaubert's life before Commanville's failure in 1875.

Although it is an exaggeration to think of the years after Flaubert's return from the Orient (1851) as spent in the absolute solitude of a recluse, his entrance into the profession of letters was, to say the least, exceptional. He submitted nothing for publication before he was thirty-five years old—no hack writing, no journalism, not even an inferior or unsuccessful book. Then, after five years of hard labor, *Madame Bovary* appeared and was followed by the trial, national celebrity and commercial success. This was, moreover, a book written in a style and in accordance with esthetic ideas totally different from those of the romantic literature on which Flaubert was nourished, and which represented a considerable evolution from his earlier unpublished works. It had been swept almost clean of purple passages, and irony replaced the earlier romantic fervor.

The *Education sentimentale*

Like *Madame Bovary*, the second *Education sentimentale* represented a return to the scene of modern life (the *Tentation* had preceded *Bovary*, and *Salammbô* was followed by the *Education*). I have chosen to go on to the *Education* and use it as my central text because in it are discernible many of the ambiguities that make Gustave Flaubert's personality and work complex, particularly his representation of his own time and of the contemporary bourgeois. The central character of that novel, Frédéric Moreau, is neither a subjectively drawn Rousseauistic hero nor an impassively observed laboratory specimen. There is much in him that is reminiscent of the youthful Flaubert and his successive incarnations in *Mémoires d'un fou*, *Novembre* and the first *Education*, much that is built, as Mme Commanville wrote, in memory of the author's own brief student days in Paris.[12] But there is much more: The *Education* is not a personal story, but the "moral history" of Flaubert's entire generation; it is his judgment of his time, his condemnation of the entire bourgeois civilization of the late July Monarchy and early Empire, an important document for the study of the evolution of the artist's alienation from society.

Throughout the composition of the second *Education senti-mentale*, Flaubert claimed to be dissatisfied with the subject of the novel. In the correspondence, the course of creation is marked by a series of protests of disgust, impatient and angry cries of being stifled and tormented by the vulgar and stomach-turning bourgeois characters and atmosphere Flaubert was compelled to study and represent as he wrote.

Decidedly, I wasn't born to write about modern things; it costs me too much to get into it. [March-April 1863]

I have planned out two books, but neither one satisfies me. The first is a series of analyses and mediocre gossip lacking grandeur and beauty. Since truth is not for me a primary consideration in Art, I can't be resigned to writing such drivel. As for the second [*Bouvard et Pécuchet*], I like the over-all idea of it, but I am afraid of being stoned by the population or deported by the government, not to speak of some frightful difficulties I foresee in carrying it out. [May 1863]

After much hesitation, I have begun work on a great novel that will take *years* and that has a subject I hardly care for at all. [May 1865]

It will be mediocre, for it was badly conceived. I shall take my revenge in another where there will be no more bourgeois, for they make my gorge rise with disgust. [August 1866]

. . . at present I am lost in a desert. . . . To paint the modern French bourgeois gives me a strange stink in the nose. And besides, it might perhaps be time to have a bit of fun in life and to take subjects that are agreeable for an author. [December 1866]

What really distresses me is the conviction I have that I am doing something useless, that is, something contrary to the purpose of Art, which is a vague exaltation. As it is, with the scientific requirements we have now and with a bourgeois subject, the thing seems radically impossible to me. Beauty is incompatible with modern life. So this is the last time I meddle with it. I've had enough. [December 1866]

. . . I shall no longer undertake such tasks. This moral cohabitation with bourgeois obsesses and exhausts me. I feel the need for living in cleaner surroundings. [July 1868]

But I shall not start portraying the bourgeois again. Oh no! Oh no! It's time I had some fun. [October 1868] [13]

These violent assertions cannot quite be taken at their face value. One mitigating circumstance, which Thibaudet stresses, is that Flaubert wrote his letters late at night, when he was at work on a novel.[14] The letters are therefore partly the result of fatigue and disappointment after a long day's struggle with the *affres du style*. Moreover, writing was for Flaubert a sort of masochistic act, a combination of pleasure and torment, with the pain of it outweighing the pleasure on some days, and on others, the pain stimulating, augmenting or constituting the pleasure. This is a diagnosis Flaubert himself formulated and expressed several times in his letters:

As for my passion for work, I might compare it to a kind of itching skin disease. I scratch while I scream. It is simultaneously both pleasure and torture.

I lead a bitter life, barren of all exterior joy. There is nothing in it to sustain me save a sort of permanent fury, which sometimes weeps for impotence, but is uninterrupted. I love my work with a frenzied and perverted love, as an ascetic loves the haircloth that scratches his belly.[15]

The discouragement and bitterness of letters Flaubert wrote while he was working on *Madame Bovary* and *Salammbô* may suggest that his complaints were inspired more by the pain and labor of composition than by the bourgeois subject of the *Education*. Here, however, we must perceive a distinction. However discouraged Flaubert was about the progress and perfection of his work on *Salammbô*, he did not revolt from the subject of that novel. In all that he wrote before the *Education*, there is only one work that evoked similar outbursts of nausea and anger, and that work also had a modern bourgeois subject. Here are some of the things Flaubert had to say about *Bovary*:

What I'm writing now risks sounding like Paul de Kock, unless I give it a profoundly literary form. But how can one compose trivial dialogue that is well written? [September 1852]

What I am required to do is to speak of the very commonest people in a literary style. [September 1852]

Each paragraph is good in itself, and, I am sure, there are some perfect pages. But precisely because of that, *it doesn't go.* . . . I am exhausting myself in realizing an ideal that in itself is perhaps absurd. Perhaps my subject does not permit this style. Oh! the happy times of *Saint-Antoine*, where are you now? Then I could put every bit of myself into writing! [January 1853]

To pronounce vulgarities simply and correctly! This is atrocious! [March 1853]

They won't get me to write about bourgeois things again. The fetidity of the foundation of this makes me sick to my stomach. [April 1853]

The vulgarity of my subject nauseates me at times, and I am terrified by the prospect of writing well about so many such commonplace things that are still ahead of me. . . . What is distressing is the thought that even a perfect success can be only tolerably fair and will never be beautiful, because of the very nature of the subject. I am producing the work of a clown. [July 1853] [16]

There can be no doubt that Flaubert's wrestlings with style, his relentless search for the *mot juste*, tired him, made him impatient, irritated and despondent; but in these two series of quotations there is a special and different kind of resentment, a feeling of "nausea" that is specifically related to the bourgeois subject. "This evening I am so beat I can't even hold my pen. It's the result of the vexation I had at the sight of a bourgeois. The bourgeois is getting *physically* intolerable for me. He almost makes me scream aloud." [17]

Flaubert often described *Madame Bovary* as a sort of experiment, the subject of which would be subordinated to the style, without love or hate of any of the characters. He maintained, in fact, that he was able to continue the novel only because its "mediocre" subject was an asset. Without any temptation to identify himself with the characters, with no vision of beauty to unleash his troublesome propensity for purple passages of lyric prose, he felt that his direct approach to the problem of style was unimpeded by personal or confessional obstruction. In one well-known letter, he went so far as to deny absolutely the value of the subject in a work of art. "Subjects are neither beautiful nor sordid and . . . taking the point of view of pure Art, one might almost hold it as axiomatic that there are no subjects at all, since style is in itself an absolute manner of seeing things." [18]

This position is comparable to that of Duranty and his group, as they presented it in the short-lived journal *Réalisme* (November 1856–March 1857). Bent on the unique study and exact representation of contemporary reality, they maintained that there are neither *beautiful* nor *ugly* subjects, but only *true* ones—a position that both resembles and differs from that of

Flaubert. The similarity resides in the fact that both accept an absolute standard of quality, which is or should be totally independent of the writer's feelings about the subject and indeed be apart from the subject itself. The difference lies in the identification of this quality or value. For the "realists" it is reality; for Flaubert it is "art," a beauty that is not a function of the subject, but of style.

Flaubert did not pretend that he could or wanted to suppress his feelings; he maintained rather that they should not manifest themselves in the "objectively" or "impassively" created work of art. Even so, there is considerable doubt that he succeeded in doing this in *Madame Bovary*, in which the style is often transparent to the writer's estimate of such characters as Emma and Homais. The second *Education* is somewhat more complicated, for it is even less than *Madame Bovary* a work with a purely "bourgeois" subject.

Nevertheless, it would seem at first glance that he had only reasons for avoiding what Gide called this "epic of disgust." [19] Flaubert swore during the writing of *Bovary* that he would never write another bourgeois novel. After the exotic interlude of *Salammbô* and less than a year before he began work on the *Education*, he was still protesting that his disgust was unabated. "I had taken a subject from antiquity in order to eliminate from my system the disgust that *Bovary* made me feel. It didn't work at all! Modern things are still just as repugnant to me as before! Just the anticipation of portraying bourgeois turns my stomach." [20] One would think that there were enough subjects to pick from without Flaubert's having to condemn himself to five more years of torment, writing a novel "contrary to the aim of art" about people and an era that were "unexalting" and "incompatible with beauty." Surely, the esthetic ideas that were presumably the guiding principle behind *Bovary* could have been satisfied without Flaubert's having to tickle his gorge over and over again.

But disgust had its compensations; Flaubert enjoyed the oratorical frenzies of his correspondence and wallowed in his vomit. Moreover—and this is much more important—the word bourgeois fails to describe the subject of the *Education* adequately. It was also a novel of love and, to some extent, Flaubert's own love at that. "For a month now I have been harnessed to a novel about modern life in Paris. I want to do a moral history of the men of my generation—'sentimental' history might be more exact. It is a book about love, about passion, but only the kind of passion that is possible nowadays, that is, inactive passion." [21]

"I want to do it": The wish is strongly expressed. In his project are two elements that Flaubert, the stylist, might have rejected, but that Flaubert, the moral historian and the romantic, was deeply concerned with. (Despite his dedication to pure Art and his hatred of his time, Flaubert was a self-righteous, preaching moralist, who, if he could have endured the sight of a mass of bourgeois congregated before him, might have been at home in the pulpit.) These two elements are the compelling interest in his own time—violently negative, but real for all of that—and the persistent appeal of the phantoms of Trouville.

Like most of the great novels of the nineteenth century, the *Education* is both a psychological novel and a novel of manners. These two aspects are joined in Frédéric Moreau's love for Marie Arnoux, which is not only a refashioning of Flaubert's own early passion for Elisa Schlesinger but also a symbol of Frédéric's weakness, which in turn is a symptom of the manners of his time. "The kind of passion that is possible nowadays, that is, inactive passion"—this is a formula reminiscent of Stendhal's and even of Balzac's criticisms of love in the nineteenth century. (Stendhal: "There are no longer any true passions in the nineteenth century; it is because of that that there is so much boredom in France." [22] Balzac: "Passion is a martyrdom. One aspires to the ideal and the infinite, and on all sides people want to improve themselves through love. . . . This hypocrisy, which is the character of our time, has put a gangrene into gallantry." [23]) But it recalls even more vividly Flaubert's own description of love in *Madame Bovary*: "It is an uninterrupted depiction of a bourgeois life and an inactive love, a love all the harder to portray for its being both timid and profound. But, alas! no inner extravagances, because the gentleman has a temperate disposition. There was already something analogous in the first part. My husband loves his wife a bit in the same way as my lover. They are two mediocrities put into the same setting, and yet I must make them different from one another." [24]

All the great Flaubert novels—*Madame Bovary*, *Salammbô*, the *Education*—are love stories, in which the hero's or heroine's love represents a failure to realize the ideal. (Bouvard's and Pécuchet's embarrassing and painful skirmishes with the fair sex are on a totally different plane from that of the love stories of Emma Bovary, Matho and Salammbô and Frédéric Moreau.) One may legitimately ask to what extent these stories are "impassively" recounted bourgeois adventures and how much they are reflections or transpositions of Flaubert's own youthful romantic dreams and yearnings. In their composition Flaubert exploited two kinds of sources, the external and the internal, and his characters therefore have two kinds of ambiguities. There is the kind described by Taine in a letter to Flaubert: "Your characters are exact specimens of the average modern bourgeois in France. They are all mixed beings, at times vulgar, refined at others, simultaneously good and bad, with intermittent desires. . . . Every real, living man is only an approximate, a hybrid, a mixture of whims and inconsistencies. To write with truth is to create the man in flesh and blood and not some energetic and grandiose character my imagination would take delight in contemplating." [25]

But when Taine, in the same letter, declares that Flaubert's choice of characters was accomplished by his having cast a net over the boulevard and hauled in a number of chance and average passers-by, we must disagree. This was not the way the character of Frédéric Moreau was created. The "hero" of the *Education* is the kind of modern mixed being Taine describes, but he is also endowed with virtues and weaknesses, ambiguities in short, which are common only to the extent to which Flaubert himself was an average young romantic bourgeois in 1840.

Frédéric Moreau is a bourgeois observed partly from within and partly from without. He cannot settle down to any steady productive work or get rid of many of his silly juvenile illusions. He is, however, potentially more noble than many of his friends and certainly on a much higher plane of contemporary bourgeois life than an Homais, a Roque or a Dambreuse. He is capable of an enthusiasm, of a fresh and naïve hunger for beauty and passion—qualities which Flaubert never really condemned. In this respect Frédéric resembles Emma, who, whether or not Flaubert ever said "Madame Bovary, c'est moi," was also a partly sympathetic character for Flaubert.

Baudelaire perceived this first and most acutely (although his curious feelings about sex and women required him to insist on the masculinity of Madame Bovary's qualities).

To put a final finishing touch to this *tour de force*, all that was left was for the author to abandon his sex (within reasonable limits) and to turn himself into a woman. The result of this has been wondrous. Despite all his zest for the role, he could not prevent himself from infusing virile blood into the veins of his creation. Madame Bovary, for her energy, her ambition and her penchant for reverie, remains very much a man. Like Pallas Athene, springing fully-armed from Zeus's forehead, this bizarre androgyne has, in her charming feminine body, kept all the seductiveness of a virile soul.[26]

Flaubert was not displeased by this comment. He replied: "Your article has given me the *greatest* pleasure. You have penetrated into the secret heart of my work, as if my mind were your own. You have understood and felt it perfectly." [27]

The bourgeois aspect of the *Education* was repulsive to Flaubert, but the story of Frédéric's attachment to Madame Arnoux, with its opportunities for the evocation of Flaubert's old romantic sensibility and lyricism, was attractive to him; at the same time, he sought to control both and subordinate them to the superior demands of style. "Neither monsters nor heroes!" he once wrote to George Sand, in definition of his art.[28] He said about the first *Education:*

> Literarily speaking, there are two distinct fellows in me. One of them is infatuated with windy gab, with lyricism and great eagle-like flights, with all the sonority of expression and the peaks of thought. The other digs and rummages in truth as much as he can, likes to give as much weight to the little facts as to the big ones, and would like to get you to feel in an almost *material* way the things he reproduces. This one enjoys laughing and takes pleasure in the animal side of man. Without my knowing it, the *Education sentimentale* [the 1845 version] was an effort to fuse these two tendencies of mine.[29]

Two months later, substantially the same idea reappears in connection with *Madame Bovary:* "Whatever value my book has, if any, will reside in its success in keeping to the narrow path just between the two abysses of lyricism and vulgarity (which I want to combine in a narrative analysis)." [30]

Both these forces of attraction and repulsion, however, are counteracted: Flaubert wanted to study contemporary social reality, and Frédéric's passion was weak, inactive and gradually atrophied by his "sentimental education." The result of the novelist's divided sentiments is that although the novel may seem to be a "realistic" representation of contemporary moral history, Frédéric's resemblances to the adolescent Flaubert make this story of conspicuous weakness and undermined virtues seem more like a pathetic personal drama than a detached satire or a moral comedy. The bitterness and disgust of Flaubert's inflamed correspondence conflict in the novel, as in his own feelings, with an inner compulsion, a personal commitment, to return again and again to the themes of his youthful confessional novels and revive in Frédéric his own dreams, passions and frustrations.

Frédéric Moreau—"Homme de toutes les faiblesses" [31]

Frédéric Moreau is introduced to the reader of the *Education* as an adolescent romantic of 1840. Some essential remarks about this, and the relevant citations from the text, have been made by Louis Biernawski in the concise critical study he wrote for the Conard edition of the novel.[32] Biernawski observes that not only Frédéric, but all his friends as well, are set in milieux that around 1840 were particularly susceptible to romantic influence: They are students and the children of professional bourgeois and minor civil servants, a group similar to that studied by Louis Maigron, whose material covers approximately the years of Frédéric's (and Flaubert's) adolescence.[33]

There are numerous striking resemblances between Frédéric's romanticism and Flaubert's own. Biernawski was concerned with demonstrating Flaubert's intention to recall

the ideas and sentiments of his generation, to write its moral
—or sentimental—history, by portraying in Frédéric a bourgeois adolescent *type* of the 1840's. There can be no doubt
that this is partly so. A question that concerns us more
directly, however, is the degree of sympathy that is established
between Flaubert and his young hero and, moreover, the
extent to which the novel is, if not pure confession or autobiography, the re-creation of Flaubert's own early sentiments
and state of mind. Frédéric is not Flaubert; no strict identification is possible; the novelist turns away from his hero, dis-
credits him, mocks him, attacks him. Yet there is much sympathy and much resemblance.

Briefly, the romantic elements Biernawski identifies in
Frédéric's moral and intellectual formation are the following:
Frédéric would like to be an artist or a writer ("the Walter
Scott of France"). His literary heroes are Werther, René,
Lara, Lélia. He does not produce much, but lazily dreams.
His ambitions, which are many and grandiose, are not matched
by his accomplishment; when work is the next step, Frédéric
finds a new subject for his dreams and abandons the old. He
falls in love with Mme Arnoux because of her resemblance to
the heroines of romantic books. He is a "maniac of exoticism—
that tendency of the imagination to emigrate in space or in
time, because one feels uncomfortable in one's country or in
one's age." [34]

Frédéric's central role in the *Education* is that of a lover.
He falls in love with Mme Arnoux in the first pages of the
novel, and this love is maintained as a unifying link throughout the book—which otherwise is very much a succession of
vignetted tableaux. There are, moreover, other women in
Frédéric's life—Louise Roque, Rosanette and Mme Dambreuse—contributing in diverse ways to the young hero's
"sentimental education." There are, in particular, three aspects
of Frédéric's manner of loving that seem to relate him inti-

mately with the Flaubert of *Mémoires d'un fou, Novembre* and the first *Education:* These are the linkings-up of love with adultery, with reverie and with money. A cursory examination of the importance of these matters in both the *Education* and the earlier works may demonstrate that Frédéric Moreau is neither a despised nor a "realistically" observed contemporary bourgeois; nor is he a totally sympathetic romantic hero; rather he is a hero who is weakened by being both romantic and bourgeois, and a bourgeois who is elevated by being both romantic and a sort of reflection of Flaubert himself.

Adultery: An Aspect of Romantic Ambiguity

The early attacks on the importance of the theme of adultery in *Madame Bovary* hit closer to the mark than admirers of Flaubert have been willing to admit. Flaubert held that morality has no place in art, and he was doubtless sincere when he said this. Thus, the argument that *Madame Bovary* is a book *against* adultery, because of its detailed revelation of the horrors that are its consequences, is not valid except for courtroom defense, where the main object of an argument is acquittal. It would also be a mistake to maintain that *Madame Bovary* was written to encourage the practice of adultery, although it is certain that the theme had a curious fascination for Flaubert.

Almost all of the novels, both the early and the later ones, include some form of forbidden love. Frédéric Moreau's love for both Marie Arnoux and Mme Dambreuse is adulterous, as is Henry's for Marie Renaud (in the first *Education*). Perhaps

—although this is straining the argument—Matho's passion for a girl who has renounced worldly relations and dedicated herself to the service of the virgin goddess Tanit is also in a way akin to adultery. Flaubert's own feelings about Elisa Schlesinger and his affair with Louise Colet were unquestionably adulterous. It may seem that these are frivolous and superficial *rapprochements;* there is more beneath the surface.

The early quasi-autobiographical writings—*Mémoires d'un fou* and *Novembre*—are crammed with erotic images and desires. The young Flaubert's incarnation of woman and mistress usually takes standard romantic forms: the mysterious and enchanting actress, separated from her adoring child lover by the magic barrier of the footlights; the untutored beauty of a girl in a fishing village; an Oriental houri, enveloped in misty veils and surrounded by silken cushions. In both works, however, another conception of love is outstanding: This is the passion for an older, married woman, mingling within it the attraction to her mature charms and the resentment (almost Oedipal) aroused by the boy's awareness of his exterior and inferior position with respect to the husband or the established lover.

This is no new theme in French literature. But adultery is more easily identifiable as cuckoldry in the seventeenth century and as libertinism in the eighteenth. In the nineteenth it becomes a serious and a sentimental kind of love. Two implications of the adulterous sentiment are evident in Flaubert's writings. One is that love of a married woman represents or creates a resentment or even rebellion against the institutions of society. Adultery, as Flaubert discovered, sitting on the bench of the accused, is regarded by organized society as an act undermining one of the most precious articles of bourgeois morality. The romantic in revolt was fond of expressing his contempt for the institution of marriage; but at the same time, knowing that his was an outlawed kind of love, he felt himself removed from society, a victim of fate, condemned either to sin or to frustration, though perhaps forgiven or even ennobled before a higher law. The lover of the married woman feels himself both superior and inferior to the husband, superior because of his sentiment, inferior because of his situation. Like Dumas' Antony, a host of young romantic heroes find themselves too sincere, too seriously in love to act the gay libertine, and even at times too sympathetic with the husband to turn him into the traditionally comic *cocu*.

The other element of this sort of illegitimate passion lies in the protective maternal attraction of the older woman. No doubt the prototype of this kind of seduction is Rousseau's relationship with Mme de Warens.[35] A similar situation is found in Stendhal's novels (Julien Sorel and Mme de Rênal, Lucien Leuwen and Mme de Chasteller, Fabrice del Dongo and the Duchess of Sanseverina) and in those of Balzac (Felix de Vandenesse and Mme de Mortsauf, Lucien de Rubempré and Mme de Bargeton). But none of these heroines is quite so much the married, the maternal, type as are Flaubert's numerous reincarnations of Mme Schlesinger.

In earlier writings Flaubert expressed his sentiments passionately. The youthful hero of *Mémoires d'un fou* reaches his moment of greatest ecstasy when he sees Maria nursing her infant child. The scene is intense, almost maniacal. "Oh! the unmatched ecstasy I derived from the sight of that breast! How I devoured it with my eyes, how I should have liked just to touch that bosom! It seemed to me that had I touched my lips to it, my teeth would have bitten it in fury, and my heart swooned with delight to think of the pleasure that kiss would bring."[36] The hero's ardor is also spurred by the contemplation of his successful rival, who has the enormous and unfair advantage of being married to the object of his passion: "I thought of her husband, that vulgar, jovial man, and the most hideous visions came before my eyes. It was like being put into a cage to starve to death in full sight of the most exquisite dainties." [37] In this tantalizing situation, the hero experiences a combination of feelings that had been matched in pre-Rousseauist literature only by the heroines of Racine. It is peculiarly romantic to indulge luxuriously in such self-imposed torments, to blend with passionate desire the conviction that individual fulfillment is a social crime. No doubt, the Church had always condemned the appetites of the flesh; but the tragic romantic hero laicized the older injunction. To yield to his temptation might even constitute a realization of divine intention (if love constitutes its own higher law), but it was most certainly a violation of human, social and, perhaps particularly, bourgeois morality.

Another, equally romantic aspect of this young man's situation is his inability to realize his desires, the complete separation of dream and reality. "La femme idéale que chacun poursuit dans ses songes" must be, if not unreal, at least unattainable. Part of the perverse voluptuousness of Flaubert's hero's passion depends on his being denied; this kind of pleasure must also give pain.

Although the heroine of *Novembre* is also called Marie, there is no literal reproduction of the seashore episode of Trouville. Nevertheless, part of the voluptuousness of the amorous adventure of *Novembre* is derived from the contrast between the hero's virginity and Marie's maturity. This experience is preceded in the text by many pages of reveries and lyrical longings inspired by "the demon of the flesh." One passage in particular seems remarkable: "From then on there was for me one word that seemed fair among all human words. Adultery—an exquisite sweetness glides vaguely over it and a singular magic embalms it. All the stories we tell, the books we read, the gestures we make, they all eternally pronounce and elucidate that word in a young man's heart. He drinks his fill of it and finds in it a supreme poetry, a blend of malediction and voluptuousness." [38]

The poetry of adultery has its practical problems too. Youth is poor and cannot pay for its pleasures, and this imposes its own bitterness and restraints. In another passage in *Novembre* that seems directly inspired by Flaubert's visits to the Schlesingers in Paris, the narrator protests his distaste for the love of a woman whom another man keeps. Following a general statement of this sentiment, the description becomes very precise: "To desire a married woman, and because of that to become her husband's friend, to clasp his hand with affection, laugh at his jokes, sympathize with his business troubles, run his errands, read the same newspaper he does—in a word, to commit more base acts and pronounce more platitudes in a single day than ten galley-slaves do in all their lives—that was something too humiliating for his pride, and yet he still loved several married women." [39]

This is exactly the situation in which Frédéric Moreau places himself shortly after his arrival in Paris. (For that matter, it is also comparable to the situation of Léon and Rodolphe in *Madame Bovary*.) Even though, in the later work, Flaubert makes something of a fool of his hero, inducing in the reader feelings of impatience with Frédéric's doglike attachment to the Arnoux, the fact that this behavior mirrors the words of an earlier, more personal hero seriously blunts the edge of detachment and establishes a firm and undeniable sentimental union. To attack one's generation in toto is quite different from attacking it through one's own person and through the heroes whom one has created passionately and sincerely in one's youth. Frédéric's love for Marie Arnoux is no ordinary bourgeois emotion; it is a special feeling from Flaubert's own past. Though it sometimes seems a caricature of reality, it has not entirely lost a lyric and poetic and even youthful quality. This is nowhere more evident than in the language of Frédéric's dreams.

Dreams: A Romantic Retreat from Reality

Another aspect of Flaubert's dogged retention in later works of the themes, language and action of his juvenilia is Frédéric Moreau's association of dreams of passion with dreams of the Orient. This is already evident in the first chapter of the *Education* when, struck by a sort of romantic *coup de foudre*, Frédéric Moreau falls in love at first sight. Mme Arnoux is immediately put into a colorful and exotic setting, not only in the imagination of the character Frédéric, but by the will of the writer. It is Frédéric who imagines Marie Arnoux to be of Creole or Andalusian origin, and who thinks she may have brought her maidservant from the distant isles of the West. But Flaubert decided that the servant should be a Negro; it was his choice that the violet and black and rose of Mme Arnoux's costume should be set against a boat rail and an open blue sky. Flaubert himself invented the long-haired harpist who sings and plays an Oriental romance. If Frédéric seems a silly, romantic dreamer, it is partly because Flaubert loaded the dice by creating circumstances especially favorable to his dreams.

During his first stay in Paris, Frédéric begins his visits to the Arnoux. Stimulated by frequent encounters with the woman he loves, the young man's imagination creates a series of exotic daydreams as he wanders about the city. This episode is a reworking of pages from *Novembre* and the first *Educa-tion*.[40] (Any understanding of the sentimental authenticity of the second *Education* must begin with the rejection of the comment that the editor of the Conard edition offers the readers of the first *Education:* "This work has nothing in common with the one published in 1869.")

Everything that Frédéric sees in his tour of the streets, parks and museums of Paris, is experienced as a function of his desire to possess Marie Arnoux. "It penetrated down into the depths of his temperament," comments Flaubert, "and became almost a general manner of feeling and a new mode of exist-ing." [41]

In Frédéric's mind's eye the Jardin des Plantes and the Louvre undergo romanticized transformations. The sight of a palm tree suggests the Orient, and Frédéric imagines himself and Mme Arnoux, traveling together, "on the backs of dromedaries, under the canopy of an elephant's howdah, in the cabin of a yacht amidst blue archipelagos, or side by side mounted on two mules that ring bells as they stumble in the grass against the remains of ancient columns." At the Louvre, Frédéric substitutes Mme Arnoux's face for those in the portraits of past centuries, in scenes of the Middle Ages, in the splendid panoramas of ancient Rome, on the cushions of an Arab's harem. "And everything that was beautiful, the twinkling of the stars, certain melodies, the turn of a phrase, a contour, made him think of her again in a sudden and imperceptible manner." [42]

This assemblage of romantic bric-a-brac, of ancient ruins, of the brilliantly colored and heavily perfumed Orient, with its strange and exciting fauna and flora, is not an unsympathe-tic caricature of the dreams of romantic adolescents. The studied rhythms of these jewel-studded sentences communi-cate a genuine lyricism and intoxication. The composite imagery, richly appealing to the senses, suggests comparison with the contemporary poetry of Baudelaire, Gautier, Leconte de Lisle and some of Hugo's *Orientales*. What is more, this imaginary voyage is no literary novelty for Flaubert; it is rather, on the contrary, a constant refrain in his work. It even makes its appearance in *Madame Bovary*, at a moment when Flaubert and the reader are warmly sympathetic with the unfortunate Emma, enclosed by ugliness and boredom, and longing for the passion and beauty she knows only from her childhood novels of love. Dreaming awake in her bed beside her snoring husband Charles, Emma imagines an elopement with Rodolphe. An enchanted, unreal countryside unfolds before the lovers as they flee southward on galloping horses, past domed cities, through forests of lemon trees and flowered streets to an idyllic fishing village by the blue sea.

We can go farther back to writings in which these imagined paradises are not the escapes of unhappy, disoriented and futile fictional characters, but are instead Flaubert's own. This language was not freshly invented for the impassively written novels of later life; it was taken from the dreams of Flaubert's youth, built on reminiscences from books like *Paul et Virginie*, *Les Natchez* and *Les Orientales*. "Oh, how my childhood was full of dreams," confessed Flaubert in 1838.[43] "I used to give myself over unrestrainedly to limitless reveries," he wrote four years later;[44] and in 1845, in the first *Education*, Jules asks Henry: "Do you remember our passion for India and for camels striding across the desert and the roaring of lions?"[45] In the profusion of dreams of flight and distant voyages through composite and panoramic landscapes with which the earlier writings are filled, the reader recognizes the images and objects, the exotic fauna and flora, that excite the imagination of Emma Bovary and Frédéric Moreau: palm trees and ruined columns, elephants and camels and galloping horses, primitive canoes and gondolas and ancient galleys and, above all, dark-skinned, passionate women who enfold the young hero in the mysterious embrace of the Orient.

The exoticism and lyricism of Flaubert and his heroes constitute a sort of measuring stick—not an absolutely sure one, but one that is of some use—for ascertaining the degree of sympathy between Flaubert and the heroes of later books. When Biernawski calls Frédéric a "maniac of exoticism," he is right; however, this is not simply Flaubert's objective diagnosis of the weaknesses of a generation of nineteenth century youth: It is that of *his* generation and of himself. Moreover, Flaubert's feeling about this lush romantic lyricism—this hunger for storybook love and dreaming about camels and elephants and the palm trees and pagodas of the East—is judged ambiguously. It is something he is trying to get away from, yet it is also something he remembers with nostalgia and even respect. He has tried to get into a different sort of art, purer and more impersonal, but he also connects his youthful enthusiasm with a state of moral integrity, of honest passion, and with an innocent vision of beauty.

As early as 1842 Flaubert already was aware and critical of the purple passages in *Novembre*. The bulk of this passionately confessional text, written in the first person, is highly colored and romantic. At the end, the young author appended a commentary, written in the third person, in which he not only terminated the interrupted narrative, but also criticized the style of the preceding pages. He is troubled by the excessive rhetoric, the many "metaphors, hyperboles and other figures of speech." He makes the following observation about the author: "During his early youth, he devoured the writings of very bad authors, as can be seen from his style. As he got older, he lost his taste for them, but really good writers never again gave him the same enthusiasm." [46]

The man who wrote these lines seems already in the process of becoming the author of *Madame Bovary* and the second *Education,* the man who subordinated life, the subject matter of art, to art itself. Still, mingled with his criticism and disapproval of the juvenile excesses in the text of *Novembre* is a feeling of nostalgia and regret for an age that, if it was more innocent and naïve, was also more active and "enthusiastic"—a regret that has its counterpart in Flaubert's disparaging comments about "inactive love." The real Flaubert replaced his lost youthful enthusiasm with a regimen of hard work, dedicated to the production of an art more difficult and exacting than his earlier lyric outbursts. Yet this was a productive process totally lacking in youthful abandon, an art that was hard in all senses of the word. Like Mallarmé, Flaubert complained of being blocked and sterilized by the kind of art he pursued. He once wrote to George Sand: "I have contradictory *ideals.* Because of that, I am obstructed, checked and impotent." [47]

Frédéric Moreau's life ends in failure. Having begun with many of the same qualities and defects as his creator, he submits to and participates in his own corruption. Society and the events of his time transform him into a "bourgeois," in Flaubert's own special unfavorable sense of the word. The study of this degradation made Flaubert's gorge rise; but it was necessary, he thought, if he were going to write the moral —or sentimental—history of his generation. And for those who wanted such a history to have a more attractive conclusion (than the ironic "those were our best times"), he had nothing but contempt. Flaubert is said to have remarked to the novelist, Henry Céard: "The public wants books that will exalt its illusions, whereas *L'Education sentimentale. . . .*" Whereupon, related Céard, "he turned his big hands downward, and indicated that all his unfulfilled dreams were tumbling hopelessly down into nothingness." [48]

The decline, sentimental atrophy or "bourgeoisification" of Frédéric Moreau can perhaps be illustrated best by relating his sentimental life to his conception of the kind of bourgeois life he wanted to lead and to the importance he attached to the role of money in that life. Like all the important characters in Flaubert's novels of modern life, Frédéric Moreau is inescapably a nineteenth century bourgeois, even though he is, like Emma Bovary, different from others because of his sensibility and his addiction to romantic dreams.

Love and Money

Frédéric comes of a modestly well-to-do provincial *rentier* family, is of vaguely aristocratic origin on his mother's side and has expectations of a comfortable inheritance from a rich uncle who has made his money in business. Frédéric and his mother are ashamed of the rich uncle because of his debasing commercial activities; nevertheless, they feel no qualms about looking forward to his death and the inheritance of a fortune that will enable Frédéric to pursue a socially esteemed career like diplomacy. When, very early in the novel, Uncle Barthélémy does die and surprise the Moreaus by willing all his money to Frédéric, there are no tears wasted on him. The Moreaus are unreservedly overjoyed; their ship has finally come in.

Frédéric's financial history is an acknowledgement of the essential importance of money to himself and his mother. Money regulates their social relations with neighbors in Nogent; it is necessary for the preservation of an elevated status, to which Frédéric's mother clings, and for the realization of both his and her dreams for his future. To be sure, they are not avaricious or inclined toward the crude accumulation of wealth in the manner of various other bourgeois in Flaubert's novels—Roque, Dambreuse, Homais, Lheureux. These are the men who rise in Flaubert's fictional world and whose energy, aggressiveness and success constitute, shamefully, its major social dynamics. Frédéric Moreau is another kind of man. He has no great taste for making money, no real ambition for a trade, a profession or a career. This is of course, suggestive of Flaubert's own feelings about a career at the time he left college, and also those of his hero of *Novembre:* "When it became necessary for him to choose a calling, he hesitated before a thousand repugnant possibilities. . . . And besides were things like these [criticism, literature] really *professions? You have to get established; find a position in the world; man is born to work:* Care had been taken to repeat often to him these maxims so difficult to understand." [49] Soaked, like Emma Bovary, in his romantic dreams, Frédéric thinks of money only when threatened by its loss and faced with the prospect of being toppled from his high style of *rentier* living with all its pleasures, prestige and privileges. (On the great day of his inheritance, Frédéric informs his mother of his firm desire to return to Paris. "To do what?" she asks. "Nothing!")

There are curious associations in Frédéric's mind between money and his misty love for Marie Arnoux. His half-hearted and inactive courtship of this married woman must be accompanied by signs of a comfortable bourgeois way of life. Like the hero of *Novembre*, he is ashamed of a social and economic position inferior to that of the husband of the woman he loves. His first reaction to unexpected wealth is the joyful thought of how it will affect his relations with Mme Arnoux. The course of Frédéric's sentimental evolution can, in fact, be traced by reference to some crucial moments of his financial history.

The first crisis arrives when Mme Moreau informs her son that as a result of various misfortunes he will inherit an income of only 2,300 francs a year. Although, at the time, many workingmen were obliged to support a family on less than 1,000 francs, Frédéric is crushed by the news. ("Ruined, stripped, lost!") He curses his fate and savagely wishes to relieve his feelings by beating someone up.

Frédéric's first concern in connection with this revelation of poverty is for his relations with Mme Arnoux. He feels his friendship with the Arnoux is based on his insinuations of great expectations, that Mme Arnoux will despise him as a liar and a fraud. Poor, he can never see her again. "He could not always live up on the fifth floor, with the door-keeper for his servant, and come calling on her wearing his old black gloves worn blue at the finger tips, a greasy hat, the same frock coat for a year! No! No! Never!" [50]

His despair gives rise to fresh dreams. Frédéric reminds himself that others have been and are as poor as he. He loathes himself for attaching so much importance to money. Without it, he will have all the more reason to accomplish great things. And he already sees himself feverishly at work in a garret, while Mme Arnoux, far from scorning and abandoning him, will be moved to new tenderness by his trials, and admire his energy and courage. This is silly romantic dreaming; Frédéric will never be able to work, and Flaubert despises him for it. What is significant in this action is that one of Frédéric's ideals is unrealizable without wealth, and that another, that of the self-pitying, martyred romantic hero, is awakened by his destitution. Frédéric would never be happy if he were poor. But he has read enough and knows enough about the structure of contemporary society to feel guilty toward those less fortunate than he and to have the feeling, if not the conviction, that money is despicable, is a corrupting influence and is not necessarily related to merit. His relations with Deslauriers, for example, who is poorer—and bitterer—than he, are marked by his feelings of guilt about his social successes and more comfortable situation.

It is again of Mme Arnoux that the hero of the *Education* first thinks when he hears a few months later that he will inherit his uncle's fortune. His immediate reaction to the news takes the form of a dream of the imagined future. "An income of twenty-seven thousand francs! He was convulsed in a frenzy of joy at the idea of seeing Mme Arnoux once again. With the clarity of a hallucination, he saw himself at her side in her apartment, bringing her some gift wrapped in tissue paper, while before the door stood his tilbury—no! rather a coupé! a black coupé with a manservant in brown livery. He could hear his horse pawing the ground and the clinking of its curb-chain mingling with the murmur of their kisses." [51]

At this early stage of Frédéric's youth, wealth symbolizes a way of life, that of the elegant, idling dandy, the same sort of life to which Lucien de Rubempré aspired in the second part of *Les Illusions perdues*. There is the added complication that this way of life is important to Frédéric mainly as a requirement for his continued courtship of Mme Arnoux. Frédéric does not seek actively to enrich himself; his material well-being is important to him primarily for sentimental reasons.

Money is also an important factor in Frédéric's relations with Louise Roque and Mme Dambreuse, two women whom he courts but does not love. In both of these affairs, his interest is more selfish and his sentiment is less ethereal. Nevertheless, neither of these relationships is totally exempt of elements that were already present in Flaubert's youthful writings.

Frédéric courts Louise Roque for one reason: He has lost 60,000 francs on the stock market and has thought of recouping his losses by making a good marriage. Deslauriers reminds him that Louise is available, whereupon Frédéric sets out immediately for Nogent-sur-Seine. There he discovers that both his mother and Louise's father favor the marriage and that the girl is ardently in love with him. Once more, however, it is clear that Frédéric is not uniquely concerned with material gain. He hesitates to reply definitely to Louise's own proposal of marriage and is disturbed and embarrassed by the violence of her passion. Other factors complicate the situation: Frédéric is once more welcome at the Dambreuses; Rosanette seems ready to become his mistress; and he is nostalgic for Paris. Feeling that he is being given no time to come to a decision which presumably he had made before his arrival, Frédéric leaves everything in the air and returns to Paris.

Once back, with a safe distance between himself and the field of action, he is able to deal with the matter in a way that can have no consequences: He dreams about it. "The idea of getting married no longer seemed exorbitant to him. They would travel, they would go to Italy and to the Orient! And he pictured her standing on a little knoll, viewing the countryside, or clinging to his arm in a Florentine gallery. . . . Once outside her surroundings, in a little time she would make a charming consort. Besides, he was tempted by M. Roque's fortune. Nevertheless, such a consideration repelled him as a weakness, a degradation." [52]

This action has an element of baseness in it. Frédéric's approach to Louise because of her money is relieved and tempered by his embarrassment, his consciousness of the ignobility of what he has started to do and his inability to carry out his first intentions; but mingled with this combination of weakness and virtue are Frédéric's snobbish feelings about Louise's social origin and her rusticity, her total lack of the maturity of Mme Arnoux, the verve of Rosanette and the sophisticated worldliness of Mme Dambreuse. Thus his rejection of Louise is only partly motivated by virtue; it is also connected with his snobbishness, vanity and indecisiveness.

Mme Dambreuse is quite a different woman, as well as a different social type, from all the others whom Frédéric courts. He had admired her for years before she became his mistress. It was chiefly her social grace, all that she represented of a world above his own, that attracted him to her. This is still the only charm she exerts over him when he becomes her lover and then husband.

> It seemed to Frédéric, as he descended the staircase, that he had become another man, that he was being steeped in the perfumed warmth of a hothouse and was definitively entering the higher society of patrician adultery and lofty intrigue.

> His joy at possessing a rich woman was spoiled by no contrast. The sentiment harmonized with the setting.[53]

This is evidently an echo of Flaubert's earlier lyric dreams of adultery in *Novembre*. Here, of course, he ironizes the sentiment and does not associate himself personally with Frédéric's juvenile vanity and social *arrivisme*. It is at this moment of the action, it would seem, that Flaubert withdraws most of what little sympathy he had retained for his hero.

Frédéric is at first charmed by the novelty of his mistress' social graces. He admires her coolness and aplomb when they are together in company. He contemplates with delight the elegance of her attire and is impressed by the expensive and tasteful gifts she sends him. But these spurs to his senses are soon blunted and ineffective. It becomes particularly disillusioning to see Mme Dambreuse in dresses that display her meager endowments. Frédéric is compelled to counterfeit passion by imagining in their place the fuller charms of Rosanette or Mme Arnoux.

To be excited by the idea of possessing a rich lady of fashion may be an adolescent emotion, yet it is not necessarily a base one. The disillusionment of Frédéric's senses, however, is accompanied by what Flaubert calls a sentimental atrophy. "This atrophy of the feelings left his head entirely free, and more than ever he thought ambitiously of a high position in society. Since he had his foot on such a stepping stone, the least he could do was to make use of it." [54] Frédéric's subsequent marriage is a calculated act, devoid of sentiment. That Dambreuse had left his widow no money is Frédéric's ironically just punishment. Had he married Louise, whose attractions were not entirely limited to her fortune, Frédéric might have fared a bit better, even if she too had been impoverished.

An incident in which Maxime du Camp played a major role is said to have inspired this part of the action of the novel.[55] This is not difficult to believe. Here alone, out of all Frédéric's sentimental adventures, is the pursuit of money and of social position unrestrained by the hero's feelings of disgust, guilt or contempt for his own behavior and untempered by the admixture of other motives and considerations that might evoke some sympathy from the reader. Once again, it is true, he delivers himself to his habit of dreaming. But this time, both the setting and the substance of his dreams are unsympathetic and revolting. M. Dambreuse has just died, and at his deathbed his wife has proposed to Frédéric. He accepts and begins at once to picture his future life of wealth, the furnishing and redecoration of Dambreuse's house—a reverie interrupted by only a brief moment of remorse for his crude thoughts.

In short, Frédéric's capacity to love sincerely has been corrupted by the material values of bourgeois society. His potential nobility, his dreams of beauty, are relics of childhood, attenuated or transformed into indecision, the inability to work and a welter of out-of-date juvenile illusions.

Frédéric has neither revolted against society nor been integrated into it in a solid and productive way.

Flaubert himself admired a certain kind of bourgeois competence. In the character of Dr. Larivière, who attended Emma Bovary at her deathbed, he raised a memorial to his father, a competent, respected physician, dedicated to the highest ideals of his profession. Some of the virtues of this man were transmitted to his bourgeois-hating son. Flaubert too was dedicated to his work and practiced it with the laboriousness and conscientiousness that distinguished his father's exercise of the profession of medicine. Mme Commanville relates that when she was a little girl, she thought vaguely that the words "Madame Bovary" were a synonym of work.[56] He won the battle that raged within himself, conquering what he considered his juvenile impulses and subjecting himself to a rigid and painful discipline. In Frédéric he paints a man whose will and desires were weaker and who retained only the illusions of his youth.

It would, however, be inexact to maintain that Flaubert had "homogenized" his own personality or that Frédéric had become a totally despicable character. Though Flaubert steeled himself to the labor required by his pursuit of "style," he did not work with the complacent pleasure of naïve confidence or self-satisfied vanity. He often confessed feeling inadequate to the tasks he had set himself and even claimed his ideals were contradictory. And Frédéric, despite his basely motivated marriage to Mme Dambreuse, still finds himself sentimentally attached to Mme Arnoux and is still innocent enough to be shocked by the workers' desertion of the socialists, by Deslauriers' marriage with Louise and by the turncoat Sénécal's, killing Dussardier.

Although invested with none of the solitary greatness of the poet or even with the honorable and respectable dignity of a Larivière, Frédéric is, nevertheless, far from being a bourgeois villain, and is less of a mediocrity than an Arnoux, a Charles Bovary or a Martinon. Like Emma Bovary, he is partially redeemed from total mediocrity by his sensibility and the idealism of his youthful desires. (Thibaudet, rightly seeing in Emma Bovary a "heroine" in contrast with characters like Sancho Panza and Homais, whom he calls counter-heroes, attributes her heroic value to her sensuality. "Everything in her is mediocre, except her desire and her feelings." [57]) Though by no means represented with total sympathy by Flaubert, Frédéric seems distinguished and, in a negative way, even moderately "heroic," in contrast with the more savagely hated bourgeois, Roque, Lheureux and Homais.

The "Bourgeois"

These three men are almost caricatural representatives of a new kind of bourgeois and incarnate most exactly Flaubert's most pejorative and contemptuous conception of the word. Unlike Frédéric, they are successful and in progress toward still greater future triumphs. They represent, not a numerically limited social class, but an evolutionary type Flaubert felt he could detect on all levels of contemporary society.

Despicable though a Dambreuse is, he does not belong to this group, but rather represents the financial bourgeoisie of the July Monarchy, a sort of aristocracy of its time. Larivière too is described as of a generation that disappeared with the July Monarchy. Like Stendhal and Balzac, Flaubert is fond of contrasting the ignoble present with the past and of observ-

ing decadence and degradation in the democratization of
modern France. He is capable of a feeling of respect for the
bourgeoisie, but when he speaks of it in this way, it is with the
understanding that the finer, old bourgeoisie is dead: "Bourgeois *no longer even means bourgeois,* for since the invention
of the omnibus, the bourgeoisie has been dead." [58] It is
customary to feel that society has entered a moral decline in
one's own lifetime. Stendhal found 1789 a line of demarca-
tion, terminating an era of grace and elegance and beginning
a new reign of boredom and hypocrisy. Balzac entertained a
similar conception of the importance of 1830. Flaubert went
a step farther: "The year 1789 demolished royalty and the
nobility, 1848 the bourgeoisie and 1851 *the common people.*
There is *nothing* any more save low and imbecilic impos-
ture." [59] But if in 1848 the bourgeoisie (in a nonpejorative
sense) had been suppressed, what sort of bourgeois survived
the debacle to be attacked by Flaubert throughout his lifetime?

Doubtless Flaubert's most familiar definition of the bourgeois is the one reported by Maupassant, who claimed his
master had not meant to vilify a particular class, but rather a
kind of mentality. "He made this word *bourgeois* the synonym of *stupidity* and defined it thus: 'I call anyone who thinks
basely bourgeois.' His quarrel was therefore in no way with
the bourgeois class, but with a particular sort of stupidity that
one most often encounters in that class. He had, moreover,
just as much contempt for the 'people.' But being less in contact with workers than with the upper classes, he suffered
less from lower-class stupidity than from the stupidity of
'society.' " [60]

This is confirmed by Mme Commanville, who wrote in the
"Souvenirs intimes": "He had a hatred for the 'bourgeois'
and constantly made use of that term. But in his mouth it was
a synonym for being mediocre, envious, for living virtuously

only on the surface and insulting all greatness and all beauty." [61]

Actually, these restatements of Flaubert's position reproduce fairly well what Flaubert himself said many times. He too maintained that the object of his contempt was, in principle at least not limited to any social or economic group. "As for me, I include in this word 'bourgeois' the bourgeois in overalls as well as the bourgeois in a frockcoat. It is we and we alone, that is to say the literati, who are the People, or better, the tradition of Humanity." [62] He declared often that he hated the masses, the crowd, the herd; maintained that the idealized conception of the popular man or worker was as worn out as that of the monarchy. [63] He was profoundly disillusioned by Louis Napoleon's easy victory over the French people and spoke slightingly of socialism afterwards. He wrote in 1853: "It was only on the days of rebellion that I liked the crowd, and even then! If one only saw what was at the bottom of things! In all that there were plenty of leaders and agitators. It's perhaps more contrived than we think." [64]

Flaubert's feelings about the masses are also clear in the *Education,* in which he expressed contempt for both the people and the socialists who sought to better their condition. There is certainly nothing impassive about the description of the sacking of the Tuileries. "Since they had won, didn't they have to have a good time!" "An obscene curiosity made them rummage through all the closets. . . ." "Convicts thrust their arms into the princesses' beds and rolled around on top of them to console themselves for not being able to rape their former occupants." When Hussonnet suggests to Frédéric that they leave this scene of wild and drunken material destruction, there is no doubt that Flaubert sympathizes with his comment, "Let's get out of here . . . these specimens of the lower classes disgust me"; while it is equally clear that Frédéric's reply was meant to sound naïve and juvenile: "I don't care," said Frédéric, "*I* think the lower classes are sublime." [65]

Not fully disabused during the rioting and elections of 1848, Frédéric has still not taken the measure of the people he says he adores, even as late as the December *coup d'état*. Flaubert seems deliberately to have indicated his personal contempt for both workers and bourgeois in his narration of an incident that takes place December 3rd. Frédéric has taken no part in the political action of the preceding days, being too concerned with his personal affairs. Stepping out into the street at last, he is surprised that the passage of an armed patrol evokes only jokes and insults from groups of people clustered on the boulevard.

> "What! Aren't you going to fight?" Frédéric asked a worker.
> The man in the worker's smock answered: "We're not so stupid as to get killed for the bourgeois! Let them settle it!"
> And a gentleman, looking sidewise at the workingman, muttered: "Socialist filth! If only, this time, we could exterminate them!"
> Frédéric didn't understand at all so much rancor and silliness. His disgust for Paris increased, and the day after next he left for Nogent on the first train.[66]

In this incident, as in Stendhal's narration of Lucien Leuwen's adventure at Blois, Flaubert's sympathy with his hero is mixed. He mocks Frédéric's naïveté, but also views the situation partly through his hero's eyes and judges it with Frédéric's sensibility; in Frédéric's reaction, he expresses his own disgust and contempt for the baseness of the Paris populace. And though this incident is mockery of Frédéric's innocence, the young man does not come off worst. His surprise and disgust are in a way the reaction of an external observer, a Zadig or a Gulliver, whose innocent question is posed only to create an occasion for revealing the author's judgment of mankind, which in this instance is severely critical of both worker and bourgeois. The incident, then, is really an attack on two species of the Flaubertian "bourgeois,"—worker and gentleman—in a man characterized (in this incident) by rancor, stupidity and lack of devotion to principles.

Of all the characters in Flaubert's novels of modern life, Homais, Lheureux and Roque, and perhaps Bournisien, are the most outstanding symbols of what Flaubert hated and meant most by the word bourgeois. These men are not purely imaginative creations. Real life models have been identified, and besides there are the earlier examples provided by Balzac and Monnier. (Henry Monnier, in fact, saw in Homais a character closely akin to his Prudhomme and asked Flaubert's permission to act the role on the stage.) But their significance is broader than as literal representations of reality. They stand for the new world in which the moral sense is on the wane and in which meanness and mediocrity are triumphing; they are the bourgeois who are coming into possession of the present and are to inherit the future.

There is in the fictional world of Flaubert a faint echo of the violent social dynamism of the *Comédie humaine*, in which the evil characters plot the downfall of the innocent and the good. Frédéric Moreau and the two Bovarys are hardly ideal heroes, yet they are relatively sympathetic characters. In *Madame Bovary* the decline of the Bovary family is reciprocal to the rise of Lheureux (who profits from Emma's foolish purchases and debts) and of Homais (who profits by taking over Charles's medical practice). Moreover, neither of the pair profits and rises in an ethical way: Homais's medical activities are illegal; Lheureux's business practices are sharp and unrespectable. Homais, though shrewd, is neither competent nor intelligent. He was really responsible for Charles's dreadful operation on Hippolyte's clubfoot. Larivière, exposed to his conversation, judged him a fool. Yet, at the end of the novel these two men, symbolizing *la bêtise humaine*, are triumphant, a conclusion that is vividly indicated by Flaubert's sudden change of tenses. All the action of the novel is related in the past tense. But suddenly, in the last few lines, the reader becomes aware that he has reached the present: This is *now*. Berthe, Charles' and Emma's little child, *is* poor and works in a cotton mill; while Homais *has put* three doctors to flight in Yonville, *is protected* by public opinion and *has just received* (final irony) "the Cross of Honor."

There is a comparable, though not an identical, opposition between Roque and the Moreaus. The fortunes of Frédéric and his mother are on the decline, whereas Roque's star is rising. Like the "bourgeois" of Yonville, he is a cruel, ruthless man. Dambreuse is not handled by Flaubert in exactly a kindly fashion, but compared with Roque, he is a gentleman and even an aristocrat. The latter is definitely condemned by Flaubert in a horrible scene in which Roque fires his rifle point-blank into the face of a young revolutionary who, from behind prison bars, begs him for bread. If there had previously been the feeblest spark of sympathy for any word or gesture of Roque's, Flaubert made sure it would be extinguished at this moment.

These men are all frauds. Homais is no scientist; Bournisien —who must fall into this group—is neither a respectable nor a competent priest. Flaubert is attacking neither Voltaireanism [67] nor religion in their persons, for they are not meant to represent men with sincere convictions, whether right or wrong. Emma and Frédéric are weak and silly, and they are failures; but they are sincere and sensitive, and, contrasted with these monsters of modern times, as Flaubert conceives them, they are almost hero and heroine.

Flaubert's exaggerated and almost caricatural disgust for the humanity of the Second Empire is related to a general pessimism, a generally negative attitude toward life. It would be beyond our powers to attempt to ascertain the relationship between his pessimism and the undiagnosed malady from which he suffered, but it seems certain that there was some correlation, that what happened to him in the winter of 1843-44 colored his emotions for the rest of his life. His feelings about mankind, society, life, are not altogether those of a well man. But this is not to say that Flaubert's argument was wildly conceived; it is rather to suggest that his conclusions were aggravated and darkened by his own personal condition. His argument is still basically reasonable. His time was one which favored strong doubts of the excellence of democracy—at least, of the limited democracy based on property that existed under the *monarchie censitaire* and of such sudden and untutored universal suffrage as existed under the Second Republic. It seemed to him—and he was perhaps not wholly wrong—that mankind was coming to be governed by its lowest common denominator. Moreover, as the son of a scientist who had come into close contact with the medical realities of death, and as a representative of an era in which science was rapidly becoming immensely important, he was compelled to reject the concept of an anthropocentric universe and to view man in his true material proportions. He wrote in 1857 to that spiritually troubled lady, Mlle Leroyer de Chantepie:

> Like you I have a constant spleen, which I try to appease with the great voice of Art. And when this Siren's voice happens to fail me, I suffer from an inexpressible dejection, irritation and ennui. What a poor thing humanity is, is it not? There are days when everything appears lamentable to me and others when everything seems grotesque. Life, death, joy and tears, it's all the same, ultimately. From up on the planet Saturn, our universe is a little spark. I know we should try to think as though we were up among the stars. But that isn't easy, not all the time.[68]

This is about the substance of Laforgue's *farce éphémère*, a life in which man is "a dreamy louse on a pitiful miniature world," although that ironic young man had not been born when the above lines were penned. But Flaubert was not altogether alone in his own generation. One of his contemporaries was the distressed Matthew Arnold of "Dover Beach"; another was Baudelaire, whose thought, despite the curious religious orientation of his mind, was in many ways in accord with that of the author of the *Education*. Like Flaubert, Baudelaire had come to think that a government based on democracy was absurd and feeble, and was exasperated by contemporary Voltaireans.[69] Flaubert felt that in "L'Albatros" and "Spleen" the poet had reproduced his own innermost thoughts. "*Le Spleen*," he wrote, "is heart-rending, so exact is its shading. Ah, you understand what a horrible bore existence is!"[70]

Flaubert and the Bourgeois Public

Given the special feelings that Flaubert had about both art and humanity, it is not difficult to accept his disdain for a public composed of contemporary bourgeois. He commented often on the decadence of the public of his time and pessimistically predicted the continuance of what he regarded as an unfavorable trend. Like Stendhal and Balzac before him and, for that matter, like most of the serious writers of the nineteenth century, he despised the mass public and claimed to write for an elite and, *à la rigueur*, for himself alone.

What in hell does the mob care about Art, poetry and style? It doesn't need any of that. Give it vaudeville shows, treatises on the work of prisons, on communities for workingmen and the material interests *of the moment.* . . . Why are Dumas' novels so prodigiously successful? It's because no initiation is required in order to read them, and their action is entertaining. Thus, one is distracted while reading them. Then, when the book is closed, since no impression is left and it has all gone through you like clear water, you can *get back to your business.*[71]

We are all sunk at the same level in a common mediocrity. Social equality has taken control of us. We put out books for the millions, Art for the millions and science for the millions, the way we build railroads and public warming-rooms. Humanity is crazed with moral debasement, and I am resentful for being part of it all.[72]

These letters sum up common trends of thought. In them Flaubert re-expresses observations that had helped to develop a sentiment of solitude among older artists who also had felt isolated in the midst of an uncomprehending society. From them emerge not only disdain for the general mass public, but also indifference to publication and contempt for the publishers and writers who pleased that public's taste.

But Flaubert's protests, indebted though they are to earlier expressions of solitude, superiority and alienation, are new and of his own time. His isolation is not inspired, even partly, as was Rousseau's, by feelings of apartness created by being a foreigner, a Protestant and, most important, of humble origin. Flaubert does not suffer from René's *mal du siècle;* the changes taking place in his world are only distantly caused by the Revolution of 1789. Flaubert's conception of art (for art's sake) is different from Vigny's presentation of the artist's situation in *Chatterton* and his revulsion from the industrial ugliness of modern civilization in "La Maison du berger."

The concept of a bourgeois who symbolizes "all humanity . . . including the common people" [73] is foreshadowed in Balzac's use of the expression "bourgeois masses," but Flaubert's extension of the word's meaning reflects social and cultural changes beyond the situation as Balzac knew it. By the bourgeois masses, the author of *César Birotteau* meant a petty bourgeois group, still close to a peasant and working-class origin and still distinct from the bourgeoisie proper. Flaubert perceives a more important and more general cultural leveling process taking place in the society of the Second Empire. What had formerly been the lower fringe of the reading public was then becoming, at least numerically, the dominant group. And instead of Prudhomme's elevation to the level of a Thiers, Flaubert saw Thiers assuming the stature of a Prudhomme.

Gautier had attacked the imposition of utilitarian principles on art as early as 1835, when *Mademoiselle de Maupin* first appeared, equipped with its formidable preface. But there is a profound difference betwen the target of his attacks and that of Flaubert's. *Mademoiselle de Maupin* appeared in an age of Saint-Simonian ascendancy. The Saint-Simonians had envisioned art as the handmaiden of human and social progress, the poet as a seer and mage who would lead an inspired public to the promised land. No poet who voluntarily espoused this conception of art need have been ashamed of his vocation.

Flaubert attacks utilitarianism of a different kind, the self-interested pursuit of personal material profit. This is not the kind of utilitarianism which generously asks the artist for a vision of human welfare and ennoblement; it asks instead for recipes for personal success, food for conversation and practical hints on the art of living. Flaubert once advised Mlle

Leroyer de Chantepie not to read, as children do, "for the fun of it," or, as the ambitious do, "for the sake of education," but rather to read *"to live."* [74]

For Flaubert, the bourgeois reader was not the bourgeois of the eighteenth century, or even that of the July Monarchy. He was the direct precursor of the twentieth century cinema public; that kind of reader and spectator who undertakes "serious" reading to be "informed" and "improved," while his artistic entertainment, furnished by the so-called mass communication media, must be trivial and ephemeral. In his conception of the representative bourgeois of his time, whose cultural level was to determine that of the twentieth century mass-man, Flaubert offered a justifying argument to those sensitive artists who retreated from the general literate public. Even though *Madame Bovary* (unlike *Un Coup de dés* and *La Jeune Parque*) could be read by all, it would have been Flaubert's contention that the nuances and delicacies of its style were perceptible only to a tiny elite. Flaubert did not take the way of hermeticism, but rather of a subtly polished art, the peculiar perfection of which is apparent only to the refined adept of style. The contrast between the kind of public he despised and the ideal public he might have respected is well put by Maupassant:

> Gustave Flaubert was before and above everything else an artist. The public of today scarcely perceives what the word means when it pertains to a man of letters. The feeling for art, a flair so subtle, so delicate, so difficult, so elusive and indescribable, is essentially a gift of intelligent aristocracies and can barely be claimed by democracies.
>
> In the preceding century, on the other hand, the public judged with great delicacy, was hard to please and carried to the extreme that sense for the artistic which is now disappearing. It would take passionate delight in a sentence, a verse, an ingenious or daring epithet. . . . It would hunt for what lay

beneath or inside the surface of a word, would penetrate the author's secret motives, would read slowly, passing nothing by, and always searching, after having understood a sentence, to see if there remained nothing more to discover. The minds of that time, slowly prepared for the perceptions that literature has to offer, were capable of undergoing the secret influence of that mysterious power that puts a soul into a work of art.[75]

In and Above the Bourgeoisie

Despite the evident sincerity of both Maupassant's and Flaubert's estimate of their contemporary public, however, there is more than meets the eye in these persuasive, absolute formulations. The public of the eighteenth century accords with Maupassant's description only partly. There were then no writers like Flaubert or Baudelaire; nor was there a public which could have appreciated them in the same way as their contemporary elite public. Flaubert is a late nineteenth century phenomenon and cannot be compared to a Montesquieu, a Diderot, a Voltaire, or a Rousseau. Even though the eighteenth century texts were dense and polished and best read slowly and leisurely, they were primarily communicative; the conditions responsible for the development of an art produced for "art's sake" did not yet exist. The art of writing clear and energetic prose was cultivated by all educated gentlemen, and the eighteenth century novelist wrote for his intellectual peers; he did not fancy himself a "poet," apart from other men, creating a "style" that would enclose and subordinate the subject of his writing, a style whose very perfection would symbolize the vast difference between literary levels.

Moreover, Flaubert's claim that he wanted to write only for himself was at least partly a pose. One cannot go so far as to call it hypocrisy; but the fact remains that had he genuinely renounced an approach to the public at large, he would have circulated his manuscript among his friends and let it go at that. As Vigny put it, "There is only one thing for a self-respecting man to do: publish, see nobody and forget his book." [76] But no. Flaubert wanted to sell his work: He not only wanted it published; he also wanted a good price for it. When he pretends otherwise (as he often does in the correspondence) he is dishonest, perhaps as much with himself as with his reader.

We cannot expect Flaubert to have wanted to appeal to the "liberty of a classless public," an impossible and utopian ideal, as Sartre himself admits. But, it seems to me, Sartre is perfectly right when he maintains that a writer like Flaubert "lives in contradiction and bad faith, since he knows and at the same time does not want to know *for whom* he writes." [77] Flaubert knew into whose hands Lévy, and later Charpentier, delivered his books. He accepted the commercial situation of writers of his time, as well as the bourgeois book-buying public. Furthermore, whereas some of his fellows might plead in their own defense that they needed the money, this was decidedly not so for Flaubert—at least, not before 1875.

It is hardly my object to take Flaubert to task for not having exercised his talent in the service of the oppressed. But I do find a subtle and not altogether honest sort of legerdemain in his use of the word bourgeois to isolate himself verbally from his class, while his way of life, his intellectual formation and even his art and "style" were all products of a highly cultivated bourgeois minority culture of the nineteenth century. The fault is not altogether his. Flaubert was led to use this word "bourgeois" as he did by the example of preceding generations of writers and caricaturists. Nevertheless, by not choosing instead some word free of a distinct class meaning, he seems to insinuate that he is not really a full-fledged bourgeois himself, although he half admitted that that was not so in a very questionable assertion: "Yes, I maintain (and that, for me, must be a practical dogma in an artist's life) that we have to divide our existence in two: live like a bourgeois and think like a demigod. The satisfactions of the body and of the head have nothing in common." [78]

Flaubert has no quarrel with what is comfortable and pleasant in nineteenth century bourgeois life: He wants its material comfort. Profoundly rooted in him is the bourgeois reverence for property; he is shocked by its destruction, by disorder, by the undisciplined rise and revolt of the masses. Are these traits of his character totally divorced from his life in art, or are they not related to his own heavy suppression of the romantic elements of his character? He rejects the romantics' socialism, their idealization of the man of the people, adopts a haughty and aristocratic attitude toward society, refusing his respect to a kind of "bourgeois" that is admittedly more common among the people and petty bourgeoisie than among those of his own social group. He scorns art designed to please or to instruct, himself producing and respecting only a luxury product, whose value is solely esthetic. Yet, he reveres hard work, competent productive labor, and denigrates the frivolous dreaming to which he himself was formerly so addicted and the appeal of which he still cannot totally deny.

Flaubert's certainty and dogmatism jar uncomfortably against his confusion and contradictions. He is hardly the spokesman of any dominant political or economic group of the bourgeoisie. His feelings of superiority are not quite those of a Nietzsche, and the kind of order he wishes for society is neither Proudhon's, nor Comte's nor Maurras's; yet there are resemblances and foretastes. Flaubert's position at the end of the nineteenth century is somewhat like Stendhal's at the beginning, with the major difference that the author of the *Education* lived in a more complex and troubled world in which the disparate and confusing elements of the society of Stendhal's time had been increased and compounded, while none had completely disappeared. As Stendhal's situation in literature constituted a sort of bridge between the eighteenth and nineteenth centuries, so is Flaubert's a natural introduction to the problems of the writer's attitude and class alliances in the twentieth.

V · Anti-Bourgeois Sentiment and Mass Culture

The Unheroic Hero

Realism and the heroic ideal clashed bitterly in the late romantic novel, and a new type of hero emerged from the conflict. Too bourgeois to be heroic, too lonely and sensitive to be bourgeois, the contradictory unheroic hero is a tragic misfit in modern society. All the heroes of Stendhal, Balzac and Flaubert are not alike. They do not have to be. It is not individual character but a common situation that identifies the many appearances of this new bourgeois hero. If he is vigorous and determined, he may succeed, like Julien Sorel or Eugène de Rastignac, good men playing the game as they have learned it. Most nineteenth century heroes are made of weaker stuff, however, with less will power than Sorel, and more sensitive than Rastignac. Their lives are a series of protests and minor compromises.

On final examination, of course, it turns out that there is no intrinsic contradiction in the work of art. The ambivalence and complications of the unheroic hero mirror the contradictory situation of the anti-bourgeois writer and can even be derived from contrary currents within bourgeois society itself. It is perfectly consistent for ambivalence to breed ambivalence.

Like most anti-bourgeois writers, Stendhal, Balzac and Flaubert could not rid themselves of the notion that in the eighteenth century their situation would have been clearer and more flattering. They did not like their bourgeois century and tormented and consoled themselves with the occasional thought that they did not quite belong. Yet they knew that they themselves were bourgeois, and, moreover, they knew why and how they were bourgeois. Perhaps this is what they resented most.

From the poets and novelists who felt uncomfortable in the age of the bourgeois the twentieth century writer has inherited a vision of his own situation in a society in which he often sees the same trends of progressive vulgarization and subjection to material success. He has also absorbed the ironic and embarrassed relationship between novelist and hero that Rousseau, perhaps, and certainly Stendhal helped establish as a literary tradition. This is one of the chief reasons why so many twentieth century literary heroes are introspective bourgeois youths whose will power and ambition are weakened by a sense of estrangement from society, and why many others, though capable of action, tend to undertake it in terms of compromise or revolt.

Other factors were introduced later: the effect of World War I, the seductive lessons of Nietzsche and Gide, new guilt about being bourgeois and fresh sympathy for the proletariat, homosexuality and Freudian complexes. But to bear the weight of these added burdens, the anti-bourgeois sentiment had already prepared a skeletal character, a personality split by considering the problems of sincerity and hypocrisy, conformity and dissent, commitment and indecision, loneliness and complicity. We might call that character the unheroic hero.

A simplified conception of the classic Cornelian type of hero might interpret a Cid, or a Horace or even a Polyeucte as the product of a stable society in which the poet has no ideological quarrel with his public. Such a hero may be subject to conflicting feelings and desires, but his course of action, however dramatic, is clearly charted according to the demands of a conventional social morality. This morality requires the willful suppression of individual passion or interest in favor of the performance of a duty imposed on the hero by his situation in a hierarchically constituted society. He is a class hero, and his action maintains and is obedient to the ideal code of his class.

On the other hand, such extravagantly romantic heroes as Manfred, Karl Moor, and Chatterton are primarily concerned with the fulfillment of their own personal ideals. They are nonconformists, archindividualists, in reaction against an unjust and oppressive society; they believe themselves superior to the common run of men and are isolated by their superiority and by unique personal feelings that no one else can fully share. They express confusedly the concept of the autonomy of the individual and preach the doctrines of self-achievement and the pursuit of personal happiness (though it be difficult or even futile) on this earth.

The heroes of Stendhal, Balzac and Flaubert are not clearly set in the mold of these extreme types. Not one of the three novelists found the character of his age palatable; but not one of them was a revolutionary—not even on paper. Many of their heroes submit to contemporary modes of moral humiliation, but their submission, even at its worst, is usually an indirect accusation of society. Stendhal was closest to the violently romantic times, and it is not surprising that his heroes are the most strongly alienated from the bourgeoisie—closer to being enemies and accusers of society, social outcasts and rebels than are the later heroes of Balzac and Flaubert. Even when Stendhal mocks the naïveté of his hero and shocks him with the grimy realities of situations in which he involves him, the reaction of a Lucien Leuwen, a Julien Sorel, a Fabrice del Dongo, is an outsider's observation, a criticism and a rebuke. At such moments the hero is not unlike the curious and innocent voyagers of eighteenth century philosophic tales in which the author, shielding himself by a superficial detachment from his hero, uses him to expose those aspects of contemporary life which arouse his resentment.

This (admittedly secondary) function of the Stendhalian hero is maintained to some extent in the action of Lucien de Rubempré and Eugène de Rastignac. At various times both of these talented young provincials, innocent but apt pupils, fall under the spell of the romantic hero-villain Vautrin and take lessons in the art of conquering the Paris of the Restoration and the July Monarchy. Though neither of them is accorded the unmixed sympathy of Balzac, both roam the sort of money-dominated Babylon that Balzac depicts under the name of Paris; they are open-eyed observers and critics of what they see, and their first visit to the capital is an apprenticeship in the art of social success, a moral and a sentimental education. Each episode provides fresh material for an indictment of their time.

The same may be said of Frédéric Moreau, who, like most of the Stendhalian and Balzacian heroes, is a provincial inno-cent. Moreover, Frédéric shuttles back and forth between Nogent and Paris, just as Flaubert divided his time between Croisset and the capital. Each return requires a new reorienta-tion to the big city and provides an opportunity for an advance in Frédéric's education, a new blunting of his sensi-bilities and a new exploitation of his fundamental weakness.

Unlike the Usbeks, Gullivers and Candides of the eighteenth century, however, the new bourgeois heroes do not enjoy the comfortable, detached situation of a philosophic tourist. All three novelists were highly sensitive to historical and social change and professed some notions of fidelity to the idea of realism in art. In situation, at least, their heroes had to fit into the décor and not be too jarringly anachronistic or foreign. They are as bourgeois as they can be without putting too much of a strain on the novelist's sympathy. Like the writer himself, they are averse to seeking "normal" bourgeois careers in medicine, law or commerce; instead, they have vague ideas about becoming writers, diplomats or gentlemen of leisure. They all require a comfortable minimum income and are distressed by the thought of relative poverty, but are not competent at enriching themselves by hard, steady and patient work. This occupational inertia is sometimes due to laziness and juvenility and is not viewed kindly at all by diligent workers like Balzac and Flaubert. Nevertheless, it is hard for the post-romantic novelist to cast his heroes in roles that compel them to perform degrading tasks in what he considers a materialistic, unscrupulous and penny-grubbing bourgeois world.

The half-engaged bourgeois hero is not free to pursue his selfish interests without first overcoming inner restraints. Lucien Leuwen tries to conform outwardly, but holds himself in reserve inwardly. It takes a lecture from the cynical Vautrin to decide Eugène de Rastignac. Lucien de Rubempré and Frédéric Moreau are demoralized far more easily and languish in inaction, compromising themselves more and more. The bourgeois hero is therefore a hero of ironies—one whose ideals, desires and feelings are in disharmony with his adult conception of reality. Nourished by romantic literature, inspired by conflicting eighteenth century ideals, he is uncomfortable in the society in which, alas, he must make his living. But he lacks the raw courage to dissociate himself from it. He values *rentier* status partly because of its material comforts and prestige, and partly because it offers him more liberty than any other condition; he cannot entirely surrender his chance to achieve or maintain it. He does not emigrate to a new world; he does not dedicate himself to the defense of the people's cause; he does not retire from life into art. He consigns himself to a life of weak protest, of pseudo-disengage-ment and momentary feelings of shame, regret, guilt and complicity.

It would also seem that these troubled young men of the bourgeois monarchy and Second Empire must drift and even decline if they are to retain the sympathy of the novelist. Ordinary worldly success may be a condemnation in itself, the sign of a pact made with bourgeois society, a proof of acceptance of its values. Stendhal's heroes intermittently achieve worldly success, but only at the expense of an inner feeling of shame and disgust with themselves. Balzac was warmer toward the idea of success. Yet, in the *Comédie humaine* there are few men of uncompromising virtue who succeed and many honest men who fail (César, Rabourdin, David Séchard). In the vice-ridden world Balzac created, success is more often accompanied by degradation, inhumanity and an uneasy submission to all that is worst in a corrupt bourgeois society. The successful *arrivistes* of the modern novels of Flaubert are the blackest villains, the most atrociously "bourgeois" characters of all.

Pessimism and the Triumph of the "Bourgeois"

The "pessimism" of an artist is a vague and intangible matter, and any sort of enlightening discussion of it is bound to get extremely delicate and complex. Any man's pessimism is probably largely personal and usually suggests an unhappy childhood; but this is only one dimension. There are broader and more general causes for a pessimistic attitude among artists and intellectuals of the mid-nineteenth century: political disappointments and letdowns in 1815, 1830 and 1848; the inheritance of a taste for lugubrious and sepulchral romantic novels and sad, sentimental love poetry; the romantic conception of the poet as a solitary, superior genius; the possible effect of the writings of the Marquis de Sade; the spread of a scientific materialistic conception of the universe and an accompanying loss of the consolations of religion. Certainly, a good deal of the pessimism of Vigny, Flaubert, Leconte de Lisle, Bouilhet and the Goncourts can be attributed to another factor: a growing disbelief in the idea of social perfectibility and the conviction that the Darwinian jungle of society was permitting only the survival of *Homo burgensis,* a new low, coarse and anticultural product of the nineteenth century triumph of the bourgeoisie.

Already in the novels of Stendhal, there is some intimation of the rise of a vulgar new bourgeoisie and of the need for a sensitive soul to assume some sort of protective coloration for his own defense. Balzac manifested a particular contempt for the "bourgeois masses," as he called them in *César Birotteau.* In *Madame Bovary* and the *Education sentimentale,* Flaubert rose to new pinnacles of disgust and implied the inevitable triumph of selfish calculation and hypocritical unscrupulousness in a society in which everyone was tending to find a common level on a low, bourgeois plateau.

On the popular level, the portrait of the crooked bourgeois had an astonishing success, as in the various theatrical incarnations of Robert-Macaire. In *L'Auberge des Adrets,* this comic hero had been simply an escaped convict. But in *Robert et Bertrand,* a vehicle for the vaudeville talent of the famed Frédéric Lemaìtre, Macaire becomes, in successive acts, a campaigning politician and a capitalist organizing a stock company. Lightly disguised beneath the farcical action is the idea that politicians and financiers are all really out to cheat their stockholders. ("There is no financier who doesn't jump a little in his skin when someone yells: 'Here come the cops!'") It is no wonder that Karl Marx, comparing the July Monarchy to a stock company with Louis-Philippe as its director, pictured the citizen king as "Robert-Macaire enthroned."[1]

Although many critics of French bourgeois culture were liberals, Saint-Simonian socialists and, later, Marxists, such men as Flaubert were not purely moralists, or advocates of social and economic justice. It was not just a matter of problems to be solved or causes to be supported. Even Leconte de Lisle, who was politically liberal and active, can be called pessimistic because, like Flaubert, he doubted that moral decline and the reign of Moloch, "the golden-bellied idol," could be arrested within his lifetime.

> Un air impur étreint le globe dépouillé
> Des bois qui l'abritaient de leur manteau sublime;
> Les monts sous des pieds vils ont abaissé leur cime;
> Le sein mystérieux de la mer est souillé.[2]

For Flaubert, as for Renan, the crowd would always be hateful. Not a foolish snob like Balzac, Flaubert was nonetheless contemptuous of the common herd, which he felt was only in its place when it bowed before the mandarins—a title he had found for the artistic and intellectual elite long before Simone de Beauvoir. The reader of his correspondence is less impressed by his regret for the decay of the aristocracy of blood, for the collapse of a socially aristocratic world like that of Proust's, than by the extension of *la bêtise humaine* to all classes and by the isolation and impotence of superior intellects like his own.

Indeed, there is some justification for Brunetière's assertion that Nietzsche's aristocratic ideal was anticipated by Flaubert and by Renan (in the *Dialogues philosophiques*). When Flaubert said the superior man (himself) should live like a bourgeois, but think as if he were a demigod, he was implying a double standard of morality, one for the artist and another for the common bourgeois. In other words, some minds are capable of only petty and mediocre ideas and need stricter rules to govern their behavior. "Only a few persons," said Renan, "have the right not to believe in Christianity." This, says Brunetière, is precisely Nietzsche's idea of addressing his doctrine to only a chosen few and leaving the rest of humanity to live in faith and obedience.[3]

Such an attitude does not necessarily imply tyranny and oppression, but it does imply a selfish and ungenerous cult of the individual and an aristocratic disdain for the irreparably inferior multitude. Brunetière was probably excessively fearful of individualism (in general he is not a very good guide to what was being written in France at the end of the century), but the question is a thorny one and not easily settled one way or another. The idea that some men are beyond good and evil is a perilous one, even when sustained by an artist. A work of art is a *thing*, but it is also an act, and as an act, it may be attributed a moral value.

There is some fuzziness and a not altogether sincere play on words in Flaubert's insistence that he, at least in thought, was not a bourgeois. Of course, in a sense, he would have agreed that he came of a bourgeois family and was educated and culturally formed in a bourgeois tradition. He was right too in stressing the differences between the "bourgeois" of his day, as he defined them, and the bourgeois elite of the eighteenth or even the seventeenth century. But Flaubert was not an eighteenth century man. His horror of the masses, the importance he granted property and his intense concern for order and his propensity for hard work make him seem very bourgeois himself today. His rupture with the bourgeoisie was, as Sartre says, a mythical one; his *déclassement* was more symbolic than real.[4] Flaubert found comfort in the idea that by bourgeois should be meant, not a social class or group, but a kind of mentality, a *Weltanschauung*, possible at any social level. Still, even as he thundered against the bourgeois, did he not adhere to fundamental elements of bourgeois morality? And was it really perspicacious on his part to lump bourgeois and workingman together under a common title, implying that both shared exactly the same guilt and were accomplices in society?

Flaubert's impatience aside, there is an element of truth in his vision of society. The industrial revolution took place in France in the nineteenth century, when the bourgeoisie was in power. Whatever the hostility generated by the conditions under which the industrial proletariat was formed, the lower classes were still obliged to take the bourgeoisie as a cultural model. Indeed, it is chiefly because of the tardy development of efficient methods of mass production in France that the life of a workingman is still so different from that of the middle classes. This, of course, is a special question, complicated by feelings of class loyalty and by a long heritage, encouraging the maintenance, even in strife, of a traditional social structure. It is only in the United States of America that the workingman's taste in literature and art is almost indistinguishable from that of his employer. But the creation of media of mass communication in mid-nineteenth century France transferred enough of the bourgeois literary taste to the lower classes for entertainment and utility to become general criteria of the excellence of art.

Thus, the potential public of the nineteenth century was subjected to vulgarizing influences from the moment it crossed the threshold of literacy. Esthetes like Flaubert sought to aggravate, rather than palliate, their estrangement from *le grand public*. The writer of the seventeenth or eighteenth century was much less resentful of the fact that he could be appreciated only by a tiny minority of France's population.

He was aware that the cultural elite that read books was largely identical with the social, economic and political elite. The nineteenth century esthete had no such conviction and therefore resented the incomprehension of the general public. He widened the gap by his own movement in the direction of esthetic rather than intellectual refinement and by launching insulting attacks on the public, either in the text of his book or in a polemical preface. (Flaubert once complained to the Goncourt brothers that they had been too conciliatory toward their readers in the preface of *Soeur Philomène*.) [5] Accepting the axiom that the bourgeois hates literature, such a writer made his work as inaccessible as possible to the popular reader.

"The ruling classes," writes Arnold Hauser, "are often filled with the choking feeling of their own imminent destruction." Hauser considers Flaubert's pessimism a function of his own identification with "the classes doomed to destruction." [6] In a sense, this is true; Flaubert in no way identifies himself, as Zola did, with the rising lower classes. Yet one must at least credit Flaubert with a refusal to equate "ruling classes" with "cultural elite." He does not unreservedly admire the topmost political elements of the Second Empire or regret nostalgically the reign of the Orleanist bourgeoisie. Nor are the rising classes whose success fills him with horror a revolutionary proletariat or the beneficiaries of gradual socialism. His feelings about the Paris Commune should not be allowed to overshadow the lesson of his earlier writings. His central target is the calculating, egotistical, ambitious and unscrupulous "bourgeois." And if material gain and individual progress in society were the chief motivations of an Homais, it was not the proletariat but the bourgeoisie that gave him the sense of their value. Flaubert's hatred for his own time cannot be attributed purely to the changes that took place in French society after 1848. Part of his pessimism and disgust must be traced back to earlier romantic discontent with the bourgeois triumphs of 1789 and 1830. Moreover, more recent attacks on cultural trends of the twentieth century have sprung from the same old source, even though their authors may not have cared to acknowledge the connection.

From the Bourgeois to the Mass-Man

The sort of discontent fanned in the nineteenth century by the evolution of a raw, new bourgeois society has continued to give rise to little flurries of protest and retains considerable vigor today. One important change, however, is that the bourgeois seems to be slipping off the scene. The French bourgeoisie has obviously lost most of the robust coarseness of its youth. The most conservative French sociologists agree it is a class in its decline. As a term of rebuke, the word "bourgeois" scarcely scratches the skin any more. It is a mild reproach, and has been duly mummified in the official dictionary of the language. Almost the only people who can still put some of the old fervor and bitterness into it are the Marxist slogan-writers. In fact, when the Russian communists denounce "decadent bourgeois culture" and the *l'art pour l'art* esthetes, all the old bourgeois-haters, the sworn enemies of Babbitts and philistines, have to recognize that they too are included in the general anathema. Ironically, the communists have turned the Soviet Union into the most stuffily bourgeois of all modern nations, and now officially sponsor the ultimate in anecdotal, moralistic "bourgeois" art.

Anti-bourgeois sentiment still manifests itself very strongly in France,[7] but in this age it is more likely to be directed against the bourgeois as a capitalist, an exploiter, stubbornly protecting his vested interests. Already in the nineteenth century, many writers who were hostile to the bourgeois for political and economic reasons were attracted to the masses. George Sand, Sue and Hugo, among others, created heroes of the people for humanitarian and socialistic reasons. Others, including the romantic Jeune-France and the aristocratic Goncourts, found an esthetic appeal in the study of the lower classes. For the earlier group, the people had much the same charm as the Napoleonic grenadier; they were endowed with innocence, spontaneity, drama, color, energy and originality.[8] The Goncourts, however, treated their lower-class characters much as an exotic, curious kind of humanity that lived in a different world from their own.[9] For such literary minds, an attraction to the lower depths of society was corollary to their boredom with the class of their origin.

In the novels of Hugo and George Sand there is a warm humanitarian sympathy for the popular hero and the miserable oppressed poor he represents, but the hero is still conceived in the romantic style and idealized and sentimentalized. It is really only after Zola and in the twentieth century that important novelists stop romanticizing the lower classes and also create bourgeois characters who feel ashamed of their class and sympathetic with the workingman, without turning into frustrated individual enemies of society. To be sure, the kind of action that effectively expresses the moral sympathy of a *fils de bourgeois* for the proletariat is not undertaken without mistakes, frustrations, defeats, personal regrets and inner conflicts. On the whole, however, French intellectuals since World War I have been men of good will, with a strong strain of optimism in their character.

Our view of anti-bourgeois sentiment, however, has been restricted to attacks on the moral and esthetic crudeness of a new mass bourgeois society. Those twentieth century writers who stress the guilt of the bourgeois and who sympathize with the proletariat have followed another line of feeling. Of course, it has not been a completely independent line. Simone de Beauvoir, for example, includes among the many problems she has packed into *Les Mandarins* that of the Leftist intellectual whose culture separates him from the proletarians he would like to help. Her Henri Perron and Dubreuilh are stalwartly determined to remain on the side of the working classes. Nonetheless, they are unable to deny that there may be no place for their own books in the society they foresee for the future.

By and large, those who have cried "Fire!" loudest in our century are men of a more conservative temper—men who, like Stendhal and Flaubert, are nostalgic for the past and reluctant to gamble on the future. As in the nineteenth century, a fair amount of snobbishness and an excessive fondness for old aristocratic elites is mixed into the present outcry against the so-called reign of the mass-man. Esthetes, avant-garde writers and artists, unsuccessful in the market place, contemplate with envy, contempt, or a mixture of both, the prosperity of those who have signed up with the big magazine combines, the book clubs, the cinema and television, and feel about them much as Flaubert did about Paul de Kock and Eugène Sue.

Regardless of how one feels about the protests against mass culture and industrialized art, there are striking resemblances between the era of the common man and the older age of the bourgeois in France. Obsessed—and perhaps compelled to be obsessed—with the acquisition of money and with buying the tinselly products of an industrial civilization, the common man of today, like the bourgeois of the Second Empire, looks to art for entertainment and self-improvement. To succeed, he must be better "educated," relaxed and better adjusted. For all its mechanical monotony, his life is so tense and rapid that he must crave rest and forgetfulness, passively imbibed entertainment, for his ever-increasing leisure time.

Nineteenth century writers heaped abuse untiringly on the editors and publishers of their day. We have their counterparts in our century among the board chairmen, the men of power, who buy and dispose of words and pictures—neatly fitted to their scientific measurements of public taste and subtly concocted to mold opinion in accordance with their designs. They employ armies of writers who discover and apply their recipes for success and learn to handle the anonymous styles that have become the trademarks of the companies that hire them. Such a writer's attitude toward all this is not uniform. He may feel quite innocent of compromise; he may compromise with soul-splitting anguish and despise himself, seriously or humorously, or be frankly or secretly cynical; he may lead a dual life, writing one sort of thing for little magazines and in more or less unsuccessful books, and another sort for the "mass media of communication." He may also be an optimist like Zola, who had no great esteem for the *feuilleton*, but accorded it some value as a field for a poor young writer's apprenticeship and as a means for initiating *le grand public* into the higher mysteries of literature.[10] All these attitudes are familiar to the reader of *Jérôme Paturot*, *Illusions perdues* and the correspondences, little reviews and memoirs of the middle decades of the nineteenth century.

The American Century?

Flaubert's prophecy of a future cultural leveling of all classes has probably been fulfilled much more rapidly in America than in Europe. The New World has almost achieved the totally "bourgeois" society he predicted with such disgust. But a similar, if slower, evolutionary process has also been at work in Europe, and it might even be sustained that the present state of American culture, with both the good and the bad that are in it, offers something of a foretaste of what may take place in post-World War II France.

Europeans who find their continent being "Americanized" today are partly right. There has certainly been conspicuous importation, not only of Coca Cola, the grapeless local wine, but also of deodorants, advertising techniques, inartistic movies from Hollywood and, in all their complexity, the mores and values of the American "way of life." We ought not to forget, though, that the reproaches currently directed westward across the Atlantic were domestic complaints in France a century ago, when the bourgeois was supreme. Americans have, in a sense, become a nation of bourgeois. There are still some poor people left, but hardly any proletarians. The way Americans interpret the history of their country, its ideals, its political principles and its myths, reinforces the idea that they are a middle-class nation in which everyone is bourgeois. No one tips his hat to his social betters in America. He has no betters and probably has no hat. Postwar Presidents look like any other man in the street and are the more highly regarded for it. Individual enterprise is everybody's dream and can come real for anybody. Business acumen is universally esteemed and commercial intelligence sought after in the nation's capital.

Both France and the United States entered the nineteenth century rich with middle-class aspirations and a heritage of bourgeois materialistic philosophy. In both countries, industrial expansion and the bourgeois conception of life, government and religion have been responsible for many substantial achievements: constitutional government, political equality, universal education and a vastly improved material standard of living. Both people have been imbued with many of the ideals that help explain both the qualities and the shortcomings of the French bourgeois: progress, success, self-improvement, security and middle-class morality.

For various reasons, the most important of which may be their bewildering technical achievements and present prosperity, Americans are still more attached than are Europeans to the nineteenth century idea of progress and perhaps even to the eighteenth century notion of perfectibility. Perhaps because of the importance of Protestantism, and certainly because of the tradition of the frontier and faith in opportunity, Americans are dedicated to the constant improvement of their standard of living, their social position and even their mind and character. They seem to flock most thickly around those spiritual seers who will banish their doubts and fears, their thoughts of failure and feelings of insecurity and inferiority, offering them "peace of mind" and recipes for "positive thinking." Success is not just money and power. It also implies an absence of guilt and anxiety; it is knocking a stroke off your golf score and not having an enemy in the world.

This Couéistic stress on success and the search for easy comfort and happiness is easily denounced, but not altogether to be disparaged. This is an attitude that encourages action and lowers barriers in the way of equality of opportunity. The idea of material and social success is not entirely hollow; to an extent, it reminds men that the physical world is fluid and can be exploited to their advantage. When, however, it is interpreted in such a way that social welfare is subordinated to individual advancement and material gain and its appearances outweigh moral virtue, there are good grounds for recalling the lesson of the anti-bourgeois moralists of the last century. Moreover, when problems of depth and complexity are superficially met with formulas of advertising-slogan simplicity and when official morality diverges from personal practice, then, as Vigny said in the *Journal d'un poète* (1832), "Charlatanism is at its peak."

There will always be opportunities and reasons for practicing hypocrisy. The last two centuries have no patent on that vice. There is still some point, though, to Montesquieu's assertion that a republic requires more *virtue* than a monarchical or despotic government. Democracy is both a challenge to integrity and a temptation to hypocrisy. And it is fully understandable that a number of aristocratic minds should have denounced the principle of universal suffrage, considering all the corruption that vote-getting entails, just as many lawyers have grave doubts of the kind of justice dispensed by juries and elected judges. The attack on the bourgeois and the mass-man is really an attack on majority democracy. It looks back nostalgically, sometimes through very rosy-tinted glasses, to eras like the golden age of Greece and the eighteenth century, as though these were times when the best people were in charge, when writers addressed their peers, without cynicism and hypocrisy. But we have probably gained more than we have lost.

Close to half a century ago, Charles Maurras, in whom some Americans and Englishmen may recognize a spiritual father of T. S. Eliot, published a little book that called for the end of the conspiratorial bourgeois destruction of an old world that had, he said, been based on faith and honor. He condemned the post-Dreyfus pattern of French culture and proposed a holy crusade to bring about a triumphant resurgence of discredited authoritarian institutions that would turn back the pages of time and restore in France the ways of a nobler past. With some justice, he identified various social and political hypocrisies and faults of bourgeois democracy. Like him, but with considerably more finesse and intelligence, Eliot has laid bare some of the wounds of democratic society. Like Maurras, too, he has disclosed a curious nostalgia for a past distinguished partly by a deeper religious faith, but also by a rigid hierarchy of social groups—and, let it be said, by untold human misery, by social, political and economic injustices that men of good will should hope have disappeared forever from modern France and other democratic countries.

Great though the underground anxiety of the modern individual may be and impatient though he may be with the faults —or at least the problems—of modern bourgeois democracy, it would be sad indeed if he were to allow himself to be persuaded that the only solution required a return to the past. In assessing the gains and losses that bourgeois industry, ingenuity and acquisitiveness have been responsible for, it would be rash and cruel to underestimate the success they have achieved in reducing physical misery. The horror of the nineteenth century factories is almost over. In those countries where man has become most "common" and most "bourgeois," he is also freest from poverty, disease and famine—indeed, war is the only major physical evil that remains of those that are not essential ingredients of man's fate; we are even beginning to do something about the weather. These benefits we cannot relinquish or forget. Perhaps man has been noblest and his tragedy clearest in defeat, but posterity is usually most grateful for his successes.

It would be almost as arrogant to denounce unequivocally

the so-called mass communication media that sprang up in France in the 1830's and have so expanded today that in many countries they now overshadow all commercially distributed literature. Certain unpleasant facts are all too evident. American comic books, it has been observed, are produced less to satisfy a "need" or to provide a medium of expression for artists and writers, than to keep pulp mills in operation and lumber interests prosperous. In a series of articles, first published in the *New Yorker* and later as a book, Lillian Ross followed the production of a Hollywood "prestige" film and reached the conclusion, confirmed by many off-stage comments through the years, that movies are mostly made to pay dividends to stockholders. However artistically a production is conceived, the final decisions on what is cut and what is retained are made, not by the writer, not by the director or even the producer, but by the astute businessmen who are responsible to the stockholders.[11] As in the early days of the *feuilleton* and *La Presse* and *Le Siècle*, there is money for the artist in the new media—much more, in fact, than ever before. But in return for his pay, the individual artist must often sacrifice control of his "product." He must slant what he writes to fit the market, and, even then, commercial interest will often require last-minute changes.

Artists have always been confronted with the problem of pleasing their public. Censorship, overt or hidden, has always hobbled writers and imposed on them some of the dictates of public morality or of the caprices of powerful groups and individuals. To their great credit, book publishers have struggled hard to remain free of censorship and commercial standards. Even they, however, have not been immune to the impact of a vastly enlarged public. It is hard to blame them. For a book to pay its way in the United States, it must sell upwards of 6,500 copies. It is evidently a very hard job to find that many people willing to buy a book that has not followed some standard recipe for success.

This is no question of pure greed or dark intrigue. Like all other industrial production, the phenomenon of mass-produced art and literature cannot be wholly separated from social and economic progress. The very fact that workmen have been able to get a comfortable living wage and achieve a sort of bourgeois estate has contributed to depriving us of certain luxury products that were more readily available when artisans and laborers were underpaid. The increased wages of printers, binders, and the like, make limited printings of books prohibitively expensive and frustrate the authors of books that, though they may be good, have no general appeal. To regret this should not make us condemn industrialism and mass production. Even if all Fords are alike (although, alas, no longer black), we can be grateful that the assembly line has given us all a chance to own a car. The sacrifice of variety in literary produce is a far graver loss; yet—and here is the rub—we cannot in good conscience begrudge to the workman in the book manufacturing trade the same decent standard of living enjoyed by the men who make automobiles.

An ingenious idea was recently expounded by the Belgian economist Robert Triffin (in a public lecture at Yale University). Confronted with the contrast between the variety of European products and the uniformity of American ones, he proposed what he called the hypothesis of the *petite clientèle*. Americans, he suggested, are not content with maintaining a business, commercial or industrial, that caters solely to the needs of its clientele. They are always seeking expansion. This has its advantages: It may sharpen competition, improve the product, reduce costs and prices and create additional employment. The European producer—and particularly the Frenchman—will more likely (not always by design, but often because of fear of the risk and resistance to change) be out to please the taste and satisfy the needs of a small group. The effort to sell more broadly, to expand the clientele, may require the elimination of idiosyncrasies that, for that small group, were virtues. His customers, unlike the Americans, are not convinced that the car the greatest number of people want is necessarily the one for them.

Now, these are certainly a number of thorny economic points that this hypothesis must surmount. There is the Marxist view that all capitalistic economies, including the French, must inevitably seek expansion. There is also the argument that France's slow industrialization, its discontented proletariat, its low material standard of living, are not chiefly due to the individualistic character of its inhabitants. Nevertheless the idea is appealing and no doubt isolates a factor that is of great importance in accounting for the diversity of literary works published in France. It is a fact that French publishers, like other entrepreneurs, often manage with very little capital, limited facilities and a very slim profit on 2,000-copy printings of many of their books. No one gets very rich this way, but a greater proportion of French writers get a public hearing, and numerous *petites clientèles* are able to buy what amounts to a limited edition of the sort of book that hardly any American publisher can afford to print very often, whatever his conviction about the merit of the manuscript.

On the other hand, despite a much greater diversity in book, magazine and newspaper publication in France, publication for a mass public is very conspicuous. The French newspaper with the widest circulation is *France-Soir*, in which one can always find the full and gory details of hatchet-murders, love-nest scandals and criminal trials. Like most profitable American and British dailies, it is also highly pictorial, carrying an extraordinarily heavy load of comic strips and illustrated serials (historical and biographical narratives, condensations of novels). Like American tabloids, this is what sells best, what the mass-man prefers to read. (French proletarians evidently like this sort of reading much better than the communist paper *L'Humanité;* its loss of circulation has become something of a party scandal.) Novels are less revelatory of popular taste, although there have been few greater commercial successes in postwar years than *Caroline chérie* and the French translation of *Forever Amber*. Neither of these works has had the help of any of the numerous literary prizes (which seem to boost sales considerably). They derive their appeal from the same bosomy charms that have enlivened the historical novel in America. Among magazines, the story is clearer: *Sélection* (the French version of the *Reader's Digest*) claims the largest circulation of any periodical in France. Television, although still too dear for most Frenchmen, launched its Gallic career with nightly telecasts of boxing, wrestling and *le catch*.

Such details confirm D. W. Brogan's view that the common man is something of a factor in the reduction of intellectual and literary currency to its lowest terms in Europe as well as in the United States.[12] It seems likely that if the taste and mentality of the mass-man fail to dominate publication in Europe as much as in the United States, it is partly because his buying power is more limited and because his labor is still cheap enough for publishers and film producers to exist marginally and make a slim profit on products that have a limited appeal. There are other factors, including the survival of a class structure that, although crumbling and in transformation, still allows the intellectual writer the great prestige he has always had, even during the worst days of artistic hostility toward the bourgeois. This is, in turn, related to the relative conservatism (or quality) of the French educational system, and the role played by the universities in the production of an intellectual elite viewed less suspiciously, entrusted with greater responsibility and allowed a larger voice than the corresponding elite in America.

Dedication to the ideal of economic progress and to the task of ending material insecurity should make us more tolerant of the intellectual leveling process that has accompanied the extension of the benefits of democratic government and industrialization to an ever increasing proportion of humanity. But it is hard to suppress entirely the feeling that things are not going well. Even among "bourgeois" Americans, there seem to be signs of a deep and cruel distress. Europeans like to dwell on the mounting population of insane asylums and the immense popularity of psychoanalysis in America. More significant perhaps is the divergence between public myth and individual reality in American life revealed by such books as Mills' *White Collar* and Riesman's *The Lonely Crowd*. And most significant of all signs, to the literary mind at least, is the evidence of American literature, when it is honestly written with a disregard for nationalistic self-praise. From these signs we have an image of a society still in flux, pent with anxiety and, though the comfort may seem thin to some, a long way off from Huxley's brave new world where there is no place for Shakespeare.

The importance given to material success and progress, to social mobility and advancement, has had some painful effects on what, for want of a better word, we might still call the soul. Work—with all the prestige and honor that Victorian morality attached to it—has overshadowed the mystery of life's meaning. Men adopt careers, trades and professions because they hope to be successful in them, to make money, to be promoted, to climb the social ladder; but not necessarily because of any personal inclination for the work itself. Rather than mold their careers, they allow their careers to mold them. Tied for long years to their individual ways of making money, they look forward with a longing, intensified by the advertisements of insurance companies, to the moment of their release, their unharnessing, when, as they say, they can do the things they have always wanted to do. When the time for retirement comes, such men often find they do not know what to do with what we have been taught to call "leisure time."

Television, the tabloid press, the cinema, driving long distances in automobiles—these kill-time activities have served well to fill up evenings, weekends and vacations through the years. But their insufficiency becomes tragically apparent when work ceases to occupy the intervals. The pace of a life that has kept us from "really living" has encouraged the digesting and condensation of experience, devaluated idle speculation and metaphysical wonder, replaced art—considered, as Gide called it, a useless luxury and gratuitous act—with words and pictures delivered to our doors and spoon-fed into our relaxed open mouths.

There is much in such a view of the American of today to remind us of the nineteenth century bourgeois. Any number of sympathetic and comic portrayals of the shopkeeper and the *employé*, from Monnier to Maupassant, deal with the "Sundays of a Parisian bourgeois," with his retirement to the little country home he had always wanted, and with his subsequent disappointment. Freed from his harness, done with stacking coins and filling out accounts, the bourgeois felt lost, bewildered, alone. His money-making activity had constituted the only actively pursued purpose in his life; that gone, his life was empty. There is something extremely sad, a justice finally paid to the victim, in these fictional accounts of the Voltairean bourgeois who had banished metaphysical anguish from his life and is portrayed at the end in the toils of an anguish, a sense of solitude and insufficiency as great perhaps as those of the unfortunate poets who die young. This is indeed one of the levels of meaning of Flaubert's great unfinished epic *Bouvard et Pécuchet*.

The malaise of America's serious writers is also reminiscent of the nineteenth century French novelist. This is most apparent, no doubt, in the new American bourgeois' lack of sympathy for the "artistic" or avant-garde writer. His work does not satisfy the "needs" of the common man: entertainment to fill inevitable idle moments, "inspiration" to comfort him in times of doubt or despair, useful instruction to increase his earning power and solve his immediate problems. But, even excluding the incomprehensible or immoral *poètes maudits*, we still find that most good American novels and plays fail to express the relaxed companionability, the confident spirit of optimism, and the denial of the negative and the tragic that compose the current myth of the American personality. Foreign critics, as well as some of our own, have been impressed by the importance of violence, tragedy and impotence in American novels and the fundamental incommunicativeness and agonizing atomic solitude of their heroes.[13] Among postwar pieces alone, such works as *Miriam, From Here to Eternity, The Naked and the Dead, The Man with the Golden Arm, Dangling Man, A Member of the Wedding* and *The Death of a Salesman* offer an uninterrupted series of fictional characters whose alienation, isolation and anguish match or overpower the more civilized and self-analyzing tragic heroes of Proust, Mauriac, Malraux and Sartre.

At least one great American writer has given tragic depth to the decline of an authentic American aristocracy. Faulkner's Snopeses, a horde of hateful *arrivistes* clambering up toward power and wealth, bear only a superficial resemblance to the triumphant bourgeois of the July Monarchy. Nevertheless, the Sartoris novels and stories communicate a not altogether un-Balzacian and even a somewhat Proustian image of the conflict between good and evil.

Of course, native and contemporary factors prohibit any exact resemblance. Some purely American types are ideally suited for lives of tension or defeat. The advertising executive and the decadent Southerner, for example. Freud's impact in

America has been tremendous. The literary heroes who owe their troubles to an Oedipus complex are at least as numerous as those who suffer from living in a mass society. America also has a slightly older tradition of homelessness at home in the shape of Henry James, whose novels may not owe their present popularity to their literary quality alone. More suggestive of French hostility to the bourgeois, though, are the last generation's attraction to Greenwich Village and the war against the "booboisie."

Whatever the causes, American novelists seem in no danger of being lulled into smug content with their lot. Even the man in the gray flannel suit, like Babbitt, passes through his crucial moments of doubt and revolt. In some situations, maladjustment and dissent keep the best part of us alive. It is very cheering to learn that some big editors and publishers find American literature unheroic and depressing.

American writers, it has been said many times, are for the most part less intellectual than the French. They have been less concerned than the French with placing the individual problems of their characters in the context of contemporary society, with citing historical cause and precedent and reasoning eruditely about their predicament. They have remained closer to what Simenon calls the essence of the novel. Since the depression, since World War II, there has been little accusation of society, little effort to place the blame, if indeed there is any blame to place anywhere. Each unhappy character's troubles are generally limited to the sphere of his individual life, locked up within his personal history. Yet, if the technique were different, if coherent self-analysis were in order, one wonders if, among other troubles, one important diagnosis would not often appear: the paradox, the disparity between myth and reality in a crowded society in which the individual American, compelled to seem sociable and forbidden to be alone, feels isolated amid his anguished fellows, half-believing the myth and half-enraged by its devastating falseness.

In all of this, there is some immeasurable debt the modern intellectual owes to Stendhal, Balzac and Flaubert—immeasurable because there is no way of assessing how much their fictional world has become a part of our own vision of life. Through their novels they have communicated in America as well as in France a state of mind that has become part of the character of modern romantics. This is neither the spirit of individual revolt nor the cool, humorous intellect of critical reason. It combines a sympathetic understanding of the desire for public success and its corruption by the mass values of one's time with a half-secret resentment of becoming someone one had not wanted to become.

For all their many differences, these three French novelists of the bourgeois nineteenth century had a sad and even bitter sense of the improbability of any kind of clear and unambiguous heroism. To their novels the intellectual of today owes some of his uncertainty about his own thoughts and behavior. There has been introduced into his consciousness a fatal, furtive doubt of whether it is wiser to hide or to reveal his best and noblest self. After those three, we are all more hesitant to expose our most vulnerable secret virtues to a society that expects hypocrisy and is embarrassed if not angered by sincerity. On the other hand, we are humiliated when we drop into the common rut and defend ourselves in comfortable, anonymous conformity. With these preoccupations, the modern intellectual spends much of his life summoning the courage to be straightforward or the cruelty to be false; often he finds neither and slips into the middle ground of irony. In these terms, Stendhal, Balzac and Flaubert have sharpened our perception of one of the most agonizing problems of the modern intellectual and artist—isolated, but still enmeshed in a vast new mass society.

Despite appearances, I have not sought to write a brief in favor of the negative, either in life or in art. There are certain periods of history, however, when great works of art have been shaped by the artist's sense of being lost within society. The nineteenth century was one. Perhaps the twentieth is its sequel. We cannot hold Rousseau alone responsible for the unheroic hero. Bourgeois society, realism and romanticism, psychiatry and the two world wars have all helped make the tragic hero a more familiar and pitiful figure. If some modern writers' image of man seems humiliating, we can at least rejoice that they do not despise their readers enough to lie to them. As long as we continue to respect sincerity and good will, perhaps it is just as well that heroics are out of date.

Notes

Chapter I

1 Philothée O'Neddy, "Pandaemonium," *Feu et flamme*, p. 8.
2 See Armand Hoog, "Who Invented the '*Mal du Siècle*'?" *Yale French Studies*, No. 13, p. 51.
3 See Arnold Hauser, *Social History of Art*, II, 715; without specifically maintaining that 1830 initiated a new "century," Georges Matoré (*Le Vocabulaire de la prose littéraire*, pp. 17-25) finds France transformed after the July Revolution.
4 E. Beau de Loménie, *Les Responsabilités des dynasties bourgeoises*, esp. Vol. I.
5 Henry Monnier, *Les Mémoires de M. Joseph Prudhomme*, I, 2.
6 Henri Doniol, *Notes sur le passé contemporain*, p. 4.
7 Maxime Leroy, *Histoire des idées sociales en France*, II, 335-336.
8 Théophile Gautier, "Reprise de *Chatterton*," *Histoire du romantisme*, p. 154.
9 Chateaubriand, "Du Vague des passions," *Génie du christianisme*, *Oeuvres*, XI, 371-372.
10 Leconte de Lisle, "Aux Modernes," *Poèmes barbares*.
11 Leconte de Lisle, Letter to Julien Rouffet, 1839; cited by Albert Cassagne, *La Théorie de l'art pour l'art en France*, p. 403, n. 3.
12 T. S. Eliot, *Notes Toward the Definition of Culture*, p. 38.
13 Nerval, "Vers l'Orient," *Voyage en Orient*, I, 118.
14 Harry Levin, "From Priam to Birotteau," *Yale French Studies*, No. 6, p. 76.
15 See Erich Auerbach, "La Cour et la ville," *Vier Untersuchungen*, p. 28.

16 See Elinor Barber, *The Bourgeoisie in 18th Century France*, pp. 112-140.
17 Charles Morazé, *La France bourgeoise*, p. 65.
18 Paul Hazard, *La Crise de la conscience européenne*, II, 120-141.
19 *Oeuvres de Saint-Simon et Enfantin*, II, 220-221; also see Leroy, *Histoire des idées sociales en France*, pp. 380-381.
20 Cited by Leroy, p. 336
21 Stendhal, *Lucien Leuwen*, II, 234.
22 Balzac, *Gobseck, Comédie humaine*, II, 629.
23 Jean Reynaud, "De la Nécessité d'une représentation spéciale pour les prolétaires," *Revue Encyclopédique*, LIV, 13.
24 Louis Blanc, *Histoire de dix ans*, I, 6.
25 Reynaud, "Bourgeoisie," *Encyclopédie Nouvelle*, III, 45-47.
26 Hippolyte Castille, *Les Hommes et les moeurs en France sous le règne de Louis-Philippe*, pp. 263-264.
27 Paul Thureau-Dangin, *Histoire de la Monarchie de Juillet*, VI, 48-49.
28 Baudelaire, *Salon de 1846, Oeuvres*, p. 598.
29 Monnier, *Physiologie du bourgeois*, p. 10.
30 Jean-Paul Sartre, *Baudelaire*, p. 158.
31 Gautier, *Histoire du romantisme*, p. 17.
32 Arsène Houssaye, *Les Confessions*, I, 298.
33 Cyril Connolly, *Ideas and Places*, p. 136.
34 Karl Mannheim, *Ideology and Utopia*, p. 139.
35 Sainte-Beuve, "De la Littérature industrielle," *Portraits contemporains*, I, 502-503.
36 Castille, *Les Hommes et les moeurs en France sous le règne de Louis-Philippe*, p. 126.
37 Edmond Werdet, *De la Librairie française*, p. 118.
38 Hauser, *Social History of Art*, II, 666.
39 Joseph Aynard, *La Bourgeoisie française*, p. 364.
40 Joseph Bédier and Paul Hazard (eds.), *Littérature française* II, 242.
41 See David Owen-Evans, *Le Roman social sous la Monarchie de Juillet*, p. 83.
42 Heine, *Lutèce*, p. 29; also see Owen-Evans, pp. 67-89.
43 Champfleury, *Le Réalisme*, p. 116.
44 Zola, "L'Argent dans la littérature," *Le Roman expérimental*, p. 193.
45 Werdet, *De la Librairie française*, pp. 118-119.
46 Gautier, "A Jehan Duseigneur," *Poésies complètes*, III, 133.
47 Werdet, pp. 122-123.
48 Balzac, *Lettres à l'Etrangère*, I, 202.
49 *Ibid.*, I, 355-356.
50 Jules Marsan, *La Bataille romantique*, II, 57.
51 Edmond Goblot, *La Barrière et le niveau*, pp. 130-146.

52 Heine, *Lutèce*, pp. 132-134.
53 Balzac, *Lettres à l'Etrangère*, I, 273.
54 Baudelaire, *Curiosités esthétiques, Oeuvres*, p. 596.
55 Flaubert, *Correspondance*, II, 254.
56 *Ibid.*, III, 100.
57 Cited by Marsan, *La Bataille romantique*, II, 69, n. 1.
58 Cited by Jean Néret, *Histoire illustrée de la librairie et du livre français*, p. 107.
59 Flaubert, *Correspondance*, II, 320; V, 5-6, 8.
60 Balzac, *Lettres à l'Etrangère*, I, 497.
61 Heine, *De la France*, pp. 275-276.
62 Paul de Kock, *Le Cocu*, p. ii.
63 Sainte-Beuve, "Espoir et voeu du mouvement littéraire et poétique après la Revolution de 1830," *Premiers Lundis, Oeuvres*, I, 377.
64 Wallace Fowlie, "Swann and Hamlet: A Note on the Contemporary Hero," *Partisan Review*, IX, 3, p. 202.

Chapter II

1 *Le Rouge et le noir*, p. 486 (Book II, Chap. XLII).
2 *Vie de Henry Brulard*, I, 424.
3 Reproduced as an appendix to the Garnier edition of *Le Rouge* (ed. Henri Martineau), pp. 509-527.
4 *Ibid.*, p. 514.
5 Comte de Ségur, *Mémoires ou Souvenirs et Ancedotes*, I, 79.
6 Cited by Pierre Gaxotte, *Histoire des français*, II, 223-224.
7 *Lucien Leuwen*, II, 123-133.
8 *Racine et Shakespeare*, I, 26-27.
9 *Souvenirs d'egotisme*, p. 8.
10 *Vie de Henry Brulard*, I, 470-471.
11 Hauser, *Social History of Art*, I, 398-401.
12 *Lucien Leuwen*, II, 338 (n. 72, n. 74).
13 Léon Blum, *Stendhal et le Beylisme*, p. 12.
14 *Vie de Henry Brulard*, I, 133.
15 *Lucien Leuwen*, II, 263.

16 Martin Turnell, *The Novel in France*, pp. 142-144.

17 *Souvenirs d'égotisme*, p. 79; also see *Correspondance*, ed. Henri Martineau, VII, 49.

18 *Lucien Leuwen*, I, 299 (n. 62).

19 *Ibid.*, II, 347 (n. 143).

20 *Le Rouge*, p. 519.

21 *Ibid.*, p. 357; also p. 584 (n. 662).

22 "Autre avertissement au lecteur," *Lucien Leuwen*, II, 313.

23 Pierre-Aimé Touchard, *Dionysos, Apologie pour le théâtre*, p. 31.

24 Aldous Huxley, *The Devils of Loudun*, p. 324.

25 Jean-Pierre Richard, *Littérature et sensation*, p. 17.

26 "Première préface," *Lucien Leuwen*, I, xxxiii. (Italics added.)

27 *Mélanges de littérature*, II, 283.

28 Victor Brombert, *Stendhal et la voie oblique*, pp. 78-79.

29 See *La Rouge*, pp. 280-290 (Book II, Chap. VIII, "Quelle est la décoration qui distingue?"). Also see Lawrence Lesage, "Albert Camus and Stendhal," *French Review*, XXIII, 474-478.

30 See Auerbach, *Mimesis*, p. 400 (pp. 454-455 in Eng. tr.).

31 Note at the head of the first volume of the manuscript; see *Lucien Leuwen*, II, 318 (Appendix V). (Stendhal's italics.)

32 Marginal note of Stendhal's, *Lucien Leuwen*, II, 331 (n. 22).

33 *La Chartreuse de Parme*, p. 2.

34 Baudelaire, "Eloge du maquillage," *Oeuvres*, p. 903.

35 See Auerbach, *Mimesis*, pp. 400-415 (pp. 454-466 in Eng. tr.).

36 *Vie de Henry Brulard*, I, 89-90.

37 *Ibid.*, II, 116 (n. 321).

38 *Ibid.*, I, 15, n. g.

39 *Ibid.*, I, 85.

40 Hazard, *La Crise de la conscience européenne*, II, 135. (Italics added.)

41 Cited by Martineau (ed.), *Vie de Henry Brulard*, II, 116 (n. 321).

42 Baudelaire, *L'Oeuvre et la vie d'Eugène Delacroix*, *Oeuvres*, p. 871; also see Martineau (ed.) *Vie de Henry Brulard*, II, 309 (n. 1045).

43 Martineau, Introduction to *Le Rouge*, pp. i-ii.

44 See Martineau, *Le Coeur de Stendhal*, II, 72-73, 104 *et passim*.

45 See Henri Sée, *La Vie économique de la France sous la monarchie censitaire*, esp. pp. 86-114.

46 Stendhal, *Correspondance*, V, 81.

47 *Le Rouge*, p. 512.

48 *De l'Amour*, "Fragments divers," no. 93, p. 298.

49 Baudelaire, *Salon de 1846*, *Oeuvres*, p. 649.

50 Heine, *Lutèce*, p. 347.

51 "Autre avertissement au lecteur," *Lucien Leuwen*, II, 313.

Chapter III

1 Pierre Abraham, *Balzac.*

2 *La Comédie humaine* (Pléiade), I, 5.

3 See *Lettres à l'Etrangère*, I, 273-274; also André Billy, *Vie de Balzac*, I, 132-133.

4 See Balzac's letter to Mme *** (1844), *Correspondance, 1819-1850*, p. 405.

5 *Lettres à l'Etrangère*, I, 14, 360.

6 *Ibid.*, I, 512.

7 Castille, *Les Hommes et les moeurs en France sous le règne de Louis-Philippe*, p. 362.

8 Philarète Chasles, *Mémoires*, II. 150.

9 Louis Reybaud, *Jérôme Paturot à la recherche d'une position sociale*, p. 58; among similar attacks on the press is Charles Lassailly's satirical comedy *Les Taupes*, in *La Revue Critique*, No. 3 (March 1840), pp. 3-8.

10 Aynard, *La Bourgeoisie française*, p. 481.

11 Monnier, *Mémoires de M. Joseph Prudhomme*, II, 253.

12 *Illusions perdues, Comédie humaine*, IV, 1025-1026.

13 Cassagne, *La Théorie de l'art pour l'art en France*, p. 340.

14 Billy's chapter on *César Birotteau* is largely based on the resemblances he finds between the hero of this novel and the career and character of Balzac (*Vie de Balzac*, I, 297-309).

15 See Balzac's letter to Hippolyte Castille (date of composition uncertain, but first published in 1846), *Oeuvres complètes* (Conard), XL, 649.

16 Balzac, *Correspondance avec Zulma Carraud*, p. 238; cited by Billy, I, 297-298.

17 Spoelberch de Lovenjoul, *Histoire des oeuvres de H. de Balzac*, p. 112.

18 *Ibid.*

19 *Lettres à l'Etrangère*, I, 205-206.

20 *César Birotteau, Comédie humaine*, V, 366-367.

21 Beaumarchais, letter cited by Eugène Lintilhac, *La Comédie, Dix-huitième siècle*, p. 398, n. 1.

22 See above, n. 15.

23 Plato, *The Laws*, 691c.
24 *Lettres à l'Etrangère*, I, 149.
25 See Billy, *Vie de Balzac*, pp. 299, 303-304.
26 Ferdinand Brunetière, *Honoré de Balzac*, p. 110; cited by Emmanuel Failletaz, *Balzac et le monde des affaires*, p. 33.
27 Paul Louis, *Les Types sociaux chez Balzac et Zola*, p. 80.
28 Failletaz, pp. 25-37.
29 *César Birotteau*, pp. 329-330.
30 *Illusions perdues*, p. 637.
31 Abraham, *Créatures chez Balzac*, p. 202.
32 See René Wellek and Austin Warren, *Theory of Literature*, p. 228.
33 *César Birotteau*, p. 364.
34 *Ibid.*, pp. 388-389.
35 *Eugénie Grandet*, *Comédie humaine*, III, 527.
36 *Les Petits Bourgeois*, *Comédie humaine*, VII, 93.
37 *Les Employés*, *Comédie humaine*, VI, 899.
38 *La Maison du Chat-Qui-Pelote*, *Comédie humaine*, I, 22, 26.
39 *Le Lys dans la vallée*, *Comédie humaine*, VIII, 797.
40 *La Duchesse de Langeais*, *Comédie humaine*, V, 166-167.
41 *Illusions perdues*, p. 485.
42 *Ibid.*, pp. 485-486.
43 *Avant-propos*, *Comédie humaine*, I, 5.
44 Bernard Guyon, *La Pensée politique et sociale de Balzac*, pp. 78-80.
45 *Ibid.*, p. 355.
46 *Le Bal de Sceaux*, *Comédie humaine*, I, 96.
47 *César Birotteau*, p. 459.
48 *Ibid.*, p. 457.
49 *Ibid.*, p. 450.
50 *Ibid.*, p. 384.
51 *Lettres à l'Etrangère*, I, 490, 494.
52 *La Cousine Bette*, *Comédie humaine*, VI, 232.
53 *Une Fille d'Eve*, *Comédie humaine*, II, 62.
54 *La Cousine Bette*, p. 218; *Les Petits Bourgeois*, 68-71.
55 *La Cousine Bette*, p. 218.
56 See, for example, the description of the quarter around the Louvre in *La Cousine Bette* (1846), pp. 178-179; of the neighborhood of the Phellions in *Les Petits Bourgeois* (published posthumously), pp. 70-74; and of the home of the Countess Laginska in *La Fausse Maîtresse* (1842), *Comédie humaine*, II, 16-18.
57 *La Fille aux yeux d'or*, *Comédie humaine*, V, 255-267.
58 *Ibid.*, p. 264.
59 *Le Père Goriot*, *Comédie humaine*, II, 954-955.
60 *La Muse du département*, *Comédie humaine*, IV, 165-166.
61 *Le Code des honnêtes gens*, *Oeuvres complètes* (Conard), XL, 70;

cited by Guyon, *La Pensée politique et Sociale de Balzac*, p. 211, n. 1.
62 Mme de Staël, *Essai sur les Fictions, Oeuvres complètes*, II, 200-201.
63 Mario Praz, *The Romantic Agony*, esp. pp. 93-187.
64 *Les Employés*, p. 939.
65 Chasles, *Mémoires*, I, 306.

Chapter IV

1 See J.-B. Pontalis, "La Maladie de Flaubert," *Les Temps Modernes*, 9ᵉ année, pp. 1646-1659, 1889-1902.
2 Maurice Barrès, *Les Déracinés*, pp. 16-17.
3 Pierre Martino, *Le Roman réaliste sous le second empire*, p. 5.
4 Flaubert, *Preface aux Dernières Chansons de Louis Bouilhet*, pp. 282-283 (Lemerre edition).
5 O'Neddy, *Feu et flamme*, p. 2.
6 Pétrus Borel, *Rhapsodies, Oeuvres complètes*, II, 228.
7 Gautier, *Histoire du romantisme*, p. 64.
8 Emile Faguet, *Flaubert*, p. 32.
9 Dumesnil, *Gustave Flaubert*, pp. 303-312.
10 Flaubert, *Correspondance*, I, 54.
11 "Souvenirs intimes," in Flaubert, *Correspondance*, I, xxii-xxiii.
12 *Ibid.*, p. xxiii.
13 *Correspondance*, V, 90, 92-93, 175, 228, 257, 260, 383, 417.
14 Albert Thibaudet, *Gustave Flaubert*, p. 138.
15 *Correspondance*, VI, 2; II, 394.
16 *Ibid.*, III, 20, 25, 92, 140, 172, 276-277.
17 *Ibid.*, IV, 420.
18 *Ibid.*, II, 345.
19 André Gide, *Journal, 1889-1939*, p. 805.
20 *Correspondance*, V, 32.
21 *Correspondance*, V, 158.
22 *Le Rouge et le noir*, p. 293.
23 *La Cousine Bette, Comédie humaine*, VI, 218.
24 *Correspondance*, III, 86.

25 Letter reproduced in Conard edition of *Education sentimentale*, pp. 703-704.
26 Baudelaire, *L'Art romantique, Oeuvres complètes*, p. 1000.
27 *Correspondance*, IV, 229.
28 *Ibid.*, IV, 220.
29 *Ibid.*, II, 343-344.
30 *Ibid.*, II, 372.
31 *Education sentimentale*, p. 429.
32 See "Notice," *Education sentimentale*, pp. 617-623.
33 Louis Maigron, *Le Romantisme et les moeurs*, p. iii.
34 "Notice," *Education sentimentale*, p. 618.
35 Henri Peyre suggests that Phèdre's passion for Hippolyte was initiatory of the fashion ("Racine's *Phèdre*," *Tragic Themes in Western Literature*, ed. Cleanth Brooks, New Haven: Yale Univ. Press, 1955, p. 101). But surely Hippolyte's total lack of interest in his stepmother makes for an important difference. There must be a sentimental initiation for the young lover.
36 *Mémoires d'un fou, Oeuvres de jeunesse inédites*, I, 510.
37 *Ibid.*, p. 513.
38 *Novembre, Oeuvres de jeunesse inédites*, II, 193.
39 *Ibid.*, pp. 245-246; see also p. 239.
40 See *Novembre*, pp. 249-250, and *L'Education sentimentale* (version of 1845). pp. 3-5.
41 *Education sentimentale*, p. 97.
42 *Ibid.*, pp. 97-98.
43 *Mémoires d'un fou*, p. 486.
44 *Novembre*, p. 182.
45 *Education sentimentale* (1845), p. 34.
46 *Novembre*, p. 244.
47 *Correspondance*, VI, 2.
48 See Dumesnil, *Gustave Flaubert*, p. 264.
49 *Novembre*, p. 247.
50 *Education sentimentale*, p. 130.
51 *Ibid.*, pp. 139-140.
52 *Ibid.*, p. 365.
53 *Ibid.*, pp. 527, 534.
54 *Ibid.*, p. 536.
55 For an account and an evaluation of the various contributions to this hypothesis, see Dumesnil, *Gustave Flaubert*, pp. 363-370.
56 "Souvenirs intimes," *Correspondance*, I, xxvii.
57 Thibaudet, *Gustave Flaubert*, p. 94.
58 *Correspondance*, IV, 21.
59 *Ibid.*, III, 349.

60 From Maupassant's study on Flaubert, written for the Quantin edition of the works; cited in the Conard edition of *Madame Bovary*, p. 550.
61 *Correspondance*, I, xvii.
62 *Ibid.*, V, 300.
63 *Ibid.*, III, 150, 211.
64 *Ibid.*
65 *Education sentimentale* pp. 416-418.
66 *Ibid.*, p. 597.
67 Actually, Flaubert professed fondness for Voltaire: "I love the great Voltaire as much as I hate the great Rousseau . . . to me he seems ardent, eager, convinced, superb. I find his '*Ecrasons l'infâme*' like a crusader's battle cry. . . . And what makes him especially dear to me is the disgust I feel for Voltaireans." (*Correspondance*, IV, 364.)
68 *Correspondance*, IV, 231.
69 Baudelaire, *Mon Coeur mis à nu*, xxii, xxix, *Oeuvres*, pp. 1205, 1207.
70 *Correspondance*, IV, 205.
71 *Ibid.*, III, 242-243.
72 *Ibid.*, III, 349-350.
73 *Ibid.*, III, 52.
74 *Ibid.*, IV, 197.
75 Reproduced in Conard edition of *Madame Bovary*, pp. 544-545.
76 Vigny, *Journal d'un poète*, 1842.
77 Jean-Paul Sartre, "Qu'est-ce que la littérature?", *Situations II*, p. 166.
78 *Correspondance*, III, 305; also see Sartre, *Baudelaire*, p. 164.

Chapter V

1 See Karl Marx, *Les Luttes de classes en France, 1848-1850*, p. 30.
2 Leconte de Lisle, "L'Anathème," *Poèmes barbares*
3 Brunetière, *L'Art et la morale*, p. 74, n. 1.
4 See Sartre, *Baudelaire*, pp. 160-161.
5 See Martino, *Le roman realiste sous le second empire*, p. 172.

6 Hauser, *Social History of Art*, II, 792.

7 See Laszlo Borbas, "The Bourgeoisie in the Post-War Novel," *French Review*, XXVIII, 1, pp. 35-44; also "Hostilities Continue the War on the Bourgeois," *Times Literary Supplement* (May 27, 1955), pp. viii-ix.

8 See "Les Jeunes-France," *Le Figaro*, 30 August 1831.

9 See Edmond de Goncourt, *Journal*, 3 December 1871; discussed by Auerbach, *Mimesis*, p. 442.

10 See Zola, *Le Roman expérimental*, pp. 159-202.

11 Lillian Ross, *Picture*.

12 In Joseph Wood Krutch, and others, *Is the Common Man Too Common?*

13 See the chapter entitled "The Impact of the American Novel," in Henri Peyre, *The Contemporary French Novel*, pp. 263-279; bibliography of recent European comment on the American novel, p. 278.

Bibliography

Abraham, Pierre. *Balzac*. Paris: Rieder, 1929.
——— *Créatures chez Balzac*. Paris: Gallimard, 1931.
Abrégé du Dictionnaire de l'Académie d'après l'édition de 1835. Ed. by
P. Lorain. 2 vols. Paris: Firmin-Didot, 1836.
Altszyler, Hélène. *La Genèse et le plan des caractères dans l'oeuvre de
Balzac*. Paris: Alcan, 1928.
Antier, Benjamin, and Lemaître, Frédéric. *Robert Macaire*. (Includes
L'Auberge des Adrets.) Paris: Tresse et Stock, 1889.
Atkinson, Geoffrey. *Les Idées de Balzac, d'après la Comédie humaine*.
5 vols. Geneva: Droz, 1949.
Auerbach, Erich. "La Cour et la ville." *Vier Untersuchungen zur
Geschichte der französischen Bildung*, pp. 12-50. Bern: Francke,
1951.
——— *Mimesis, dargestellte Wirklichkeit in der abendländischen Lit-
eratur*. Bern: Francke, 1946. English translation: *Mimesis: The
Representation of Reality in Western Literature*. Tr. by W. R.
Trask. Princeton: Princeton Univ. Press, 1953.
Avenel, Henri. *Histoire de la presse française depuis 1789 jusqu'à nos
jours*. Paris: Flammarion, 1900.
Aymé, Marcel. *Le Confort intellectuel*. Paris: Flammarion, 1849.
Aynard, Joseph. *La Bourgeoisie française: Essai de psychologie*. 2nd
ed. Paris: Perrin, 1934.
Baldensperger, Fernand. "Sémantique et sociologie: L'avatar moderne
du 'bourgeois' ", *Letterature Moderne*, I (1950), 8-18.
Balet, Leo, and Gerhard, E. *Die Verbürgerlichung der deutschen
Kunst, Literatur und Musik im 18. Jahrhundert*. Strassburg: Heitz,
1936.

Balzac, Honoré de. *La Comédie humaine.* Ed. by Marcel Bouteron. 10 vols. "Bibliothèque de la Pléiade"; Paris: Gallimard, 1950-1951.
—————— *Correspondance, 1819-1850. Oeuvres complètes,* Vol. XXIV. Paris: Calmann-Lévy, 1876.
—————— *Correspondance avec Zulma Carraud.* Ed. by Marcel Bouteron. 2nd ed. Paris: Gallimard, 1951.
—————— *Lettres à l'Etrangère.* 4 vols. Paris: Calmann-Lévy, 1899-1950.
—————— *Oeuvres diverses,* Vol. III. *Oeuvres complètes.* Ed. by Marcel Bouteron and Henri Longnon. Vol. XL. Paris: Conard, 1912-1940.
Barber, Elinor. *The Bourgeoisie in 18th Century France.* Princeton: Princeton Univ. Press, 1955.
Bardèche, Maurice. *Balzac romancier.* Paris: Plon, 1940.
—————— *Stendhal romancier.* Paris: La Table ronde, 1947.
Bardoux, Agénor. *La Bourgeoisie française, 1789-1848.* Paris: Calmann-Lévy, 1886.
Barrès, Maurice. *Les Déracinés.* Paris: Charpentier, 1898.
Baudelaire, Charles. *Correspondance générale, 1833-1866. Oeuvres complètes.* Ed. by Jacques Crépet. Vols. XIII-XVII. Paris: Conard, 1922-1952.
—————— *Oeuvres.* Ed. by Y.-C. Le Dantec. "Bibliothèque de la Pléiade"; Paris: Gallimard, 1951.
Beau de Loménie, E. *Les Responsabilités des dynasties bourgeoises.* Vol. I, *De Bonaparte à Mac-Mahon.* Paris: Denoel, 1948.
Bédier, Joseph, and Hazard, Paul. *Littérature française.* 2nd ed., ed. by Pierre Martino. 2 vols. Paris: Larousse, 1948-1949.
Benda, Julien. *La Trahison des clercs.* "Les Cahiers verts," No. 6, ed. by Daniel Halévy; Paris: Grasset, 1927.
Berl, Emmanuel. *La Mort de la morale bourgeoise.* 6th ed. Paris: Gallimard, 1930.
—————— *Mort de la pensée bourgeoise.* Paris: Grasset, 1929.
Billy, André. *Sainte-Beuve, sa vie et son temps.* Vol. I, *Le Romantique 1804-1848,* Paris: Flammarion, 1952.
—————— *Vie de Balzac.* 2 vols. Paris: Flammarion, 1944.
Blanc, Louis. *L'Histoire de dix ans, 1830-1840.* 5th ed. Paris: Pagnerre, 1846.
Blum, Léon. *Stendhal et le Beylisme.* 3rd ed. Paris: Albin Michel, 1947.
Borbas, Laszlo. "The Bourgeoisie in the Post-War Novel," *French Review,* XXVIII, 1 (October, 1954), 35-44.
Borel, Pétrus. *Madame Putiphar.* 2 vols. Paris: Ollivier, 1839.
—————— *Oeuvres complètes de Pétrus Borel le Lycanthrope.* Ed. by Aristide Marie. 3 vols. Paris: La Force française, 1922.
Bouvier, René. *Balzac, homme d'affaires.* Paris: Champion, 1930.
—————— and Maynial, Edouard. *De Quoi vivait Balzac?* "De Quoi vivaient-ils?"; Paris: Deux Rives, 1949.

Brandes, G. *L'Ecole romantique en France.* Tr. by A. Topin. Berlin: H. Barsdorf, 1902.

Brombert, Victor. *Stendhal et la voie oblique.* Paris: Presses universitaires de France, 1954.

Bruneau, Charles. *Histoire de la langue française.* Vol. XII, *L'Epoque romantique.* Published under the direction of Ferdinand Brunot. Paris: Armand Colin, 1948.

Brunetière, Ferdinand. *L'Art et la morale.* Paris: Hetzel, 1898.

Bury, J. P. T. *France, 1814-1940.* Philadelphia: Univ. of Pennsylvania Press, 1949.

Canat, René. *Une Forme du mal du siècle—Du sentiment de la solitude morale chez les romantiques et les Parnassiens.* Paris: Hachette, 1904.

Cassagne, Albert. *La Théorie de l'art pour l'art en France chez les derniers romantiques et les premiers réalistes.* Paris: Hachette, 1906.

Castille, Hippolyte. *Les Hommes et les moeurs en France sous le règne de Louis-Philippe.* Paris: Paul Henneton, 1853.

Champfleury. *Henry Monnier, sa vie, son oeuvre.* Paris: Dentu, 1889.

—— *Histoire de la caricature moderne.* 2nd ed. Paris: Dentu, 1867.

—— *Le Réalisme.* Paris: Michel Lévy, 1857.

Charléty, Sébastien. *La Monarchie de Juillet (1830-1848). Histoire de la France contemporaine depuis la révolution jusqu'à la paix de 1919.* Ed. by E. Lavisse. Vol. V. Paris: Hachette, 1920-1922.

Chasles, Philarète. *Mémoires.* 2nd ed. 2 vols. Paris: Charpentier, 1876.

Chateaubriand, François René de. *Génie du christianisme. Oeuvres complètes.* Vols. XI, XII. Paris: Furne, Gosselin, 1836.

Collins, A. E. *Authorship in the Days of Johnson, 1726-1780; being a study of the relation between author, patron, publisher and public.* London: Routledge R. Holden, 1927.

—— *The Profession of Letters; a study of the relation of author to patron, publisher and public, 1780-1832.* London: Routledge, 1928.

Comfort, Alex. *Art and Social Responsibility.* London: Falcon, 1946.

Connolly, Cyril. *Ideas and Places.* New York: Harper, 1953.

D'Alméras, Henri. *La Vie parisienne sous le règne de Louis-Philippe.* Paris: Albin Michel, n.d.

Deberdt, Raoul. *La Caricature et l'humour français au XIXe siècle.* 2nd ed. Paris: Larousse, n.d.

Deherme, Georges. *Les Classes moyennes: Etude sur le parasitisme social.* Paris: Perrin, 1912.

Des Granges, Charles. *La Comédie et les moeurs sous la Restauration et la Monarchie de Juillet.* Paris: Albert Fontemoing, 1904.

Dictionnaire de l'Académie française. 4th ed. 2 vols. Nismes: Pierre Beaume, 1786.

Dictionnaire de l'Académie française. 8th ed. 2 vols. Paris: Hachette, 1932-35.

Dictionnaire universel des sciences morale, économique, politique et diplomatique. Ed. by M. Robinet. 30 vols. London: Librairies associées, 1777-1783.

Doniol, Henri. *Notes sur le passé contemporain, 1830-1850; la prétendue antinomie de bourgeoisie et de peuple.* Paris: 1893. (Extract from the *Compte rendu de l'Académie des sciences morales et politiques.*)

Du Camp, Maxime. *Souvenirs littéraires.* Paris: Hachette, 1882-1883.

Ducros, Louis. *La Société française au dix-huitième siècle.* 2nd ed. Paris: Hatier, 1933. Tr. as *French Society in the Eighteenth Century.* New York: G. P. Putnam, 1927.

Dumesnil, René. *Gustave Flaubert, l'homme et l'oeuvre.* 3rd ed. Paris: Desclée de Brouwer, 1947.

Eliot, T. S. *Notes toward the Definition of Culture.* New York: Harcourt, Brace, 1949.

Encyclopédie de la conversation et de la lecture. Paris: Belin-Mandar, 1833.

Encyclopédie moderne. Ed. by Léon Renier. Paris: Firmin-Didot, 1847-1852.

Encyclopédie nouvelle. Ed. by Jean Reynaud and Pierre Leroux. Paris: Gosselin, 1836-1841.

Encyclopédie ou Dictionnaire raisonné des sciences et des métiers. Ed. by Denis Diderot and Jean d'Alembert. Paris, 1751-1765.

Faguet, Emile. *Flaubert.* Paris: Hachette, 1899.

—— *Propos littéraires.* Paris: Société française d'imprimerie et de librairie, 1902.

Failletaz, Emmanuel. *Balzac et le monde des affaires.* Lausanne: Payot, 1932.

Flaubert, Gustave. *Bouvard et Pécuchet. Oeuvres complètes.* Paris: Conard, 1910.

—— *Correspondance.* New ed. In *Oeuvres complètes de Gustave Flaubert.* 9 vols. Paris: Conard, 1926-1930.

—— *L'Education sentimentale. Oeuvres complètes.* Paris: Conard, 1910.

—— *Madame Bovary. Oeuvres complètes.* Paris: Conard, 1910.

—— *Oeuvres de jeunesse inédites. Appendice aux oeuvres complètes.* 3 vols. Paris: Conard, 1910.

—— *Préface aux Dernières chansons.* In Louis Bouilhet, *Oeuvres.* Paris: Lemerre [1881], pp. 279-305.

Fournière, Eugène. *Le Règne de Louis-Philippe (1830-1848).* Paris: Rouff, 1906.

—— *Les Théories socialistes au XIXe siècle de Babeuf à Proudhon.* Paris: Alcan, 1904.

Fowlie, Wallace. "Swann and Hamlet: A Note on the Contemporary Hero," *Partisan Review,* IX, 3 (May-June 1942), 202.

Furetière, Antoine. *Dictionnaire universel.* La Haye, 1727.

Gautier, Théophile. *Histoire du romantisme, suivie de notices romantiques et d'une étude sur la poésie française (1830-1868).* New ed. Paris: Charpentier, 1884.

—— *Poésies complètes.* Ed. by René Jasinski. 3 vols. Paris: Firmin-Didot, 1932.

Gaxotte, Pierre. *Histoire des Français.* 2 vols. Paris: Flammarion, 1951.

George, Albert Joseph. *The Development of French Romanticism.* Syracuse, N. Y.: Syracuse Univ. Press, 1955.

Gide, André. *Journal, 1889-1939.* "Bibliothèque de la Pléiade"; Paris: Gallimard, 1948.

Girard, (l'Abbé). *Synonymes français.* 3rd ed. Paris: Le Breton, 1741.

Goblot, Edmond. *La Barrière et le niveau: Etude sociologique sur la bourgeoisie française moderne.* Paris: Alcan, 1925.

Goncourt, Edmond. *Journal des Goncourt; Mémoires de la vie littéraire.* 9 vols. Paris: Charpentier, 1888-1898.

La Grande Encyclopédie. Paris: Lamirault, 1885-1902.

Green, Frederick Charles. *French Novelists from the Revolution to Proust.* London: Dent [1931].

—— *Stendhal.* Cambridge (Eng.): The University Press, 1939.

Grib, V. *Balzac—A Marxist Analysis.* New York: Critics Group, 1937.

Groethuysen, Bernard. *Die Entstehung der bürgerlichen Welt und Lebensanschauung in Frankreich.* Halle: M. Niemayer, 1927.

Guérard, Albert. *Art for Art's Sake.* Boston: Lothrop, Lee and Shepard, 1936.

—— *French Civilization in the 19th Century.* New York: Century, 1918.

—— *Literature and Society.* Boston: Lothrop, Lee and Shepard, 1935.

Guérin, Daniel. *La Lutte des classes sous la première république, bourgeois et "bras nus," 1793-1797.* 4th ed. 2 vols. "La Suite des temps"; Paris: Gallimard, 1946.

Gurvitch, Georges. *Le Concept de classes sociales, de Marx à nos jours.* Paris: Centre de documentation universitaire, 1954.

Guyon, Bernard. *La Pensée politique et sociale de Balzac.* Paris: Armand Colin, 1947.

Halbwachs, Maurice. *Esquisse d'une psychologie des classes sociales.* Paris: Marcel Revière, 1955.

Hatin, Eugène. *Histoire politique et littéraire de la presse en France.* Vol. VIII (1815-1861). Paris: Poulet-Malassis et de Broise, 1861.

Hatzfeld, A., Darmesteter, A. and Thomas, A. *Dictionnaire générale de la langue française.* 2 vols. Paris: Delagrave, 1895-1900.

Hauser, Arnold. *The Social History of Art.* 2 vols. New York: Knopf, 1952.

Hazard, Paul. *La Crise de la conscience européenne (1680-1715).* 2 vols. Paris: Boivin, 1935.

────── *La Pensée européenne au XVIIIᵉ siècle, de Montesquieu à Lessing.* 3 vols. Paris: Boivin, 1946.

Heine, Heinrich. *De la France.* Paris: Michel Lévy, 1857.

────── *Lutèce.* New ed. Paris: Calmann-Lévy, 1892.

Hoog, Armand. "Who Invented the 'Mal du Siècle'?", *Yale French Studies*, No. 13 (Spring-Summer 1954), 42-52.

"Hostilities Continue the War on the Bourgeois," *Times Literary Supplement*, May 27, 1955, pp. viii-ix.

Houssaye, Arsène. *Les Confessions; souvenirs d'un demi-siècle, 1830-1880.* Paris: Dentu, 1885

Hugo, Victor. *Oeuvres.* Paris: Hetzel, 1880.

Hunt, H. J. *Le Socialisme et le romantisme en France: Etude de la presse socialiste de 1830 à 1848.* Oxford: Clarendon Press, 1935.

Huxley, Aldous. *The Devils of Loudun.* London: Chatto and Windus, 1952.

Isambert, Gaston. *Les Idées socialistes en France de 1815 à 1848.* Paris: Alcan, 1905.

Jacob, Max. *Tableau de la bourgeoisie.* Paris: Gallimard, 1929.

Jasinski, René. *Les Années romantiques de Théophile Gautier.* Paris: Vuibert, 1929.

Johannot, René. *Eloge du bourgeois français.* Paris: Grasset, 1924.

Josephson, Matthew. *Stendhal or the Pursuit of Happiness.* New York: Doubleday, 1946.

Jullien, Adolphe. *Le Romantisme et l'éditeur Renduel.* Paris: Chapentier et Fasquelle, 1897.

Kock, Charles Paul de. *Le Cocu.* Brussels: Société belge de librairie, 1837.

Kohler, Pierre. "La Bourgeoisie française et la littérature," in *Lettres de France—Périodes et problèmes.* Lausanne: Payot, 1943.

Kohn-Bramstedt, Ernst. *Aristocracy and the Middle Classes in Germany: Social Types in German Literature, 1830-1900.* London: P.S. King, 1937

Krutch, Joseph Wood, and others. *Is the Common Man Too Common?* Norman, Oklahoma: Univ. of Oklahoma Press, 1954.

Lafaye, M. *Dictionnaire des synonymes de la langue française.* Paris: Hachette, 1858.

Lassailly, Charles. *Les Roueries de Trialphe, notre contemporain avant son suicide.* Paris: Silvestre, 1833.

Leconte de Lisle, Charles Marie René. *Poèmes barbares. Oeuvres.* Paris: Lemerre, n.d.

Le Roux, Philibert. *Dictionnaire comique, satyrique, critique, burlesque, libre et proverbial.* Amsterdam: Ch. le Cène, 1718.

Leroy, Maxime. *Histoire des idées sociales en France.* Vol. II, *De Babeuf à Tocqueville.* Paris: Gallimard, 1950.

Lesage, Lawrence. "Albert Camus and Stendhal," *French Review,* XXIII (May 1950), 474-478.

Levin, Harry. "From Priam to Birotteau," *Yale French Studies,* No. 6 (Fall 1950), 75-82.

—— *Toward Balzac.* New York: New Directions, 1948.

—— "Toward Stendhal," *Pharos* (Winter 1945), 7-70.

Lintilhac, Eugène. *La Comédie, Dix-huitième siècle. Histoire générale du théâtre en France.* Vol. IV. Paris: Flammarion, n.d.

Littré, E. *Dictionnaire de la langue française.* 4 vols. and supplement. Paris: Hachette, 1863-1877.

Louis, Paul. *Le Déclin de la société bourgeoise.* Paris: Monde Nouveau, 1923.

—— *Les Types sociaux chez Balzac et Zola.* Paris: Aux éditeurs associés, les éditions du monde moderne, 1925.

Maigron, Louis. *Le Romantisme et la mode.* Paris: Champion, 1911.

—— *Le Romantisme et les moeurs.* Paris: Champion, 1910.

Mannheim, Karl. "The Crisis of Culture in the Era of Mass-Democracies and Autarchies," *Sociological Review,* XXVI, 2 (April 1934), 105-129.

—— *Ideology and Utopia.* Tr. by Louis Wirth and Edward Shils. New York: Harcourt, Brace, 1952.

—— *Man and Society in an Age of Reconstruction.* Tr. (in part) by Edward Shils. New York: Harcourt, Brace, 1951.

Marin, Henri. *Les Réflexions d'un homme de rien sur la garde nationale en général et sur la classe bourgeoise en particulier (de 1830 à 1852).* Ed. by André Lebey. Paris: Cornély, 1910.

Marsan, Jules. *La Bataille romantique.* Vol. II. Paris: Hachette, n.d. [1924].

—— *La Bohême romantique.* Paris: Editions des cahiers, 1929.

—— "L'Ecole romantique après 1830," *Revue d'Histoire littéraire de la France,* XXIII (1916), 1-26.

Martineau, Henri. *Le Coeur de Stendhal.* 2 vols. Paris: Albin Michel, 1952-1953.

Martino, Pierre. *Le Roman réaliste sous le second empire.* Paris: Hachette, 1913.

Marx, Karl. *Les Luttes de classes en France (1848-1850).* Paris: Editions sociales, 1948.

Matoré, Georges. *Le Vocabulaire et la société sous Louis-Philippe.* Geneva: Droz, 1951.

Maurras, Charles. *L'Avenir de l'intelligence*. 2nd ed. Paris: Nouvelle Librairie nationale, 1918.

Melcher, Edith. *The Life and Times of Henry Monnier*. Cambridge: Harvard Univ. Press, 1950.

Mills, C. Wright. *White Collar; the American Middle Classes*. New York: Oxford Univ. Press, 1953.

Monnier, Henry. *Grandeur et décadence de Monsieur Joseph Prudhomme, comédie en cinq actes et en prose*. Paris: Michel Lévy, 1853.

—— *Mémoires de M. Joseph Prudhomme*. 2 vols. Paris: Librairie nouvelle, 1857.

—— *Physiologie du bourgeois, textes et dessins par Henry Monnier*. Paris: Aubert et Lavigne, n.d. [1841].

—— *Scènes populaires, dessinées à la plume*. Paris: Levavasseur, Urbain Canel, 1830.

Morazé, Charles. *La France bourgeoise—XVIIIᵉ-XXᵉ siècles*. Paris: Armand Colin, 1947

Moreau, Pierre. *Le Romantisme*. Paris: Gigord, 1932.

Morienval, Jean (alias Thévenin, Henri). *Les Créateurs de la grande presse en France, Emile de Girardin, H. de Villemessant, Moïse Millaud*. Paris: Spes, n.d.

Needham, H. A. *Le Développement de l'esthétique sociologique en France et en Angleterre au XIXᵉ siècle*. Paris: Champion, 1926.

Néret, Jean-Alexis. *Histoire illustrée de la librairie et du livre français des origines à nos jours*. Paris: Lamarre, 1953.

Nerval, Gérard de. *Correspondance (1830-1855)*. Ed. by Jules Marsan. Paris: Mercure de France, 1911.

—— *Poésie et théâtre*. Ed. by Henri Clouard. Paris: Le Divan, 1927.

—— *Voyage en Orient*. Ed. by Henri Clouard. Paris: Le Divan 1928.

Nettement, Alfred. *Histoire de la littérature française sous la Monarchie de Juillet*, 2 vols. Paris: Lecoffre, 1854.

O'Neddy, Philothée [Dondey, Théophile]. *Feu et flamme; Correspondance inédite de Théophile Dondey et d'Ernest Havet*. Ed. by Marcel Hervier. "Bibliothèque romantique," No. 13; Paris: Presses françaises, 1926.

—— *Lettre inédite de Philothée O'Neddy, auteur de Feu et flamme, sur le groupe littéraire romantique, etc.* Paris: Rouquette, 1875.

Ortega y Gasset, José. *The Revolt of the Masses*. New York: Norton, 1932.

Oudin, Antoine. *Curiositez françoises pour supplément aux dictionnaires*. Paris: A. de Sommerville, 1640.

Owen-Evans, David. *Le Roman social sous la Monarchie de Juillet*. Paris: Presses Universitaires de France, 1930.

Owen-Evans, David. *Social Romanticism in France, 1830-1848, with a selective critical bibliography.* Oxford: Clarendon Press, 1951.

Pernoud, Régine. *Les Origines de la bourgeoisie.* "Que sais-je?", No. 269; Paris: Presses universitaires de France, 1947.

Peyre, Henri. *The Contemporary French Novel.* New York: Oxford Univ. Press, 1955.

—— *Les Générations littéraires.* Paris: Boivin, 1948.

Picard, Roger. *Le Romantisme social.* New York: Brentano, 1944.

Plekhanov, G. V. *Art and Social Life.* London: Lawrence and Wishart, 1953.

Pontalis, J.-B. "La Maladie de Flaubert," *Les Temps Modernes,* 9ᵉ année, Nos. 100, 101 (March-April 1954), 1646-1659, 1889-1902.

Praz, Mario. *La Crise dell'eroe nel romanzo vittoriano.* Florence: Sansoni, 1952.

—— *The Romantic Agony.* Tr. by Angus Davidson. London: Oxford Univ. Press, 1951.

Preston, Ethel. *Recherches sur la technique de Balzac.* Paris: Presses françaises, 1926.

Prévost, Jean. *La Création chez Stendhal.* Paris: Mercure de France, 1951.

Proudhon, Pierre-Joseph. *Qu'est-ce que la propriété?* Paris: Garnier, 1848.

Revue critique. Ed. by Charles Lassailly. Nos. 1-4. Paris, 1840.

Reybaud, Louis. *Jérôme Paturot à la recherche de la meilleure des républiques.* Paris: Michel Lévy, 1849.

—— *Jérôme Paturot à la recherche d'une position sociale.* Paris: Paulin, 1842. (New ed. Paris: Michel Lévy, 1873.)

Reynaud, Jean. "De la Nécessité d'une représentation spéciale pour les prolétaires," *Revue encyclopédique,* LIV (April 1832), 1-20.

Riballier, Louis. *1830.* "Les Idées claires," ed. by Noel Aymès. Paris: Nouvelle Librairie nationale, 1911.

Richard, Jean-Pierre. *Littérature et sensation.* Paris: Edition du Seuil, 1954.

Richelet, Pierre. *Dictionnaire français.* 2 vols. Geneva: J. H. Widerhold, 1680.

"The Romantic and the Bourgeois," *Times Literary Supplement,* March 26, 1954, p. xx.

Ross, Lillian. *Picture.* New York: Rinehart [1952].

Routh, H. V. *Money, Morals and Manners As Revealed in Modern Literature.* London: Nicholson and Watson, 1935.

Royaumont, Louis de. *Balzac et la société des gens de lettres (1833-1913).* Paris: Dorbon-Aîné, n.d.

Sainéan, L. *Le Langage parisien au XIXᵉ siècle.* Paris: Boccard, 1920.

Sainte-Beuve, Charles-Augustin. "De la Littérature industrielle." *Portraits contemporains.*. Vol. I. Paris: Didier, 1846.

—— *Premiers Lundis. Oeuvres.* Vol. I. Ed. by Maxime Leroy. "Bibliothèque de la Pléiade"; Paris: Gallimard, 1949.

Sartre, Jean-Paul. *Baudelaire.* "Les Essais," XXIV; Paris: Gallimard, 1947.

Sartre, Jean-Paul. *Situations II.* Paris: Gallimard, 1948.

Schuecking, L. L. *Die Soziologie der literarischen Geschmacksbildung.* Leipzig: Teubner, 1931.

Schwab, Raymond. *La Renaissance orientale.* Paris: Payot, 1950.

Séché, Léon. *La Jeunesse dorée sous Louis-Philippe.* "Etudes d'histoire romantique"; Paris: Mercure de France, 1910.

Sée, Henri. *La Vie économique de la France sous la monarchie censitaire (1815-1848).* Paris: Alcan, 1927.

Ségur, le comte de. *Mémoires ou Souvenirs et Anecdotes.* 3 vols. Paris: Eymery, 1824.

Seignobos, Charles. *Histoire sincère de la nation française: Essai d'une histoire de l'évolution du peuple français.* 6th ed. Paris: Presses universitaires de France, 1946.

Sombart, Werner. *Le Bourgeois: Contribution à l'histoire intellectuelle de la société économique moderne.* Tr. by S. Jankélevitch. Paris: Payot, 1926.

Spoelberch de Lovenjoul. *Histoire des oeuvres de H. de Balzac.* 3rd ed. Paris: Calmann-Lévy, 1888.

Staël, Mme de. *Essai sur les Fictions. Oeuvres complètes,* Vol. II. Paris: Treuttel et Würtz, 1820.

Steegmuller, Francis. *Flaubert and Madame Bovary, A Double Portrait.* New York: Viking, 1939.

Stendhal. *De l'Amour.* Ed. by Henri Martineau. Paris: Editions de Cluny, 1938.

—— *La Chartreuse de Parme.* Ed. by Henri Martineau. Paris: Garnier, 1942.

—— *Correspondance (1800-1842).* Ed. by A. Paupe and P. A. Cheramy. 3 vols. Paris: Bosse, 1908.

—— *Correspondance.* Ed. by Henri Martineau. 10 vols. Paris: Le Divan, 1934.

—— *Lamiel.* Paris: Editions du livre français [1947].

—— *Lucien Leuwen.* Ed. by Henri Martineau. 2nd ed. 2 vols. "Grands et petits chefs-d'oeuvre"; Monaco: Editions du Rocher, 1945.

—— *Mélanges de littérature.* Vol. II. Ed. by Henri Martineau. Paris: Le Divan, 1933

—— *Racine et Shakespeare.* Ed. by Pierre Martino. 2 vols. Paris: Champion, 1925.

Stendhal. *Le Rouge et le noir*. Ed. by Henri Martineau. Paris: Garnier, 1939.

—— *Souvenirs d'égotisme*. Ed. by Henri Martineau. Paris: Le Divan, 1941.

—— *La Vie de Henry Brulard*. Ed. by Henri Martineau. New ed. 2 vols. Paris: Le Divan, 1949.

Thibaudet, Albert. *Gustave Flaubert*. Paris: Gallimard, 1935.

—— *Histoire de la littérature française de 1789 à nos jours*. Paris: Stock, 1936.

Thureau-Dangin, Paul. *Histoire de la Monarchie de Juillet*. 7 vols. Paris: Plon, 1884-1892.

Touchard, Pierre-Aimé. *Dionysos, Apologie pour le théâtre*. Paris: Aubier, ed. Montaigne [1938].

Turnell, Martin. "The Writer and Social Strategy," *Partisan Review*, XVIII, 2 (March-April 1951), 167-182.

—— *The Novel in France*. London: Hamish Hamilton, 1950.

Van Tieghem, Paul. *Le Romantisme dans la littérature européenne*. "L'Evolution de l'humanité," No. 76; Paris: Albin Michel, 1948.

Veblen, Thorstein. *The Theory of the Leisure Class*. New York: B. W. Huebsch, 1918.

Véron, Louis. *Mémoires d'un bourgeois de Paris*. 6 vols. Paris: Gonet, 1853-1855.

Vigny, Alfred de. *Journal d'un poète*. Ed. by Louis Ratisbonne. Paris: Delagrave, n.d.

Weber, Max. *From Max Weber, Essays in Sociology*. Ed. and tr. by H. H. Gerth and C. Wright Mills. New York: Oxford Univ. Press, 1946.

—— *The Protestant Ethic and the Spirit of Capitalism*. Tr. by Talcott Parsons. New York: Scribner, 1930.

Werdet, Edmond. *De la Librairie française*. Paris: Dentu, 1860.

Zola, Emile. *Le Roman expérimental*. Paris: Charpentier, 1909.

Index

Abraham, Pierre, 94, 115, 219, 220
Arnold, Matthew, 177
Auerbach, Erich, 215, 218, 224
Augier, Emile, 43, 49
Aynard, Joseph, 35, 97, 216, 219

Babeuf, Gracchus, 20
Ballanche, Pierre-Simon, 105
Balzac, Honoré de, 8, 10, 11, 12, 23, 29, 38, 41, 44, 46, 49, 50, 51, 71, 90, 92, 93–131, 154, 170, 174, 177, 179, 188, 191, 212, 216, 217, 219, 220, 221
Barber, Elinor, 216
Barrès, Maurice, 134, 221
Baudelaire, Charles, 30, 31, 44, 46, 56, 79, 86, 90, 92, 130, 133, 148, 159, 177, 216, 217, 218, 222, 223
Beau de Loménie, E., 6, 215
Beaumarchais, Caron de, 98, 106, 219
Beauvoir, Simone de, 192, 198
Béranger, Pierre-Jean de, 33, 45
Bernard, Samuel, 26
Bernardin de Saint-Pierre, Jacques-Henri, 35
Biernawski, Louis, 150–151, 160
Billy, André, 110, 219, 220

Blanc, Louis, 24, 216
Blum, Léon, 65, 217
Boccaccio, Giovanni, 14
Boileau-Despréaux, Nicolas, 44
Borbas, Laszlo, 224
Borel, Pétrus, 34, 135, 221
Boucher, François, 80
Bouilhet, Louis, 135, 139, 191
Brogan, D. W., 207
Brombert, Victor, 73–74, 218
Brunetière, Ferdinand, 111, 192–193, 220, 223
Byron, George Gordon, Lord, 35, 42, 51, 71

Camus, Albert, 74
Cassagne, Albert, 100, 215, 219
Castille, Hippolyte, 25, 32, 96, 107, 109, 216, 219
Céard, Henry, 161
Cervantes Saavedra, Miguel de, 48, 63
Champfleury, 39, 134, 216
Chardin, Jean-Baptiste, 80
Chartier, Alain, 14
Chasles, Philarète, 96, 130, 219, 221

237

Chateaubriand, François-René de, 8, 51, 53, 79, 86, 215
Coeur, Jacques, 14
Colbert, Jean-Baptiste, 17
Commanville, Mme, 138, 140, 169, 171
Comte, Auguste, 183
Condorcet, Antoine-Nicolas de, 36
Connolly, Cyril, 31, 216
Corneille, Pierre, 16, 186

Delacroix, Eugène, 86
Delavigne, Casimir, 45
Descartes, René, 16
Diderot, Denis, 35, 106
Don Juan, 77
Doniol, Henri, 215
Du Camp, Maxime, 139, 168
Ducray-Duminil, François-Guillaume, 49, 90
Dumas, Alexandre (*père*), 41, 154, 178
Dumesnil, René, 136, 221, 222
Duranty, Louis-Edmond, 144

Eliot, T. S., 9, 202, 215
Encyclopédie, 19–20
Enfantin, Barthélemy-Prosper, 21

Faguet, Emile, 136, 221
Failletaz, Emile, 112, 220
Faulkner, William, 210
Feuillet, Octave, 45, 49
Fielding, Henry, 106
Flaubert, Achille-Clophas, 138–139
Flaubert, Gustave, 8, 9, 10, 11, 12, 29, 44, 46, 49, 50, 51, 90, 92, 132–184, 188, 191, 192–196, 212, 217, 221, 222, 223
Fourier, Charles, 21
Fowlie, Wallace, 52, 217
Freud, Sigmund, 210–211
Furetière, Antoine, 15

Gall, Franz-Josef, 115

Gautier, Théophile, 4, 5, 7, 29, 41, 45, 56, 58, 96, 135, 159, 179, 215, 216, 221
Gaxotte, Pierre, 217
Gibbon, Edward, 105
Gide, André, 145, 186, 221
Girardin, Emile de, 40, 96
Le Globe, 7, 21
Goblot, Edmond, 43, 216
Goncourt, Edmond and Jules de, 133, 191, 195, 197, 224
Gosselin, 37
Greuze, Jean-Baptiste, 80
Guizot, François, 25
Guyon, Bernard, 120, 220, 221

Hauser, Arnold, 32, 63, 195, 215, 216, 217, 224
Hazard, Paul, 19, 86, 216, 218
Heine, Heinrich, 39, 43, 49, 69, 90, 216, 217, 218
Helvétius, Claude-Adrien, 36
Holbach, Paul-Henri, Baron d', 36
Hoog, Armand, 215
Houssaye, Arsène, 30, 216
Hugo, Victor, 16, 29, 34, 41, 42, 50, 81, 106, 159, 197
Huxley, Aldous, 70, 208, 218
Huysmans, Joris-Karl, 130

James, Henry, 211

Karr, Alphonse, 41
Kock, Paul de, 33, 41, 44, 45, 46, 49, 90, 91, 95, 217
Krutch, Joseph Wood, 224

Labiche, Eugène, 43, 49
La Bruyère, Jean de, 16
Laclos, Choderlos de, 90
Ladvocat, 37, 42, 114
Laforgue, Jules, 177
Lamartine, Alphonse de, 33, 50
Lassailly, Charles, 219

Lavater, Jean-Gaspard, 115
Law, John, 26
Leconte de Lisle, Charles, 8, 133, 159, 191, 192, 215, 223
Le Nôtre, André, 80
Le Poitevin d'Egreville, 93
Le Roux, Philibert, 17
Leroy, Maxime, 215, 216
Lesage, Lawrence, 218
Levin, Harry, 11–12, 215
Lévy, Michel, 46
Lintilhac, Eugène, 219
Littré, Emile, 17
Louis, Paul, 112, 220

Maigron, Louis, 150, 222
Mallarmé, Stéphane, 161
Mannheim, Karl, 31, 216
Marie-Antoinette, 80
Marsan, Jules, 43, 216, 217
Martineau, Henri, 68, 85, 88, 217, 218
Martino, Pierre, 134, 221, 223
Marx, Karl, 192, 223
Matoré, Georges, 215
Maupassant, Guy de, 171, 180, 209, 223
Maurras, Charles, 183, 202–203
Mills, C. Wright, 208
Molière, 15–16
Monnier, Henry, 7, 27, 39, 97, 135, 174, 209, 215, 216, 219
Montesquieu, Baron de, 90, 105, 202
Morazé, Charles, 19, 20, 216
Moreau, Gustave, 130
Moreau, Pierre, 38
Murger, Henri, 87, 134
Musset, Alfred de, 51, 54

Napoleon I, 76, 87–88, 9, 123
Néret, Jean, 217
Nerval, Gérard de, 4, 5, 10, 29–30, 47, 83–84, 135, 215
Nietzsche, Friedrich, 183, 186, 192–193

O'Neddy, Philothée, 135, 215, 221
Oudin, Antoine, 15
Owen-Evans, David, 216

Pascal, Blaise, 16
Peyre, Henri, 222, 224
Pigault-Lebrun, 49
Plato, 108, 220
Poe, Edgar Allan, 130
Pontalis, J.-B., 221
Praz, Mario, 130, 221
La Presse, 40
Proudhon, Pierre Joseph, 21, 26, 183
Proust, Marcel, 120, 192

Quinet, Edgar, 105

Rabelais, François, 14
Racine, Jean, 15, 222
Renan, Ernest, 192
Renduel, Eugène, 37
Reybaud, Louis, 96, 219
Reynaud, Jean, 22–24, 87, 216
Richard, Jean-Pierre, 70, 218
Richelet, Pierre, 15
Riesman, David, 208
Rops, Félicien, 130
Ross, Lillian, 204, 224
Rousseau, Jean-Jacques, 12, 20, 35–36, 79, 80, 136, 154, 178, 186, 213, 223
Rubens, Peter Paul, 116, 119

Sade, Donatien Alphonse, Marquis de, 191
Saint-Simon, Claude-Henri, Comte de, 21, 25
Sainte-Beuve, Charles, 6, 32, 39, 42, 44, 50, 89, 216, 217
Salvagnoli, Count, 55, 90
Sand, George, 50, 57, 81, 106, 197
Sartre, Jean-Paul, 28, 182, 193, 216, 223

Scarron, Paul, 16
Schiller, Friedrich, 71
Schlesinger, Elisa, 146, 154
Scott, Walter, 151
Scribe, Eugène, 43, 45, 49, 90
Scudéry, Madeleine de, 15
Sée, Henri, 218
Ségur, Comte de, 217
Sismondi, Léonard, 6
Sombart, Werner, 113
Soulié, Frédéric, 41
Spengler, Oswald, 105
Spoelberch de Lovenjoul, Charles de, 103, 219
Staël, Mme de, 53, 129, 221
Stendhal, 8, 10, 11, 12, 23, 30, 49, 50, 51, 53–92, 93, 94, 97, 154, 170, 177, 184, 186, 187–188, 191, 212, 216, 217, 218
Sue, Eugène, 41, 44, 49, 95, 197

Taine, Hippolyte, 53, 147–148
Talleyrand, Charles-Maurice de, 56
Thibaudet, Albert, 142, 170, 221, 222
Thureau-Dangin, Paul, 26, 216
Touchard, Pierre-Aimé, 69, 218

Toynbee, Arnold, 105
Triffin, Robert, 205
Turnell, Martin, 66, 218

Urfé, Honoré d', 15

Valéry, Paul, 77
Vaugelas, 16
Vernet, Horace, 90
Véron, Louis, 96
Vico, Giambattista, 105
Vigny, Alfred de, 7–8, 9, 23, 30, 38, 50, 54, 125, 178, 182, 191, 202, 223
Villon, François, 80
Volney, Constantin, 105
Voltaire, 17, 79, 90, 116, 223

Walpole, Horace, 70
Warren, Austin, 220
Watteau, Antoine, 80
Wellek, René, 220
Werdet, Edmond, 32, 41–42, 95, 216
Wordsworth, William, 79, 106

Zola, Emile, 39–40, 106, 197, 199, 216, 224